Asperger's Syndrome FOR DUMMIES®

by Gina Gomez de la Cuesta, PhD and James Mason

Foreword by Dr Judith Gould
Consultant Clinical Psychologist and Director,
The National Autistic Society Lorna Wing Centre for Autism

WILEY

A John Wiley and Sons, Ltd, Publication

Asperger's Syndrome For Dummies®

Published by
John Wiley & Sons, Ltd
The Atrium
Southern Gate
Chichester
West Sussex
PO19 8SQ
England

E-mail (for orders and customer service enquires): cs-books@wiley.co.uk

Visit our Home Page on www.wiley.com

For general information on our other products and services, please contact our Customer Care Department within the U.S. at 800-762-2974, outside the U.S. at 317-572-3993, or fax 317-572-4002.

For technical support, please visit www.wiley.com/techsupport.

Wiley also publishes its books in a variety of electronic formats. Some content that appears in print may not be available in electronic books.

British Library Cataloguing in Publication Data: A catalogue record for this book is available from the British Library

ISBN-13: 978-0-470-66087-4 (paperback), 978-0-470-66915-0 (ebk), 978-0-470-66465-0 (ebk), 978-0-470-66466-7 (ebk)

10 9 8 7 6 5 4 3 2 1

About the Authors

Gina Gomez de la Cuesta, PhD is charming, vivacious, hyperintelligent, and hates writing about herself, so this was written by the Goth! She went to school, studied psychology at Oxford, then did a PGCE, becoming a science teacher. She decided to do a PhD in autism at the Autism Research Centre, Cambridge (Oxford *and* Cambridge, I know!), before going to work for the National Autistic Society as their Action Research Leader. She used to have a more conventional name, but then she got married to a Spaniard (the Goth used to have a normal name, too, but that's explained below). She enjoys long walks in the countryside, exercising her Spanish-speaking skills and going on holiday, especially to remote, sunny places (don't we all!). Gardening and watching wildlife are her new-found hobbies which make her feel remarkably middle-aged!

James Mason the Goth has been called the Goth on three separate occasions by three entirely unconnected people, so it must be appropriate. He doesn't wear black or write vampire fiction. He has High-Functioning Autism, which was diagnosed at the age of 34. He went to a mainstream comprehensive, then went travelling. He has studied physics, maths, psychology and linguistics. He continues to study a wide range of more and less obscure subjects in between reading any novels that people recommend. He works for the National Autistic Society editing and producing *Asperger United* magazine, and also reviews autism-related books, edits translations, sits on the web-steering and employment committees of Research Autism, is a member of the Autism Accreditation standards body and provides training and gives talks about autism to those on the spectrum, parents and professionals. All of this work, directly or indirectly, came his way because of his diagnosis. Before his diagnosis he worked, when he worked, in the civil service, in personnel and insurance administration (still awake?). He enjoys walking (especially when there's wildlife) and socialising (especially over a pint of Mr Harry). If you've read this far you'll realise that he knows a lot more about himself than he does about Gina. When he was 19 he learnt Tibetan, which is bound to come in useful soon.

Stefan Gleeson is a consultant psychiatrist practising in Hampshire, although he grew up in Italy. His experience of autism-spectrum conditions stems from working in child guidance clinics, Learning Disability Services, autism diagnostic clinics and work with street children in Guatemala. He's also published work on schizophrenia, personality disorders and social inclusion. In the face of overwhelming distractions from his four children, guitar, wife and church, he's attempting to complete an MA in Medical Education. He says he will one day succeed. He remains hopeful.

Dedication

Gina dedicates this book to all who've encouraged her with studying and writing, and all the families and people on the autism spectrum who've inspired her (the Goth being one of them!). Thanks to Ramon, my long-suffering husband, for putting up with my inability to do anything else useful while writing this book and for his constant support.

The Goth dedicates this book to all those who, knowingly or otherwise, helped him to stop seeing the world as such a scary and bewildering place. Heartfelt thanks to Boojum, Krissy, Lynn, the Raven, Leila, Carol, Bottom, Mary, Mat, Sara, Tony, Pat, Ellen, Andy, Steve and Alison.

Authors' Acknowledgments

Many people have helped with information for this book or with stuff elsewhere in our lives so that we could get on with the book. The book could not have been written without their kind support and incredible knowledge.

We would especially like to thank Carol Povey (that's Gina's boss) and Kathryn Quinton (that's the Goth's boss) for letting us take on this crazy project and supporting us with it throughout.

We would also like to say a warm thanks to Alison Green, Carly Oberheim (whose experience of supporting people and understanding people were invaluable), Beth (who helped enormously with the woman's perspective), Ramon Gomez de la Cuesta and all of our friends who helped with both the writing part and the moral support part during the roller coaster ride of writing. We couldn't have done it without you!

Our sincere gratitude goes to all individuals who helped contribute small or large parts of the book. Thanks to Stefan Gleeson (super psychiatrist and really nice guy), David Perkins, Sarah Hendrickx, John Booker, Laura and Scott Brougham, Anne, Jack, Elizabeth and Paul Wady, Judith Gould, Lorna Wing, Dave, Sarah, and Tony's wife (who didn't wish to be named). Thanks also to Meng-Chuan Lai and Teresa Tavassoli for their helpful comments on our writing.

Huge thanks also to Nicole Hermitage, Simon Bell and everyone at Wiley for their incredible patience and hard work to enable this book to get finished!

Thanks to people we've accidentally missed out from these acknowledgements. If we have, we are sincerely sorry — please accept our deepest thanks.

Publisher's Acknowledgments

We're proud of this book; please send us your comments through our Dummies online registration form located at www.dummies.com/register/.

Some of the people who helped bring this book to market include the following:

Commissioning, Editorial, and Media Development

Project Editor: Simon Bell

Commissioning Editor: Nicole Hermitage

Assistant Editor: Ben Kemble

Copy Editor: Kate O'Leary

Publisher: David Palmer

Production Manager: Daniel Mersey

Cover Photos: © iStock/Shilpa Talluru

Cartoons: Ed McLachlan

Composition Services

Project Coordinator: Kristie Rees

Layout and Graphics: Cheryl Grubbs, Joyce Haughey

Proofreader: Melanie Hoffman

Indexer: Claudia Bourbeau

Contents at a Glance

Table of Contents

Foreword

You may think "Not another book about Autism!" Rest assured, this book is different and offers a new dimension to a fascinating subject.

I have specialised in the field of Autism for around 40 years and thought I knew a great deal. However, this book provides some fresh insights into the complex enigma of autistic conditions. The book collates a broad range of information to interest and inform a wide audience, using the accessible style of the *For Dummies* series of books.

The writers have sensitively woven together details of potential strengths and difficulties commonly experienced by anyone who fits into this pattern of behaviour, and have highlighted how this affects other people within their family and broader social network. The book skilfully relates potential causes and theoretical explanations of the condition to real-life, practical day-to-day situations. The authors give clear direction about management techniques and ways to understand how a person and their family cope in a confusing, unpredictable and often socially alien world.

Importantly, the book emphasises the individual ways in which autism spectrum conditions impact on each person. It can still be hard to obtain a diagnosis and sadly, clinicians attribute diagnostic labels at times without sufficient assessment of each individual's specific needs. To quote from the book "autism spectrum conditions are just that: a spectrum. This means that people are affected differently and each person is unique". This is too easily forgotten when discrete labels are used in isolation, and there is a danger that general assumptions about autism may be applied to all people on the spectrum.

Another valuable reminder is that often those with Asperger's syndrome do not ask for help, which can lead to problems perpetuating to a marked degree. The book takes a proactive stance and signposts the reader as to where to get support and appropriate help.

My favourite chapters were those describing how to interact with a person with Asperger's syndrome. No-one can make general assumptions, and we all need to be aware of just how differently a situation may be perceived by those with Asperger's syndrome. We need to take a fresh perspective for each individual and ensure we behave and react in the ways that meet their individual presentation. This is a challenge we must all embrace.

Throughout the book, the authors make important references to sensory issues. This has often been a neglected area in the past, although increasingly we are now recognising the tremendous environmental implications. Highlighting these concerns in this book is much applauded.

A personal interest of mine relates to the ways in which autism conditions present in women and girls. The chapter relating to this was fascinating and illuminating. I could relate the different 'types' of behaviour described in the women to my clinical work. This area is one in which we need to reflect and learn much more and it was positive to see attention has been given to such an important topic. Clinicians do need now to move away from just considering the male-dominated descriptions of Asperger's syndrome and embrace the differences between genders, particularly if they are to support women and girls in effective ways.

Overall, this book should help any reader get closer to understanding, respecting and valuing the differences between individuals within this broad spectrum. The insider perspective is rightly emphasised. Our understanding of this complex pattern of behaviour is undoubtedly incomplete, but reading this book may move us further forward in such a quest.

Dr Judith Gould
Consultant Clinical Psychologist
Director, The National Autistic Society Lorna Wing Centre for Autism

Introduction

Asperger's syndrome is a form of *autism spectrum condition* that affects a person's ability to communicate and interact with other people. As the term suggests, *autism spectrum conditions* are not a single thing but several closely related things. Like a rainbow, the autism spectrum is made up of a range of conditions, including Asperger's syndrome (AS). And like a rainbow's colours, identifying exactly where one condition ends and the next begins isn't possible. Often, diagnosticians disagree about exactly which autism spectrum condition (ASC) to diagnose somebody with.

Because it's part of a spectrum, it's thus impossible for us to write a book solely about AS. At first, recognising the similarities between some of the conditions on the spectrum is difficult. This book helps you to understand why these conditions are grouped together, and also why people with these conditions can seem so different to each other. If you or those you care for have an ASC, we hope you find this book useful.

No one's done a recent study of how common AS is. A study looking at the prevalence of all forms of autism in children found that 116 people in every 10,000 were on the autism spectrum (that's roughly 1 in 100). A similar prevalence rate was estimated for adults with an ASC. These results suggest that more than 700,000 people in Britain have some form of autism. This number sounds a lot, but many specialists believe that some people on the spectrum, particularly adults and women with Asperger's, are being overlooked, so this number is probably an underestimate.

About This Book

As well as being informative, this book sets out to be *autism friendly*. That is, we've written it using language and in a way that should be easier for people on the autism spectrum to understand. To achieve this ease of understanding we've had to allow for literal interpretation of language, black-and-white thinking, and difficulty with understanding humour. So, in complete contrast to most writers, we avoid elegant and clever descriptions in favour of direct, simple, repetitive language, and we try to make the *For Dummies*' trademark humour clear and obvious. Most of the jokes and the passages in which we're being a little light-hearted are indicated with a liberal use of exclamation marks.

We've written a book about AS, but it also covers other forms of autism that come under what some would call the patronising term "higher-functioning forms of autism". Basically, what you can do in terms of learning, therapy, drugs, diet and everything else has to be individually tailored, no matter what the diagnosis.

If you want more detail on helping someone with "lower-functioning autism", *Understanding Autism For Dummies* by Stephen Shore and Linda G. Rastelli (Wiley) may be more suitable.

Avoiding confusion over terminology

You may well come across quite a number of terms used to describe people with AS or another form of autism. Sometimes the terms can be used interchangeably, but not always. Collectively, they're sometimes called autism spectrum disorders or autistic spectrum conditions. So let's spell a few things out.

Pervasive developmental disorder, *autism* and *autism spectrum disorder* all mean the same thing (regardless of the number of hyphens you may see added in). The word *autism* is also used for what is, strictly speaking, called *childhood autism*. The term *childhood autism* is very confusing because adults can have it, so even doctors usually just say *autism* or *classic autism* when they mean childhood autism.

Diagnostic terms

The autism spectrum is usually broken down into several groups:

- ✓ Childhood autism
- ✓ Regressive autism
- ✓ Childhood disintegrative disorder (CDD), which sounds really scary, but is very rare; many professionals avoid using this term and use the broader term "regressive autism" to include CDD.
- ✓ Asperger's syndrome (also known as Asperger syndrome, AS and Asperger's disorder)
- ✓ Pervasive developmental disorder—not otherwise specified (PDD—NOS)
- ✓ Atypical autism

Personal terms

When people talk about themselves and their loved ones, they tend not to use the diagnostic labels but to call themselves Asperger, Asperger's, Aspergic, Aspergian or Aspie so you'll find all of these terms in books on autism and AS. Because "Asperger" has a capital letter, some people like to put Autie, Autist and Autistic on an equal footing. Because Asperger's is a form of autism, some people with AS like to call themselves autie, autist, autiste (if they're female) or autistic — they see the connection between all people with autism as more significant than the differences between the diagnoses.

You may be wondering why the Goth calls himself that. He doesn't wear black, but even so, people have chosen to name him "the Goth", and after the third time it happened he decided to adopt it as his name. More details of this story are provided in the "About the Authors" section at the front of the book and also in Chapter 6.

Our terminology

The existence of all these terms means we have to make a choice and also try not to offend anybody with the words we use — which actually is impossible. We choose to use the terms:

- Asperger's syndrome (which we sometimes abbreviate to Asperger's or AS)
- Autism spectrum condition (or just ASC)
- Person who has AS or person who has an ASC
- Person on the (autism) spectrum
- Autist
- Autistic

We make these choices because when you shorten Asperger's syndrome to Asperger's it's logical, but to shorten Asperger syndrome to Asperger's is not. The readers of *Asperger United*, a quarterly magazine by and for people on the autism spectrum, chose "autism spectrum condition" in preference to "autism spectrum disorder", and "person on the spectrum" is one of the preferred phrases of the National Autistic Society. Sometimes when the Goth is writing from the perspective of a person on the spectrum, he uses the terms autist and autistic, because many people on the spectrum object to the politically correct "person first" language that uses phrases like "person with AS". Instead of "person with AS" we sometimes use the term "person who has AS", which is somewhat less offensive. Chapter 6 has more on political correctness. We do not intend to cause offence with any of the terms used in this book.

Offering a short explanation of the autism-friendly approach in this book

People with any form of autism have more problems with reading, language and understanding than most people, so we try to be clear in a way that people on the autism spectrum will understand. All *For Dummies* books contain humour, but because people on the spectrum find understanding whether or not something is a joke particularly difficult, we've taken special care to make it clear when we're joking.

For those with visual problems, we've avoided using single quote marks where possible and use longer dashes (called em dashes) than is usual in modern books.

Conventions Used in This Book

We use the following conventions to help you get the most from this book:

- We use *italics* for emphasis, to highlight titles of books and films (such as *The Sign of Four* by Sir Arthur Conan Doyle), and to draw your attention to new words or terms that we define.

- We use **boldface** to highlight key words or phrases in bulleted lists like this one.

- We use `monofont` for web and email addresses so that they're easily identified.

- We use sidebars — see "Why sidebars are called sidebars" for more on these grey boxes.

Foolish Assumptions

This book makes the following assumptions, which we hope aren't really that foolish.

We assume that you have AS, another ASC, are the parent of someone with an ASC, or someone else affected by an ASC personally or professionally. We assume that you or the person you care for may not have a formal diagnosis, and even if you do, that diagnosis could be any condition on the autism spectrum.

Why sidebars are called sidebars

You're doing it now. Reading a sidebar, that is. But it's at the bottom of the page, not the side.

Originally, sidebars were used in magazines to "enliven" the text, and they were placed down the sides of wide magazine-style pages. So they were at the side and narrow, hence the name. To a lot of people on the autism spectrum, these features are just confusing and pointless, especially when the main text doesn't tell you when to read them. However, they're part of what makes a *For Dummies* book a *For Dummies* book, and here they're shaded grey and appear at the top or bottom of a page. So some would say they should have a different name like "topbars", but we're going to stick with the traditional name here and make every effort to make sure that every one is referred to in the main text.

Every sign and symptom of ASCs, such as poor social skills, is found "throughout the general population", as psychologists say, and that's everybody. What qualifies a person as having a form of autism is the sheer number of signs and symptoms they display. So, even though this is a book about AS, anyone on the autism spectrum will find it useful.

We assume you want to learn a lot about AS, including what it is and why it is (as far as anyone can tell), and that you want to be able to understand, or at least look up, the technical terms used by medical professionals.

How This Book Is Organised

This book is split into five parts, plus the contents, this introduction and the index. These last three elements are there to help you find exactly the information you need, without having to read the whole book. Each chapter has been written to be complete, so it doesn't rely on information in previous chapters. Where a chapter does mention something which is described elsewhere in the book, we add a reference such as "more on this can be found in Chapter 9". Nevertheless, we realise that many people with autistic traits are going to want to read the book from cover to cover, so we've attempted to arrange the chapters and parts in the most logical order. Here's a brief explanation of what appears in each part.

Part I: Understanding Asperger's Syndrome (AS)

We hope that what you need to start with is an overview of what AS is, the history of AS, its causes and what it's like to have it. We go on to explain the biological causes and psychological theories of AS, how it's diagnosed, how to obtain a diagnosis if you want to, and how to decide whether you want to.

Part II: Living with Asperger's Syndrome

If you're reading this book, you're probably already living with AS! This part draws a picture of life from the point of view of people with AS: how to understand (and maybe even cope with!) family, friends, school, relationships, work, college and living independently. Part II also deals with self-advocacy, the benefits system and autism rights. This is an enormous subject area, but all the essentials are here.

Part III: Supporting People with Asperger's Syndrome

You may need to support someone on the autism spectrum even if you bought this book because you yourself have Asperger's. We try to cover everything you need to know to make that person's life, and your life, better. From parenting a child with Asperger's to managing stress, coping with sensory difficulties, managing other people, joining a support group and relating to people with AS — it's all here.

Part IV: Discovering Therapies, Medication and Diet

Part IV covers the different approaches that parents and individuals can look into that may help with communication, social skills, behaviour and well-being. These approaches fall into three main groups: therapies, medication and diet. We provide an overview of each, along with pointers to further information.

Part V: The Part of Tens

Here's the part you find in every *For Dummies* book. It includes three short chapters, each listing ten of something: helpful organisations, good things about AS, and famous people and characters who might have had AS.

Icons Used in This Book

The icons used in this book highlight particular paragraphs. The different icons represent the different reasons for highlighting the paragraphs.

This icon highlights information that will help you deal with problems, hassles and irritations. Of course, the whole book should help you too, but the tips are short and easy to implement.

This icon highlights information that you need to bear in mind; the sort of stuff that everyone who wants to know about autism should know.

This icon highlights suggestions for things you might like to try. These suggestions are a bit more involved than the Tips, and some can result in considerable changes to your life; others, however, are just fun.

 This icon highlights the fine details of a given subject. None of this information is essential, but reading it will round out your knowledge of the subject and deepen your understanding. Feel free to skip it, though, especially on your first reading of this book.

 This icon highlights information about potential risks of any course of action. Please pay attention to the warnings we give in this book. We've phrased them to be as autism-friendly as possible, so in places we've gone into quite a lot of detail about exactly what we mean.

Where to Go from Here

"Follow your nose" is the saying. From an autist's point of view, that instruction's either obvious — what else can you do? — or deeply confusing. No one ever explains what they mean. Well, for once we are going to explain. This expression means "let your desire or your interest lead you towards something you want". The expression "to sniff out" comes from the same idea: following an interesting scent to its source. So if you really want to find out about a specific subject, look it up in the contents or the index now and start reading the book there. Otherwise, also "following your nose", just turn the page and keep reading. When you get to the end of the book, don't stop! An appendix lists other books you may want to read, and a glossary explains some key terms.

Chapter 1

Introducing Asperger's Syndrome

*W*hen people first hear about autism or Asperger's syndrome (AS), they often think about the film *Rain Man* — the one in which Dustin Hoffman's character could memorise all the numbers in the phone book and do difficult maths in his head really fast. Some people on the autism spectrum have these amazing abilities, but not all. In fact, only about one in ten people on the spectrum have a so-called *savant skill* — an incredible ability in a particular area. Misconceptions like "all people with autism have an amazing skill" are some of the false impressions of AS we deal with in this chapter.

One thing about *Rain Man* that was quite an accurate portrayal of the autism spectrum was the character's dislike of change. He liked to stick to his routines and know what was happening when, and had certain obsessive interests. He also found social interaction hard to understand and sometimes had difficulty communicating. So the film covered some of the key characteristics of the autism spectrum: dislike of change, obsessive interests, difficulty with social interaction, social communication and social imagination.

In this chapter, we introduce you to AS as part of the autism spectrum. You can find out how it was discovered, what life with AS is like and how AS is diagnosed.

Describing What Asperger's Syndrome Is Like

Describing a person with AS at key stages in his or her life is probably the best way to explain the condition. We've invented a fictional character here (called Robert) to help you understand what life is like from the perspective of someone growing up with AS.

Robert as a young child

Robert didn't like being cuddled as a baby. He didn't really enjoy playing peek-a-boo with his mother and didn't smile very much. However, the rest of his development was fine: he learnt to both walk and talk at the right times. In fact, he was really good at language, often using really complicated words that were advanced for his age. Robert was interested in light bulbs as a young child. He learnt the names of each brand and each type of bulb, and had an extensive collection in his bedroom. He could talk about his collection for hours to whoever would listen! Robert didn't play with other children at nursery school. He preferred to draw pictures of light bulbs on his own, rather than join in with games. At this age, Robert also hated the noise of the vacuum cleaner. His mum had to wait until he'd gone to nursery before she could do the hoovering.

People on the spectrum are often extremely sensitive to sensory stimuli; sudden noises, for example, can be a particular difficulty, as can bright lights and certain smells. For more on senses and autism spectrum conditions (ASCs), go to Chapter 12.

Like anyone, Robert found changes in his life stressful. And some changes he seemed to find much more stressful than most people did. High stress levels can make anyone suffer and retreat into the safety of routine, and very small children displaying some rigidity which they then grow out of is completely normal. When Robert and his parents moved house, everyone found the experience very stressful. Robert's stress, however, was something special: he wouldn't come out of his bedroom for days, he made even less eye contact than usual and his hands shook continuously. His desperate need for routine and safety may have started here. His parents had to make sure he got up at 8 a.m. every day, got dressed at 8.05 a.m., brushed his teeth at 8.10 a.m., had toast and jam for breakfast (using exactly the same plate, knife and fork and eating the same brands of bread and jam), and so on. If anything had to change for some reason, he'd throw a really big tantrum.

Routine is very important for some people on the spectrum. If you're a parent looking for more information on routine, see Chapter 9.

Robert at school

Robert was bright, so he went to a mainstream primary school. He enjoyed learning but really struggled with break and lunch times. He'd often hit and kick other children who wanted to join in with what he was doing. He'd spend a lot of time standing at the edge of the playground, walking along the lines marking out the football pitch. This habit often got him into trouble when other children were playing football! Robert was still really interested in light bulbs and would switch the school lights on and off when he could, to see how the lights flickered. He was often in trouble with the teachers.

Break and lunch times can be particularly difficult for children on the spectrum. Teachers may need to provide extra support during these periods or provide alternatives to going out in the playground, such as going to the library or a quieter, less busy area of the school. For more information on school and AS go to Chapter 11.

At secondary school, Robert became fascinated by history, particularly the world wars. He memorised lots of facts, details of uniforms and dates of battles. In fact, his history teacher used to get quite cross with him because he'd shout out the answers to every question she asked in class. He didn't give the other students a chance to answer. Robert got bullied a lot at secondary school because he was different. Bullies pick on people who don't have friends because no one tries to stop them. Robert wasn't interested in girls and didn't relate to the social chit chat teenagers enjoy. He didn't understand why the other students would spend ages chatting at break and lunch time instead of doing something constructive like maths or reading about the Second World War in the library. He had one friend with whom he played card games, but the other children didn't like him because all he'd talk about was world wars. Nevertheless, Robert did well at school academically (though he did struggle with English literature and foreign languages) and got a place to read history at university.

People with AS aren't intellectually impaired. They may be of average intelligence like the rest of the population, and some people with AS are exceptionally bright.

Robert as an adult

At university, Robert wanted to make friends and have a girlfriend, but didn't know how. He liked one girl and so followed her to all her lectures, but the girl got cross and told him to leave her alone. Robert became miserable, because he hadn't made any good friends, and he wasn't enjoying lectures. Though he loved history, there were too many people in the lecture hall. Someone would always be coughing, which was a noise he couldn't stand, and he found it difficult to concentrate on what the lecturer was saying because of the traffic noise outside. Other people in his classes teased him because he'd always wear the same T-shirt (it felt nice, and didn't scratch his skin). He often couldn't tell when people were being friendly or not, because he couldn't recognise their facial expressions very easily. Robert struggled to get his work done on time, and ended up spending more and more time alone in his room. His parents became concerned and took him to see a psychologist to determine whether he was depressed. At this point, Robert was diagnosed with AS.

You can be diagnosed with AS at any age. You have the condition all your life, but people may not realise it until you're older. For more information on diagnosis, see Chapter 3.

Having a diagnosis of AS opened the door to some support at university for Robert. He was assigned a mentor, who helped him with lecture notes and organisation. His mentor also took him along to the pub, where he began to get to know some other people in his year at university. In his final year, Robert felt much better. He left university and got a job in a library. Unfortunately, things got worse again. Robert received no support at work, and his boss was always cross with him for not being flexible enough and not dealing well with the people using the library. In the end, Robert had to leave his job. He was still living with his mother, who organised all his bills, meals and clothes.

Now, Robert is 30 and his mother is still looking after him. He has a part-time job as a library catalogue assistant, and attends some social groups run by a local charity, but his mother is worried about what will happen when she's no longer able to look after him.

Robert isn't a real person, but his story includes many facts that are common features of AS. You may find this brief description of what AS is like useful in relation to your own life or that of someone you care for.

Recognising the Characteristics of AS

Unusual behaviour is characteristic of people on the autism spectrum (see the previous section on our invented character, Robert). The autism spectrum applies to people who have difficulty with social communication, social interaction and social imagination.

We used the word *social* a lot in the previous sentence because the social aspect of ASCs is thought to be the most important in diagnosing them. We live in a very sociable world in which people often talk about the weather just to have something to say to each other. If you're asked, "How are you?", you should always reply "Fine, thanks!" even if you're feeling really unwell. Unwritten social rules and social expectations are widespread in our society. If a pause occurs in conversation, people fill it with chit chat about the weather, even if they aren't particularly interested in the weather. People ask other people if they're feeling okay out of politeness, rather than because they really want to know the true answer. These sorts of social niceties are often a mystery to people with AS. In fact, many people with AS have to learn such things by rote, if they're able to learn them at all.

If you have AS, you may have difficulties with the following things:

- ✔ Understanding social interactions, social rules and social expectations
- ✔ Recognising other people's feelings and emotions (by their facial expressions, tone of voice, or body language and gestures)
- ✔ Making friends and keeping friends, even though you may want to have friends

✔ Making conversation (knowing when to start or end a conversation and what to talk about)

✔ Understanding jokes, sarcasm, idioms and metaphors (you may take language very literally)

✔ Figuring out what other people are thinking (you may find other people confusing and unpredictable)

✔ Imagining alternative outcomes to a given situation

All these difficulties can make life a struggle for people with AS. More than half a million people in the UK have an ASC. That figure represents at least one in 100 people trying to get to grips with the very sociable world we live in. Our society can be very confusing and frightening if you don't understand it and can't predict what's going to happen next. People on the spectrum may not seem to be very interested in people and may withdraw from society altogether. This withdrawal isn't surprising — imagine having to work out what other people are thinking and feeling all the time. You may not have to imagine this scenario — it could sound very familiar to you.

Considering Other Aspects of AS

As well as the difficulties with social interaction, social communication and social imagination, people with AS have other characteristics that can make their lives tricky, as described in the following sections.

Sensory issues

People on the spectrum often have sensory sensitivities or insensitivities. For example, the label in the back of your shirt may feel painful on your skin if you have a particular sensitivity to touch. You may wear very tight clothing in order to feel "properly' clothed if you're insensitive to pressure. The noise of a vacuum cleaner, a baby crying or a dog barking may hurt your ears. The smell of perfume may make you feel sick. Simultaneously, some sensory input may be really attractive for you, like a fan spinning around or patterns of flickering lights. Imagine having to walk down a street being bombarded by smells, noises, lights and feelings when your senses are overloaded by the experience, and then trying to "act normal' among the people around you. You can find out more about sensory sensitivities in AS in Chapter 12.

If someone with AS wants to wear open-toed sandals and shorts in the winter, you should let them. They probably want to do that because socks and trousers make their skin feel sore, or they get too hot — yes, really!

Routines

Living in a world that you can't predict, where you can't figure out who's going to do what and when, and where sensory information is distracting, painful or overwhelming is going to make you feel stressed out. Many people with AS rely on maintaining strict routines in their lives to make more sense out of it and to have some control over what's going on. People with AS may get upset if the routine they were expecting doesn't happen. Many parents do their utmost to create order and predictability for their child with the condition.

While people with AS often need some predictability and routine, learning that things may not always work out as planned is important. If you're a parent of a child with AS, allow your child to have the routine that he or she needs, but also try to teach flexibility from time to time. See the nearby sidebar "Choosing your weapons and your battleground carefully'.

Special interests

Many people with AS have special interests. For our character earlier in the chapter, Robert, it was light bulbs and the world wars. The Goth is particularly interested in psychology, physics, linguistics, gait and poise (how people stand, walk and move), history, art, archaeology, Formula One, walking (in the countryside), maps, cricket and the autism spectrum. Not to mention the interconnections between these things! People with AS often become highly expert in a particular area such as train timetables, fossils, fashion or hairstyling (your culture tends to influence what subjects you become interested in — you can guess which of these are usually picked by boys and which by girls!). People on the spectrum may find understanding that other people may not be as interested in the things they are difficult, and may talk incessantly on the same subject without realising the person they're talking to is bored.

Special interests may take over a person's life, but don't try to stop someone from pursuing his or her interests altogether, just encourage the person to do something else some of the time. A special interest may provide a person with opportunities or even a career in the future.

Looking into the History of AS

The term *Asperger's syndrome* was first used in 1981 by Dr Lorna Wing, an expert in the autism spectrum. She drew attention to a paper written by Hans Asperger in 1944 which described people with the social, communication and imagination difficulties we talk about earlier in this chapter. To understand a bit about where the different diagnostic labels on the autism spectrum come from, you need to know a little bit about the history of Hans Asperger and another doctor, Leo Kanner.

Choosing your weapons and your battleground carefully

When the Goth was three and learning to use cutlery, he found it too difficult to use a fork in his left hand. The Goth's parents are very old-fashioned and felt that using a fork right-handedly was incorrect, so they tried to insist that he eat "properly". After several weeks and many, many tantrums, they gave up and allowed him to use his fork in his right hand and his knife in his left.

The Goth's parents used an old set of cutlery given to them by a relative. It was incomplete, and some of the knife handles had been damaged by hot saucepans and other accidents over the years. The dinner knives were larger than the side knives, so the children used side knives because they were easier for their small hands to manage. Only three side knives were left in the set, two of which had damaged handles. The Goth tried to insist on always using the "perfect" one, but while his parents eventually saw the reasonableness of using cutlery left-handedly, insisting on a particular knife was just not reasonable. The Goth tried to compromise by agreeing to use either the perfect one or the butter knife (of which there is only one in an old-fashioned cutlery set   the one with the serrated tip for scraping the butter off the rock-hard pat). This behaviour was still unreasonable. For some reason, the Goth didn't fight hard over this one, so having got used to the feel of the different handles, after quite a few tantrums he used what he was given.

Introducing Hans Asperger and Leo Kanner

Leo Kanner, an Austrian doctor working in America in the 1940s, was the first person to describe a group of children who shared a set of characteristics we now call *autism*. These children preferred to be alone rather than with others, liked playing with objects rather than other children and had problems with language. Kanner coined the term *autism* because it suggested a desire to be alone (*autos* means *self*). Children described in Kanner's paper had a desire to do the same thing over and over, and were quite rigid in their routines.

During the same period, Hans Asperger, another doctor in Austria, published a paper describing a group of children whom we now recognise as being on the autism spectrum too. These children found it hard to make friends, had one-sided conversations and had intense special interests that they could talk about for hours. Unlike the group Kanner described, Asperger's children didn't have difficulty with language and spoke fluently (they often resembled little professors as a result of the advanced language they used and their incredible knowledge about their favourite topics). No one in the English-speaking world took much notice of Hans Asperger's 1944 paper, because it was published in German. Not until Dr Lorna Wing drew attention to his paper did people start using the term Asperger's syndrome. The paper was then translated in 1991 so that people in English-speaking countries could read about Hans Asperger's work.

Nowadays, experts in ASCs argue about the differences between the diagnoses of high-functioning autism and AS. Many say that no difference exists between people with these two diagnoses; others think they are different. Arguments about diagnostic categories continue to this day, and, in fact, a new version of the diagnostic manual for doctors, due out in 2013, will include a revision of the different ASCs. Chapter 3 covers diagnosis.

Whatever your or your child's diagnosis, always remember that each person is an individual and will be different from the next person. No two people on the autism spectrum are the same. Each person's needs and interests will vary.

Whenever we say "you" or "your child" we mean "you or your child" — repeating the whole phrase each time would just be clumsy.

Understanding autism as a spectrum

You'll come across the term *autism spectrum* quite a lot when researching AS, so it's probably worth us spending a bit of time explaining what the autism spectrum is and where AS fits on it. Asperger's syndrome as a label was suggested after that of autism. *Autism spectrum conditions* is a term used to describe all people who have difficulties with social communication, social interaction and social imagination. The autism spectrum contains lots of labels, one of which is AS.

The concept of autism as a spectrum was first developed by Dr Lorna Wing, who has since worked extensively on autism and published many important research papers. The word *spectrum* implies some sort of variation, and indeed people can vary in their difficulties or abilities regarding any of the characteristics associated with ASCs. The term AS is used for people at the more able end of the autism spectrum.

If you have AS, you don't have a learning disability like many people at the lower end of the autism spectrum do (*learning disability* is when a difference exists between someone's expected performance, given their intellectual ability, and their overall achievement at school). Specific learning difficulties such as dyslexia, dyspraxia and dyscalculia (problems with reading, co-ordination and arithmetic) do affect people with AS, though, and all people on the spectrum have non-intellectual learning disabilities (sometimes called social disabilities or social learning disabilities). These non-intellectual learning disabilities mean people on the spectrum find learning the meaning of body language, facial expression and tone of voice very difficult. Some also struggle with face-blindness, which means they find it hard to recognise people from their faces.

Most people with AS have average or above-average intellectual ability. They're also usually highly able to communicate using the spoken word. Some people with AS, however, may not talk out of choice — called *elective mutism* — and some may talk less because they're not sure how to make conversation. In contrast, people on the lower end of the autism spectrum may not be able to talk at all, or may only speak in phrases. Some may communicate using symbols or express themselves by writing things down rather than using words.

These days, experts in autism like to describe ASCs as a "landscape" rather than a "spectrum", because a landscape allows for variations across many dimensions, not just one. But we'll stick to autism spectrum conditions for now (autism-landscape conditions just sounds a bit odd!). For more information on the diagnosis of ASCs, go to Chapter 3.

Looking at Where We Are Today

Researchers, parents and people with ASCs themselves have been trying to understand the causes and characteristics of ASCs for years. Thankfully, professionals have moved on from diagnosing children as being "retarded" or "emotionally disturbed", but we still need to study more and hear more people's stories to understand autism and AS fully.

Understanding the changing prevalence of autism

Twenty years ago, very few people had heard of autism spectrum conditions, let alone AS. Now they're much more widely recognised, and everyone seems to know someone who has an ASC or at least to have heard of it. Recent estimates suggest that about one in 100 children in the UK has an ASC. When you apply that figure to the whole UK population, it means over half a million people in the UK have an ASC (not all of these people will have a diagnosis though). More males than females have an ASC, and this is particularly true in AS, where the ratio is officially about 7:1. For more on the gender ratio, see Chapter 3.

You've probably noticed suggestions in the media that ASCs are on the increase. Many people blame lifestyle changes, vaccinations and other environmental factors for this rise. However, so far the evidence hasn't found any of these things to have caused an increase in ASCs. The truth is probably that ASCs are now more recognised, so more people are getting diagnosed as a result of this increased awareness. Studies all over the world have found roughly the same proportion — one in 100 — even though different countries use different vaccines (or even no vaccines), eat different diets, get different amounts of vitamin D, and expose their citizens to different levels of pollution. These differences imply that none of these things can have caused ASCs.

People with AS come from all backgrounds, religions, countries and cultures. The increase in prevalence of ASCs is a challenge for schools and service providers. The fact that more people are getting diagnosed means that more people should have access to the education, support and services that they need. We just need the system to keep up!

Correcting Misconceptions about AS

Here are a few myths and misconceptions about AS that we'd like to clear up.

If you have AS you're a genius like Rain Man

You may be extremely clever. You may have a special talent (say, in music, maths, memorising data or chess). However, not everyone with AS is a genius or has an amazing talent. People with AS can just be normal people too!

If you have AS you're stupid

This is certainly not true! Current diagnostic criteria mean that to get a diagnosis of AS you must be of average intelligence or above. Having a diagnosis of AS means you don't have significant intellectual impairments — that is, you aren't stupid (although you may have specific problems such as dyslexia or dyspraxia). You are at least average, and may be very bright indeed.

AS is the parents' fault

AS is definitely not the result of something the parents have done, or the fault of the person with AS. AS is the result of a difference in genetic make-up that makes the brain develop differently, resulting in the characteristic behaviours of AS. Parenting has absolutely nothing to do with the cause of AS, although good parenting can help children with the condition develop their skills and cope with their difficulties. You can read more about parenting in Chapters 9 and 10.

If you have AS you don't have feelings

False. Feelings and emotions affect people on the spectrum just like anybody else. You may have trouble recognising these feelings in yourself and in others, but that doesn't mean the feelings aren't there. You may feel that your emotions are so overwhelming that you *can't* express them. Or you may have trouble expressing them, often needing time for the emotions to come out. See the nearby sidebar "Merry Christmas! I hope you like it!"

Merry Christmas! I hope you like it!

One of the things the Goth hates about Christmas is receiving presents. He knows that he's expected to thank the giver warmly and look happy with the gift. "Oh, yes," you say, "everyone hates trying to look pleased when they get a present that they don't like."

But the Goth's problem is that he can't look pleased when he gets a present that he *does* like. Typically, he needs to sleep and then he can feel how happy he is to have been given the present. He doubts that he's ever managed to convince anyone that this is true!

If you have AS you can't empathise

False. Empathy between people attending social groups is visible at every social group. It's people who aren't like you that you have trouble empathising with. And that's true whether you're on the spectrum or not.

If you have AS you don't need friends

Human beings are social animals, and that's true of everybody. However, many people on the spectrum enjoy their own company more than that of others. This doesn't mean that they don't need or want friends though. Many people with Asperger's are lonely and need help making friends, but they need friends just as much as anybody else does.

AS makes you violent

You have to put up with a lot when you're on the spectrum. Daily life is more frustrating, stressful, nonsensical and infuriating than for most people. Unusual reactions to these pressures, such as shouting, meltdowns (see Chapter 6 for more on these) and banging your fist in frustration all get classed as "violent outbursts", and because of a tendency to be less concerned about what other people think, and because of the pressure people on the spectrum are under, they do these things more often, and so may seem more violent. But anyone would do these things when under enough pressure. Genuinely violent behaviour such as fighting or attacking someone with a knife is no more common in people with AS than in people in general.

If you have AS you won't ever get married

All the talk of a lack of social skills and a preference for objects rather than people suggests that people with AS won't ever form meaningful relationships. Again, this is a myth. People with AS often really want to make friends and are perfectly able to keep friends; many go on to get married or have a meaningful romantic relationship. Lots of people with AS struggle with this side of their life, though, and making sure they get the right support to work out how to make and keep friends is important. You can find more information about this in Chapter 11.

If you're able to make eye contact, you don't have AS

This is another misconception, because some people on the spectrum can and do make eye contact. Other people find looking at someone else's eyes painful, so won't do it. Some people learn to make more eye contact or work out strategies to cope with eye contact, such as looking at the side of the person's nose. Someone who makes eye contact can still have AS.

AS is something found in children not adults

Nope — AS is a lifelong condition. Often AS is diagnosed in childhood, but these children grow up into adults and they still have AS. Many adults have AS but don't get diagnosed until later on. This situation arises because AS is more widely recognised now, so people who are older may not have had the support or options for diagnosis when they were growing up.

If you have AS you're good with computers

People tend to notice unusual talents, and to most people computers are a bit of a mystery. Also, programming computers doesn't involve social interaction and follows rules, some of which are subtle and have to be puzzled over. So a disproportionate number of computer programmers have Asperger's — and an eye for detail and perfectionism tend to make Asperger's programmers among the best. Add to this detail the fact that computers have become hugely important and commonplace in the last 20 years, and everyone sees lots of people with Asperger's using computers (even though we've moved on from the days when you had to program your own). But you'll still only learn to be good at computers if you're interested in them.

Chapter 2

Discovering the Causes of Asperger's Syndrome

*H*aving just received a diagnosis of Asperger's syndrome (AS) — for yourself or a family member — probably one of the first questions you'll ask is "What caused it?" Understanding the causes of AS has exercised scientists' brains for many years, but we still don't know for sure what these causes actually are. This is because AS, like all autism spectrum conditions (ASCs), is very complex and may have multiple causes.

Luckily, with the advancement of research into genetics and biology, we know that AS is not caused by having unloving parents (as was supposed in the 1960s). More and more research is discovering that AS has a genetic basis and results from differences in the brain (what scientists call *neurobiological causes*). Having AS thus doesn't mean that you or your parents have done something wrong.

In this chapter you can discover more about the genetic basis of ASCs, the parts and functions of the brain that may be involved, and the psychological differences that have been found in people with an ASC. Heavy stuff, but important to get to grips with.

Understanding the Biology of Asperger's Syndrome

If you're trying to understand the causes of AS, starting with biology makes sense. You'll want to explore what differences there are in the brains of people with an ASC compared with those of people without. You may be wondering whether a specific gene causes ASCs. We don't know exactly the specific causes of AS, but research has come a really long way to show that genetics are involved, areas of the brain may behave differently, and hormones may play a part. As most of the research in these areas has looked at ASCs together, we'll talk about ASCs more generally rather than AS specifically. Let's start with genetics and get the trickiest bit out of the way first.

Getting to grips with genetics

Research showing that ASCs are inherited and not a result of poor parenting was an important breakthrough for parents of children with these conditions. Women who were made to feel guilty for being "cold mothers" in the 1960s no longer have to feel responsible.

Scientists believe that genetics plays a large role in all ASCs because ASCs tend to run in families (if one person in the family has an ASC, it's more likely that another person will also have it). Studies looking at twins where one or both twins have had a diagnosis of an ASC have helped scientists understand the genetics of autism. Studies show that if one twin has an ASC, then the other twin is much more likely to have an ASC too compared with normal siblings. The following list shows the different likelihoods of having an ASC between identical twins, non-identical twins and single-birth siblings:

- ✔ **Identical twins:** share 100 per cent of their genes and have a 60–70 per cent chance of both having an ASC.

- ✔ **Non-identical twins:** share 50 per cent of their genes and have a 5–10 per cent chance of both having an ASC.

- ✔ **Siblings:** share 50 per cent of their genes and have a 3–10 per cent chance of both having an ASC.

We also know that some genetic disorders such as Fragile X syndrome and tuberous sclerosis are associated with higher rates of ASCs. So, it seems that genes play a big part in ASCs.

We know that genes play a part in ASCs, but we don't yet know which specific genes are important. Scientists are working hard to solve this mystery. Researchers have discovered where we may find genes relevant to ASCs (that is, where the genes may be located), and some genes that may be important, but none of them account for all cases of ASCs, and not all of them are found to be significant in all studies.

What are genes?

You may have heard of the Human Genome Project. It created a list of all the DNA (the stuff that genes are made of) that makes up a human. A massive 30,000–40,000 genes make up the human genome, so the list is pretty long. But what actually is a gene?

Genes are lengths of DNA that contain instructions for making a specific protein. The proteins are the basis for all human development. Genetic instructions tell your body how to make all the different organs (like your heart, lungs and brain). They also determine how you look and how you behave. Genes are even involved in determining your intelligence and personality. Genes are complex, and many genes can be involved in determining a particular characteristic.

With 30,000–40,000 genes, the human genome contains loads of information — and we still don't know what lots of it does.

All people have their own unique genetic make-up (except identical twins, who share exactly the same genes). You inherit genetic information from your mum and dad (for example, you may have your father's big nose or your mother's blue eyes). This is how information is passed down from generation to generation.

We do know that it's not just one gene that causes ASCs, but many genes interacting with each other and with external factors in the environment. Experts estimate that between three and ten genes may be involved. Different genes may be involved for all the different characteristics of ASCs (social, language and repetitive behaviour). As you can see, the genetics of ASCs are pretty complicated.

No single gene causes ASCs. You can't do a test to see whether you have "the ASC gene", because no such thing exists.

Interacting genes and the environment

While genes are important in ASCs, they're not the only factor. Identical twins, who have exactly the same genetics, may have different ASC characteristics. Some people who have a gene that's thought to be important in ASC don't have a diagnosis of ASC. Some people who don't have any genes thought to be important in ASC do have a diagnosis. This situation means that lots of genes are involved (some of which we haven't found yet), and the environment plays a part too.

Epigenetics is a biological process by which genes get "switched" on and off. This process is completely normal and can happen in anyone. Scientists are currently looking at epigenetics in ASCs to see whether the switching off of genes could play a part. Identical twins who have exactly the same genes but only one of them has an ASC could be explained through epigenetics and the switching off of genes in one twin but not the other. We still don't know what things may cause a gene to get switched on or off.

Getting the genes but not the diagnosis

Genetic inheritance of an ASC is complicated. Some genes are known to be important in ASCs, but not all people who inherit those genes go on to receive an ASC diagnosis. This means that more than just one gene is involved, and that the environment must play a part too. In the figure, you can see that the mother carries a

gene thought to be important in ASCs, but she doesn't have a diagnosis herself. Her first son is the same. However, her second child (a girl) doesn't have the gene, and doesn't have an ASC diagnosis. The third child (a boy) doesn't have the gene or a diagnosis, and the fourth child has the gene and a diagnosis.

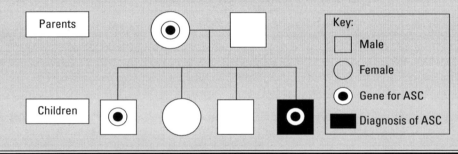

Examining the environment

So far, we don't know what environmental factors are important in ASCs, although many claims have been made. Some people think that the MMR vaccine is a cause (see the "Examining the issue of vaccinations" section later in this chapter), and others that heavy metals such as mercury, having a "leaky gut" or birth complications are responsible.

Research hasn't proved that any of these things are significant causes of ASCs. Scientists are still investigating how genes and the environment may interact with each other to contribute to the development of ASCs.

Identifying differences in the brain

After grappling with genetics, you need to consider brain bits. Scientists have been looking at the brains of people with and without ASCs to see whether any differences exist in brain structure or in how the brain works. These differences may be caused by genes, the environment or a mixture of both.

You can look at brains in a few ways: through different types of brain scan, by measuring the electrical activity of the brain from the outside (called an EEG), or through a post-mortem examination. A brain scan enables you to look inside the living brain to see all the different structures and areas. A post-mortem studies the brain of a dead person to look at brain structures. Post-mortem examination is the only way to look at differences in brain cells. Many people take part in research looking at brain imaging (called "neuroimaging") to see how the brain works. Some people donate their brains to research into understanding ASCs (see www.brainbankforautism.org.uk).

If you're interested in taking part in research into ASCs, then you can register as a volunteer at the Autism Research Centre in Cambridge (www.autismresearchcentre.com). The National Autistic Society also advertises research projects looking for participants on its website (www.autism.org.uk/research).

Spotting differences in brain structure

Researchers have found that some brain areas may work differently in people with ASCs. One difference is in how the two sides of the brain work (for the budding neuroscientists out there, this is called *lateralisation*). In ASC, the brain may also grow too much too early on in development, making lots of initial connections but then not pruning them enough at a later stage (consider a tree — if you don't prune it, it will grow too many branches, which will then cross all over the place; the information in the brain may become muddled with too many connections). People with an ASC may also have larger brain volumes (that is, bigger brains).

Looking at the brains of people with an ASC has shown many differences in specific areas too. The findings from structural brain studies are summarised in Figure 2-1. While we know these differences are there, we can't say whether they cause ASCs or are the result of ASCs.

Discovering differences in brain function

Looking at brain structures to find differences is all very well, but how the brain works is also really important. The connections between different parts of the brain, for example, seem to be significant. In those with an ASC, parts of the brain that are close to each other may be too strongly connected, and parts that are far apart may be too weakly connected. This makes relating information in different contexts quite difficult for people with an ASC. This situation resembles the London Underground: lots of Tube connections exist between different places in London, but you can't travel to Scotland.

Different structures and systems in the brain also have different functions. Lots of the structures described in Figure 2-2 are involved in processing complex social information. They're part of the "social brain". Differences in the social brain may account for some of the difficulties people with an ASC have in understanding social information.

Areas of the social brain are shown in Figure 2-2.

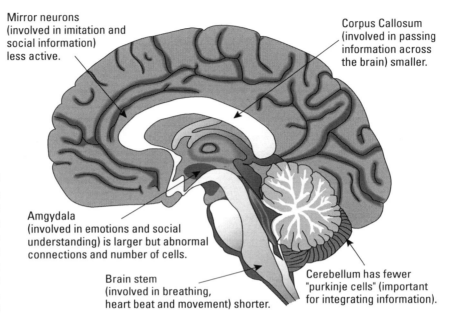

Mirror neurons
(involved in imitation and
social information)
less active.

Corpus Callosum
(involved in passing
information across
the brain) smaller.

Amgydala
(involved in emotions and social
understanding) is larger but abnormal
connections and number of cells.

Brain stem
(involved in breathing,
heart beat and movement) shorter.

Cerebellum has fewer
"purkinje cells" (important
for integrating information).

Figure 2-1:
Summary
of findings
of struc-
tural brain
studies on
people with
ASCs.

Hypothesising about the influence of hormones

Recently, scientists have found that hormones may play a part in the development of characteristics associated with ASCs. Higher levels of testosterone in the womb may influence the development of characteristics that are similar to those associated with ASCs (such as being good at mathematics, map reading and computers).

This possible association doesn't mean that testosterone causes autism. It may only be one of the factors involved.

Another hormone that scientists are investigating is oxytocin, which is involved in social behaviour and social understanding. Every woman makes oxytocin when she gives birth and breastfeeds; it helps with bonding between mother and child. Oxytocin is also produced when you're cuddled. Some genes that are involved in making oxytocin are affected in ASCs, and some studies have shown low levels of this hormone in the blood of people with these conditions. Scientists are now exploring the role of oxytocin in ASCs.

Hormone therapies for autism aren't recommended. Not enough research has been done to show whether they work and are safe, and the side effects may be nasty.

Examining the issue of vaccinations

You're probably aware of the measles, mumps and rubella (MMR) vaccination issue. The controversy stemmed from a piece of research carried out by Dr Andrew Wakefield which suggested that the MMR vaccine could cause ASCs.

This research was later discredited after several research studies found there was no link between the MMR vaccine and ASCs, and, in May 2010, the General Medical Council found Dr Andrew Wakefield guilty of serious professional misconduct and he was struck off the medical register.

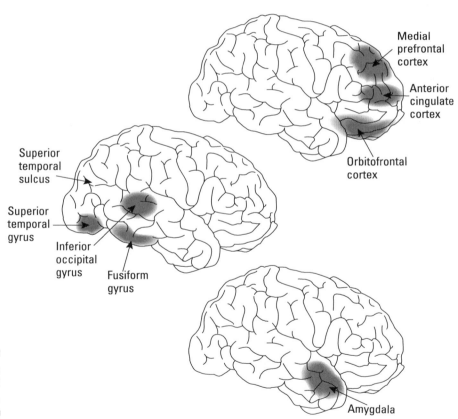

Figure 2-2:
The social brain.

Fears over the safety of the MMR vaccine have caused people to stop getting their children inoculated. As a result, the number of children contracting measles has risen dramatically. Measles is a serious illness that can be fatal.

Sussing out the Psychology of AS

This section covers how the mind works in AS. Not the biology or nitty gritty genetics, but the differences in the ways people think and see the world.

Theory of mind, empathising and systemising

When someone tells you that his or her father has died, you may feel sympathetic. You imagine how the person must be feeling. If your own father is no longer alive, you may empathise with the person, saying something like "I know how you feel." But knowing how other people feel is really difficult for people with an ASC.

Similarly, imagining yourself "in someone else's shoes" doesn't come easily. If you're at a party and see your friend look at you and then at the door, you probably infer that he or she wants to leave. People with an ASC may not pick up on this body language and eye gaze as a social hint.

The ability to see something from someone else's perspective and to imagine how the person must feel in a particular situation (and that they may feel completely differently to how you do) is called *theory of mind*. People with an ASC have difficulty with things that involve theory of mind, which means that social interaction is hard and social behaviour unpredictable (imagine not being able to know how someone is feeling and then trying to say the right thing).

People with an ASC may also take language very literally and not understand its social meaning. For example, if a teacher tells a student with AS to "pull your socks up", then that person will reach for their socks and pull them up. They won't be able to infer that the teacher really meant to say "You should work harder."

When talking to someone on the autism spectrum, use literal language and explain idioms.

Reading the mind in the eyes

Part of the difficulty of understanding other people's thoughts and feelings comes from a problem with recognising and understanding emotions. In a fun test conducted by the Autism Research Centre at the University of Cambridge, people with and without AS were asked to decide how someone was feeling based on looking at just their eyes. People with AS found this task much more difficult than those without.

On the other hand, people with AS were much better at understanding physics tests than those without. Professor Simon Baron-Cohen at the University of Cambridge thinks this outcome is because people with AS are poor at empathising (understanding and acting on emotions) but good at systemising (understanding systems, rules and logic).

Having AS makes it difficult to understand social situations. A person with AS may not have an understanding of other people's thoughts and feelings, and may find it hard to empathise. These difficulties make life in the social world that we live in very challenging.

On the plus side, people with AS may be very good (or even better than people without AS) at systemising. *Systemising* is the ability to understand systems such as those related to cars, computers, maths or physics. Things that have clear, predictable rules tend to be systems. People with AS often really like systems, and may collect model dinosaurs or take detailed notes of weather patterns. Lots of different types of system exist, ranging from train timetables to complex physics and maps. Even music is a system.

Crucially, social behaviour cannot be systemised. You may say one thing to a person and he or she may be pleased, but if you say exactly the same thing to someone else he or she may be upset or angry. Social behaviour is just not logical. You have to be able to understand other people's minds to get to grips with the social world. People with AS find this very difficult.

 If you're a parent or teacher of a person with AS, encourage the person's natural interests and ability to understand systematic things. Use such activities as a reward or as a way to build self-esteem.

Weak central coherence

Most people with an ASC have an excellent eye for detail. They can easily spot changes that may be un-noticeable to others, for example a table mat that has been shifted 1 centimetre to the left on their dining room table.

When thinking about employment, remember that tasks involving focused, detailed work can really suit someone on the autism spectrum. You can find out more about employment in chapter 7.

Psychologists call a detailed thinking style *weak central coherence*. While this helps you focus on details, having weak central coherence can cause problems. You may not be so good at getting the general gist of things or integrating information to form a bigger picture. You may have difficulty relating what you learn in one context to another context. When making decisions, people with AS may focus on the details of the decision rather than on the bigger picture or the context.

People with AS need to learn new skills in lots of different contexts. They may not relate what they learn in school to home and vice versa. They may need help to see the wider consequences when making decisions.

Language may also be affected by weak central coherence. For example, if you were to read aloud "She had a *tear* in her eye" and "She had a *tear* in her dress," you'd pronounce *tear* differently each time because of the context of the rest of the sentence. Because people with AS are more focused on the details than the whole sentence, they may pronounce *tear* incorrectly.

People with AS may take longer to understand the bigger picture or the wider context. They may get hung up on small details.

Problems with executive function

Executive function is the ability to do the following things:

- Plan
- Control your actions and impulses
- Stay on topic and not go off on a tangent
- Shift attention between one thing and another

People with AS have difficulties with tasks that involve doing these things. Problems with executive function may possibly explain the repetitive behaviour seen in those with ASCs. Having problems with executive function may mean you find it hard to organise yourself, pay your bills on time, do your homework or change activity quickly. This can really affect your day-to-day life. It may also mean you find it hard to control your impulses. If you get angry, for example, you may not be able to stop yourself shouting at the person you're angry with, even if you know that you shouldn't. Maybe you can't stop yourself from saying to the chubby lady in the supermarket, "You're fat." Alongside the social difficulties, experiencing problems with executive function can make life for people with AS very hard.

People with AS may find it difficult to concentrate on one subject, control their anger or stop themselves from saying things they've been told not to say. You can help them by being patient, and giving them more guidance and support. Needing support with day-to-day tasks such as paying the bills and planning what to have for dinner is also likely.

Strengths of the psychological theories

Psychological theories are really helpful in increasing our understanding and giving people without AS an appreciation of what it must be like to have it. The social aspect of AS is arguably the most significant. Everything to do with social behaviour — the social world, social interaction and social communication — is difficult for people with this condition. They may experience difficulties and have strengths in other areas, but understanding of the social world is the biggest issue across all aspects of their life.

Psychological theories like theory of mind, weak central coherence and executive function try to explain AS by suggesting differences in the way the mind works. Each theory has its strengths and weaknesses, but none really explains AS fully. Few explain why people with AS are more likely to have sensory sensitivities. Some don't even explain the things that people with AS are good at. Nevertheless, each theory has been valuable and has contributed something new to our understanding of how people with AS see the world differently.

People with AS see the world differently. To understand one another, we need to appreciate that different people have different perspectives.

Continuing Research into the Causes of Asperger's Syndrome

Research has come a really long way in helping us understand the causes of ASCs. Scientists are now moving forward and trying to link up different ways of explaining autism so that the biology fits with the psychology and the psychology fits with the behaviour.

Bringing together the genetics, biology and psychology

We'll only fully understand ASCs when we know how the genetics and environment work together to influence the structure of the brain, and how the brain works. We need the next Einstein to figure it all out.

A few lines of research are moving together, though. One line is the social behaviour part. We know that understanding the social world is hard for people with an ASC, and that this could be because they have difficulties with theory of mind and integrating information from parts into a whole. Scientists have found that some of the areas and functions of the brain that are different in ASCs are involved in understanding the social world. Geneticists have found genes that are important in autism are also those that are crucial for social understanding. So it looks like we're getting there with linking up life with AS, psychology, biology and genetics.

Another significant area of research involves connections across the brain. Some of the genes that are important in ASCs are those that are involved in developing connections in the brain. Some areas of the brain have been shown to have unusual connections in ASCs. We know that people with ASCs focus on detail and find it hard to integrate information to see the wider picture. Behaviour-wise, we also know that they find connecting information from one context to another difficult.

Despite these interesting findings, we're still a long way off knowing what influences the development of ASCs. In particular, we're quite in the dark about what environmental factors and epigenetic factors are important.

Looking into what we still don't know

Lots of research is investigating what causes ASCs. Without help from people with ASCs and their families, none of this could go on. Various autism research centres across the UK advertise for volunteers, in particular through the National Autistic Society website (www.autism.org.uk/research). If you're interested in taking part in research, have a look.

Understanding ASCs and their causes will enable people to appreciate the difficulties faced by those with these conditions. Knowledge and acceptance will allow people with ASCs to enjoy a good quality of life. We still don't know the half of it, and we're certain we're in for some great future discoveries.

Chapter 3

Diagnosing Asperger's Syndrome

. . . .

. . . .

*T*his chapter is about the different types of autism spectrum conditions (ASCs). It also covers the process of getting a diagnosis, either for your child or yourself as an adult. You can pick up some tips about how to ask your GP for a referral to a specialist and find out what to expect from diagnostic assessments. We also give you the info you need to spot other ASCs which are very similar to Asperger's syndrome (AS): *high-functioning autism* (HFA) and *pervasive developmental disorder—not otherwise specified* (PDD—NOS). We explore how you may feel if you've recently received a diagnosis, and what to expect afterwards.

Making a Diagnosis of Asperger's Syndrome

No blood test, brain scan or questionnaire will tell you whether you have an ASC. Although AS has a genetic basis, the genetics are very complicated and no genetic test exists that is able to diagnose it. Some research suggests that hormones may play a part in the causes of ASCs, but no test of hormone levels will tell you whether you have an ASC. So rather than a biological way of diagnosing ASCs, the diagnostic system is based purely on behavioural characteristics. What you were like as a child is important in making a diagnosis. Only qualified professionals who have expertise in ASCs (for example, psychologists, psychiatrists or paediatricians) can make a formal diagnosis of an ASC. In this section you can find out what such professionals look for.

AS is one of several ASCs. These, along with many other conditions, are described in the American Psychiatric Association's *Diagnostic and Statistical Manual of Mental Disorders* (DSM for short) and the World Health Organization's *International Classification of Diseases* (ICD). The terminology these books use can vary, but both books are describing the same conditions. Both of these books are currently being rewritten to include everything researchers have learnt since their last publication. Here we try to provide information on all the diagnoses related to AS.

All ASCs involve difficulties with social interaction, social communication and social imagination.

You may hear difficulties with social interaction, social communication and social imagination referred to as the *triad of impairments* or the *triad*. Nothing to do with Chinese gangsters, this term was first coined by Lorna Wing and Judith Gould, two important experts who first described autism as a spectrum. People still refer to Wing and Gould's triad when talking about autism, and these three areas of difficulties or differences will be covered throughout the book. For more information about the history of autism and important people who have worked in the field of ASCs over the years, read *A History of Autism* by Adam Feinstein (Wiley-Blackwell).

Social interaction difficulties

People on the autism spectrum have difficulty with social interaction. Problems with social behaviour need to be present before the age of three for a diagnosis to be made, because ASCs are developmental conditions, meaning that they exist from a very young age. Social interaction is extremely complex. It involves talking and listening to people, recognising facial expressions and body language, picking up on someone's tone of voice, and understanding even indescribable, subtle social nuances. Friendships and relationships all involve heavy-duty social interaction, and our society in general is geared towards people who are socially skilled. All people on the spectrum find at least one area of social interaction difficult. The main areas involved in diagnosis are covered in the following sections.

Eye gaze, facial expression and body language

People on the spectrum may find making eye contact uncomfortable, or they may not realise that doing so is a social expectation. So one of the key things *diagnosticians* (health professionals who make diagnoses) look out for is unusual eye contact. In ASCs, people make eye contact less frequently, or may do so in an odd or unusual way — perhaps looking at you slightly sideways or in a fleeting, quick way. Others may not know when to stop looking and may seem to be staring.

Two aspects of facial expression can be affected in ASCs. First, people on the spectrum may not be able to recognise facial expressions of emotion very easily, which makes figuring out what people are thinking or feeling really difficult. Second, their own facial expression may be inexpressive or "flat", and they may not show their feelings on their face very often.

Body language and other social clues such as your tone of voice are hard to pick up on for people with an ASC. Also, their own body language may be odd, or they may use very few social gestures such as pointing or moving their hands during conversation. People on the spectrum may have an awkward way of walking. Sometimes they may appear to lack a sense of *personal space* and may stand too close or too far away during social interactions.

People with an ASC may find eye contact difficult, so if you're talking to someone on the spectrum, don't force the person to look at you.

Friendships and relationships

Developing friendships and relationships with other people is extremely difficult for those with an ASC. Some people on the spectrum are simply not interested in other people, and would much rather spend time on their own. Children with an ASC may prefer hanging around with younger or older children rather than with their peer group, or could prefer the company of adults to that of children. Many children and adults on the spectrum really want to have meaningful relationships but don't know how to. For these people, problems with knowing how to have friendships and relationships can cause real distress.

Difficulties with making friends usually stem from a poor understanding of social expectations and a misunderstanding of social signals. For example, people on the spectrum may respond in an unusual way to other people's feelings. Some children on the spectrum may laugh when they see someone hurt themselves, while some adults may not know what to do if they see someone is upset, and thus ignore them rather than asking whether they're okay. Often, people with an ASC may not realise if they've hurt someone else's feelings and won't know what to do about it.

If you're a friend of someone on the spectrum (or anyone else for that matter), don't expect them to pick up on your feelings intuitively. Always tell them how you feel rather than expecting them to understand it from your body language, tone of voice, or facial expression.

People on the spectrum tend not to spontaneously share their enjoyment with other people. They may enjoy something very much but not feel a need to tell someone else and thus share their pleasure.

Going out in big groups of people or attending social gatherings are often really stressful for people on the spectrum, because understanding the social interactions going on around them can be very difficult. As a result, people on the spectrum may avoid social situations and prefer to be on their own or in small groups. Stress and avoidance will clearly contribute to social difficulties, and diagnosticians look out for these signs.

Misunderstanding social contexts

Most people talk quietly in a library or church and know that you shouldn't laugh during a funeral. However, these social norms are not automatically picked up on by people on the spectrum. Some people with ASCs may talk at the same volume no matter where they are, and may not change their behaviour appropriately according to the social context. Some children may not know that saying "You're fat" to a chubby person isn't socially acceptable, even if the statement is true! Many people on the spectrum have to learn social expectations and rules by rote. Some can go a long way in navigating the millions of social rules that society imposes, while others will simply not be able to.

Social stories can help children with ASCs to understand what behaviour is expected in certain social situations. For more on social stories, see Chapter 9 on parenting and check out the website of the Gray Center at www.thegray center.org.

Overall, you can see that social interaction difficulties can have a major impact on someone's life. These difficulties and lack of natural social ability pervade all aspects of a person's life and all characteristics of ASCs.

Social communication difficulties

Some people on the autism spectrum never learn to talk. Others may communicate only with symbols. People with AS, on the other hand, do learn to talk on time. By *on time*, we mean that they start to speak single words by the age of 18 months and speak in two-word phrases by two and a half. In HFA, people learn to talk, but they may be delayed in doing so.

Despite learning to produce words, people with AS, PDD—NOS and HFA do experience difficulties with the social aspects of language. They may find it hard to start a conversation with someone else and may not end a conversation appropriately. For example, instead of using a social phrase such as "nice to talk to you; see you later," they may just walk off.

During conversations, people on the spectrum may find sustaining a to-and-fro dialogue hard. Thinking of things to talk about may be challenging, and small talk may seem pointless and confusing. People on the spectrum may be able to talk for hours about their particular interests, but may not know when or how to change the subject. They may not recognise that the person they're talking to is bored with the conversation, even if the person uses less-than-subtle hints like looking pointedly at the time.

Other language differences that diagnosticians look out for are:

- **Very formal use of language or very pedantic speech:** Children with AS are sometimes described as "little professors", because the words they use are very advanced and quite formal.

- **A monotonous or unusual tone of voice:** Speech may not vary in pitch as much as other people's, and sometimes people on the spectrum speak in an unusual accent or in a child-like tone of voice.

✔ **Not modulating the loudness of speech:** People with AS may always speak more loudly than other people expect them to, or more quietly.

✔ **Difficulties understanding implied meanings of words when said with a particular tone of voice:** For example, "thank you" can mean just what it says, but has the opposite meaning when said in a sarcastic tone of voice. People on the spectrum find it hard to pick up on the subtle social undertones of speech.

✔ **Taking language very literally:** For example, if a teacher asks a student with an ASC to wash his or her hands in the toilet, the student may do just that and wash his or her hands in the toilet bowl. Idioms (for example, "a leopard can't change its spots" or "it's a piece of cake!") can be particularly difficult to understand for people on the spectrum, because they often interpret the words literally.

Social imagination differences, special interests and routines

Social imagination is the third area of potential difficulty that diagnosticians look out for when diagnosing AS. We're not saying that people on the spectrum are unimaginative (in many cases they can be extremely creative and imaginative), but the social side of imagination can be a problem. So imagining what it's like to be someone else will be really hard, whereas drawing a picture from your imagination may not be.

Problems with social imagination also refer to a preference for routine and structure. People on the spectrum often like routines, and may want to do things the same way each time. The routines usually help them to feel safe and less stressed. If a change to the routine is going to happen, a person on the spectrum usually needs lots of warning so that he or she can prepare for the change and not get stressed by it. Routines make the world more predictable and less confusing, and demonstrate to yourself that you have some control over what's happening. Young children may always want to go to school by the same route, or may get upset if they have a new teacher or if the music lesson is changed from a Wednesday to a Friday. Adults may like to structure their day according to the same pattern of activities. If the bus to work is delayed, it may make a person with ASCs very anxious or upset. Diagnosticians will look out for these characteristics when diagnosing ASCs.

Professionals diagnosing ASCs will look out for a liking for sameness and routine and a dislike of change.

People on the spectrum may also have particular special interests. They can be so interested in a particular thing that it appears to be obsessive. For example, many young children on the spectrum are so keen on *Thomas the Tank Engine* that they won't watch any other TV programme and will watch the same episode over and over again without getting bored. Other common interests in children include dinosaurs or interactive collectable card games. Interests may change over time, and sometimes are unusual (for example, being interested in lamp posts or different toilet-flushing mechanisms). Adults may also have special interests, which vary from individual to individual. These interests may form a useful basis for future careers but can become a problem if they take up too much time to the detriment of the person's well-being, or they're the only thing the person talks about when trying to make friends. Interests become a problem if they're restricted to one specific thing and the person pursues this interest to the exclusion of other important activities such as toileting, eating and basic hygiene. Obsessions can also become a problem if they stop the person living life in the way that he or she would like, or if they have serious financial impacts. For example, people with obsessive interests may not have enough money to get by day to day, because all their cash is spent on the special interests.

Diagnosis by system

The diagnostic systems DSM and ICD help diagnosticians to come to a conclusion about whether a person has a particular condition. In ASCs, a person must have at least six of the following diagnostic criteria, and at least one area should have shown abnormal development before three years of age, according to DSM-IV:

Qualitative impairments in social interaction (at least two from this list):

Poor eye contact, facial expression, body posture and gesture to regulate social interaction

A lack of peer relationships appropriate to their age

Doesn't share achievements, interests or pleasure with other people

A lack of social or emotional reciprocity

Qualitative impairments in communication (at least one from this list):

A delay in or absence of development of speech

If speaking, a lack of ability to sustain or initiate conversation

Stereotyped and repetitive use of language or idiosyncratic language

A lack of age-appropriate make-believe play or social imitative play

Restricted repetitive and stereotyped patterns of behaviour, interests and activities (at least two from this list):

Preoccupation with stereotyped and restricted patterns of interest that is abnormal either in intensity or focus

Strict adherence to specific, non-functional routines or rituals

Stereotyped and repetitive motor mannerisms (for example, hand or finger flapping or twisting, or complex whole-body movements)

Persistent preoccupation with parts of objects

Discovering other aspects of AS

In addition to the three main areas of social interaction, social communication and social imagination, people on the spectrum have other characteristics that may or may not be diagnostically significant, but certainly affect the person's life. The most important are *sensory sensitivities*. People on the spectrum are very often over- or under-sensitive to sound, touch, lights, taste and smell. This situation can really affect their quality of life. (Imagine trying to go shopping in a supermarket with a noisy tannoy and flickering lights when your hearing is super-sensitive and the lights make you feel dizzy.) You can learn more about sensory issues in Chapter 12.

Other characteristics include unusual patterns of movement, such as flapping hands, spinning around on the spot, walking on tiptoes or other repetitive movements. These are included in diagnostic criteria. People on the spectrum may enjoy these repetitive movements, and the movements can help them to calm down or give them a sense of control over their lives.

Diagnostic experts are currently reviewing the diagnostic criteria for all ASCs. Keep an eye out on the DSM 5 website (www.dsm5.org) to find out how diagnostic criteria are changing and to give your feedback on new criteria which are due out in 2013.

Professionals can rely too much on the international classification systems. Cut-offs are described, and a person may not receive a diagnosis because he or she does not fit precisely into the systems. This is why a *dimensional* rather than a categorical approach is being advocated by some professionals. The dimensional approach, which covers all aspects of development and each individual's pattern of skills and difficulties, is far more appropriate in describing that individual's needs than just saying he or she has an ASC. This approach is used at the NAS Lorna Wing Centre, and training is offered to professionals in this method of diagnosis of ASCs and all related conditions.

Uncovering the Different Types of ASC

We've run through the main areas of difficulty in ASCs, but you're probably aware that several types of ASC exist. The differences between different diagnoses on the autism spectrum can seem quite minor and can be so subtle that experts simply diagnose someone as having an ASC without specifying further. In this section we describe all the different diagnostic labels on the autism spectrum.

Autism spectrum conditions are just that: a spectrum. This means that people are affected differently and each person is unique.

Classic autism

Classic autism is also known as childhood autism, autistic disorder or just autism. When we talk about a diagnosis of classic autism we mean a diagnostician using any of these terms. Someone with classic autism very clearly meets the diagnostic criteria for an ASC, often with a "full house" of social interaction problems, social communication problems, unusual movements, unusual speech, rigid thinking and sensory difficulties along with their communication problems. A person's development needs to show differences before the age of three for classic autism to be diagnosed. In particular, language development is delayed.

Learning disabilities may be present, in which case the diagnosis is sometimes termed *low-functioning* autism. People with a very low-functioning form of ASC may not show any interest in other people and may seem in their own world. Some people with classic autism don't learn to talk using words and may not see the point in communicating. Some people with classic autism may never learn to communicate, while others learn to communicate using computers or symbols. Some do learn to talk, but only use single words or phrases. Repetitive movements, technically called stereotypies, such as body rocking, hand flapping or spinning around in circles are more common in classic autism than in others forms of ASC.

Childhood disintegrative disorder (CDD)

CDD is a scary-sounding ASC, defined as what happens when a child develops normally until two years old and then develops quite severe autism by losing some or all speech, bladder and bowel control, co-ordination, social skills and play skills. Children with CDD usually also start moving repetitively (displaying stereotypy) and developing other signs of autism. Fortunately, CDD is very, very rare, and the lost skills and abilities usually return to a degree.

High-functioning autism

The term high-functioning autism (HFA) is often used to mean any form of ASC in which the person doesn't have learning disability and has good self-care skills like being able to wash and dress in the morning with minimal help. However, HFA is also used by some researchers to describe an ASC where language developed late but then the child learnt to talk fluently and doesn't have learning disability. Experts are undecided about whether HFA and AS are the same.

Asperger's syndrome

The key diagnostic differences between AS and other ASCs are that people with AS learn to talk at the developmentally appropriate age (which is to use single words by 18 months old and phrases by two and a half) and their IQ isn't unusually low (that is, it isn't 70 or less). Nevertheless, if you have AS, then you meet the criteria for an ASC.

If you have AS, you're probably more able than others with an ASC, and you have fluent language. AS is often not diagnosed until much later than other ASCs, because children may seem okay or even very bright. Concerns tend to arise as a result of social interaction problems such as not making friends at school, avoiding social situations and so on. These sorts of issue are often not picked up until later, for example when a child starts nursery or primary school.

Pervasive developmental disorder—not otherwise specified (PDD—NOS)

You get a diagnosis of PDD—NOS if you don't meet enough of the diagnostic criteria in the DSM to get a diagnosis of childhood autism, AS (or Asperger's disorder as it's called in DSM) or CDD, because these are the only four ASCs it recognises. You may not show enough problems to meet the criteria for another ASC, or you may have developed normally and then regressed, but not severely enough for CDD, or your behaviour may have been fine before you developed signs of autism at, say, five years old. In any of these and many other cases that don't fit the other criteria, you may be given a diagnosis of PDD—NOS. You may come across the term PDDU (pervasive developmental disorder, unspecified), which is the ICD name for PDD—NOS. While this isn't a very helpful diagnosis because it's so unspecific, it can be useful if you need a diagnosis in order to get access to the services you need. See the later section "Getting a Diagnosis of Asperger's Syndrome" for more on how getting a diagnosis can help you.

Atypical autism

Atypical autism is a confusing term. It is found only in the ICD, not in the DSM and is only used by experts. Unfortunately, different experts use the term to mean different things. Some use the term atypical autism to mean PDD—NOS; others to mean a specific ASC which they can distinguish from PDD—NOS; and still others use it for yet another type of very low-functioning autism. Atypical autism is also diagnosed in people with severe problems in understanding language. So despite being specific, unlike PDD—NOS, atypical autism is so confusing that the diagnosis is really only useful for getting access to services.

Autism and autistic traits

We can probably all relate to some of the diagnostic criteria for autism to a certain degree. Lots of people sometimes dread a social gathering and would rather stay at home curled up on the sofa. Others of us may enjoy routine and get a bit worried when our lives change. But this doesn't mean we all have an ASC. The key difference between autism and *autistic traits* comes in at this point. We all may have a few (or more) autistic traits. By these we mean characteristics or tendencies that are seen in autism, but are shared by many of us, and can include, among other things:

- ✔ Not being particularly good at expressing emotions or picking up on other's emotions
- ✔ Being somewhat socially awkward and finding it hard to make friends
- ✔ Enjoying routine and predictability (sometimes being slightly inflexible)
- ✔ Preferring to be on your own rather than with others
- ✔ Noticing details that other people do not
- ✔ Liking to collect things (for example, species of beetle, cars, stamps)

People only gets a diagnosis of ASC if their autistic traits are severe and stopping them from getting on with day-to-day life.

Autism is a spectrum (a continuous range), and the spectrum carries on into people who don't have a diagnosis of ASC. These people have some autistic traits, but because they don't have very many or their traits don't affect their day-to-day life, they don't get a diagnosis of ASC.

The broader autism phenotype

The *broader autism phenotype* refers to people who have a set of autistic traits or autism-like tendencies which don't affect them living their lives, so are not serious enough to warrant a diagnosis of an ASC. People who belong to the broader autism phenotype may have several autistic traits and may show autistic tendencies. The person may have some behaviour that's like that of people with autism, but they don't have an ASC itself.

Phenotype means what a person is like on the outside (in this case, how they behave). What you're like on the outside is determined by your genes and your upbringing (nature and nurture). Broader autism phenotype means the way people are that's a bit like autism, but is not quite autism itself.

Often, the relatives of someone with a confirmed diagnosis may fit into the profile of the broader autism phenotype. Autism is known to have some genetic causes (see Chapter 2), and several researchers look into the genes involved in autism by looking at the genetics of belonging to the broader autism pheno-type. This research has helped us learn a lot about the genetics of autism.

You can get hold of various tests that measure how many autistic traits a person has, but remember that these tests cannot and do not diagnose ASCs. Diagnosis can only be done by a qualified professional, because ASCs are more complicated than a list of personality characteristics.

Other conditions associated with ASCs

Other conditions are often associated with ASCs, in the sense that if you have one of them you're quite likely also to have an ASC.

If you have an ASC, you're not likely to have one of these conditions; it's just that the chance of having one is higher than for the general population.

Some physical conditions that affect the brain and often co-occur with ASCs are:

- ✔ **Tuberous sclerosis complex (TSC):** A genetic disorder that causes benign growths, particularly in the brain, heart, lungs, kidneys, eyes and skin.

- ✔ **Fragile X syndrome (FXS):** Caused by a chromosomal abnormality, which, like Down's syndrome, can be diagnosed by a chromosomal test. People with the syndrome usually have a learning disability, a long face, protruding ears and low muscle tone. They also have mild face-blind-ness, are often shy and have problems with eye contact and memory. Because of problems with socialising, FXS can be confused with the autism spectrum, but a specialist ASC diagnostician will distinguish between the syndromes.

- ✔ **Brain damage after brain infection:** Brain infections such as encephali-tis can damage the brain permanently, and some people have developed the characteristics of ASC following such damage.

Other conditions that commonly co-occur with ASCs include:

- ✔ **Attention deficit hyperactivity disorder (ADHD or ADD):** A develop-mental disorder that affects a person's attention, concentration and activity levels. A child with ADHD may not be able to concentrate for long periods, and may be extremely active and sometimes impulsive.

- ✔ **Tic disorders such as Tourette's syndrome:** These disorders are charac-terised by involuntary twitches or shouting out words or sounds.

- ✔ **Dyslexia:** A specific learning difficulty that affects reading, spelling and word sounds.

- ✔ **Dyspraxia (sometimes called developmental co-ordination disorder):** A specific learning difficulty that affects co-ordination of movements, so that the person appears very clumsy.

Asperger's syndrome: to be or not to be?

A review of the current diagnostic system is currently underway by the American Psychiatric Association. A new version of the diagnostic manual, the *DSM-5*, will be published in 2013. Note the change from roman to arabic numerals in the title. Experts are examining the different diagnostic labels for ASCs and the behavioural criteria for getting a diagnosis. Part of the discussion has revolved around the different labels for all the ASCs. Some believe that the term *autistic spectrum disorder* should be used for all diagnoses, instead of the different labels such as AS or PDD—NOS. Rather than giving a specific name to the person's diagnosis, an emphasis will be placed on the needs and characteristics of the individual, providing a more detailed picture of how autism affects the person's life. The criteria will also include sensory difficulties for the first time. Similar discussions are determining the future of AS in the ICD (the eleventh edition, *ICD-11*), which is due to be published in 2015. While we were writing *Asperger's Syndrome For Dummies*, the debate around the label AS was continuing. Some believe that it does not add any new information about the person. Other people who have the diagnosis feel that the label is part of their identity and do not want to see it go. Log on to www.dsm5.org for more information.

In each case, the co-occurring condition or physical disorder needs the appropriate treatment, and the ASC needs additional appropriate attention. You can find out more about these co-occurring conditions in Chapter 4.

We prefer to use the term *co-occurring*, but many doctors use the more dramatic technical term *comorbid* or talk about *comorbidity*.

Getting a Diagnosis of Asperger's Syndrome

Different people react in different ways when they get a diagnosis of AS. Some people really want to know what makes them feel the way they do, or want to find out why their child behaves differently to other children. A diagnosis for these people provides an explanation and often prompts a sigh of "So that's why I feel like that!"

Other people feel that having a diagnosis is unfairly labelling them. If you have a label, people treat you differently. You may feel having a label is demoralising and suggests that you have a disability.

Whatever your feelings, the fact of the matter is that a diagnosis gives you access to services and support. A particular diagnosis acts as a signpost for health professionals, teachers and other people in your life to find the right ways of supporting, teaching and being with you. An early diagnosis may give a child access to appropriate early intervention or teaching strategies that will give him or her a better foundation for future development. If you have a diagnosis, you are legally classed as having a disability. This classification can have implications for many aspects of your life, such as employment; you're legally entitled to access to a disability employment adviser who should help you find a job that matches your skills.

In this section we go through all the aspects of getting a diagnosis: how it's done, how early you can get one (and how late!) and what to expect from a diagnostic assessment.

A diagnosis of AS can only be given by a qualified professional or team of professionals. Because AS can be difficult to diagnose, we recommend going to a professional with expertise in ASCs.

Finding out how early a diagnosis can be made

The earlier a diagnosis of AS (or any ASC) is made, the earlier you can get access to support, services and appropriate educational provision. However, getting a referral for a professional diagnosis can take many years because a lack of awareness of AS still exists among health professionals, teachers and the general public.

Getting a diagnosis as a child

In theory, a child can be accurately diagnosed with an ASC from as young as two years old. Any earlier is very difficult, because the child is too young for anyone to tell what may be causing its difficulties. AS is usually diagnosed somewhat later than lower-functioning ASCs because the characteristics are more subtle. Also, because a child with AS starts to talk on time and has no intellectual difficulties, people may not be concerned until the child is older and starts having difficulties in social situations at nursery or primary school. Often, a health professional or teacher may raise concerns with you about your child and will point you in the direction of people who can help in your area.

If you have concerns about your young child, always talk to your GP. A GP should refer you to the right specialists. Don't give up asking for referrals, because sometimes GPs don't pick up on the early signs of AS.

Getting a diagnosis as an adult

Although awareness of AS is still quite poor, it's better than it was 20 or 30 years ago. This means that many adults who have AS are still undiagnosed, because people weren't aware of AS when they were young. As children, they may have been labelled naughty or odd, or been misdiagnosed with another psychological disorder (see Chapter 4 for common misdiagnoses). You can get a diagnosis as an adult, and some people find this a real relief and an explanation for lots of problems that have occurred in their lives. However, only a few specialist adult diagnostic services are available across the UK, so getting diagnosed can be time consuming and difficult. Unfortunately, few services for people with AS are being sought by commissioners (people who buy diagnostic services from service providers). This means that service providers have no money to provide a specialist support or diagnostic service.

The Autism Act is a law recommending that local authorities provide suitable services and support for adults with autism. This means that the situation for adults with autism may improve. For more information, go to www.autism. org.uk/autismact2009.

John's diagnosis at 59 years of age

All my life, I have felt slightly out of synchronisation with the way that the world seems to operate and how people apparently think and communicate, without being able to put my finger on why.

In adult life, I held down a number of very responsible jobs in which I endeavoured to be reliable, conscientious and efficient, and was noticeably detail orientated. Each ended in disaster (not altogether of my own making) simply because I seemed to be blind to the inane complexities of company and workplace politics, and I seemed to be very easily victimised.

I had suffered periods of inexplicable depression and generalised anxiety and confusion throughout my adult life, which had led my GP to refer me to a psychiatrist in London and to a psychotherapy unit. Unfortunately, this was many years ago, before AS was better known. These referrals got nowhere: they were an expensive waste of time for everyone involved, including me. Remarkable ignorance about AS on the part of GPs, psychiatrists and mental health workers is still evident, although the situation is beginning to improve.

I was very fortunate in Liverpool to have encountered a probably unique combination of people: a very supportive social worker who was able to put me in touch with an NHS psychotherapist who knew of AS. In turn, and on her advice, I was able to approach my GP for a referral to the Liverpool Asperger Team for a clear yes/no diagnosis. My GP knows a lot about AS — she is in Liverpool, literally down the road from the Liverpool Asperger Team, and gave me a fair and thorough hearing before referring me. It turned out eventually on diagnosis that I have AS. Suddenly, a light went on in my brain and my life changed for the better.

For me, this diagnosis came as a mixed blessing. On the one hand, the scales dropped from my eyes. The diagnosis of AS was easily the most plausible explanation for the way that I am and the ways in which I had persistently "got it wrong" throughout my working, social and personal life. On the other, I found out only in late middle age when it was far too late to realistically start afresh with a new job and set of relationships armed with this knowledge. I only wish I had known about my AS earlier in my life when I might have been able to manage my life and career differently.

Knowing where to go for a diagnosis

If you suspect that you or your child may have an ASC, then you may wonder where to go to raise your concerns, ask questions and ultimately get a diagnosis, if that is appropriate. In this section we go through who to contact, what information to take, and tips to make the process easier for children and adults seeking a diagnosis of AS.

Diagnoses for children

If you think your child may have AS, you need to visit your GP and ask for a referral to a consultant psychologist, psychiatrist or diagnostic service with a good understanding of ASCs. Diagnosis is free through the NHS if your GP refers you for diagnostic assessment.

Some GPs are less knowledgeable about ASCs than others. If your GP does not refer your child for further assessment and you have concerns, then be persistent!

Take a list of behaviours that concern you and that you think indicate that your child may have an ASC to discuss with your GP. Keeping a diary of behaviours that concern you may help you to remember them and can provide evidence of any difficulties for professionals to consider.

If you are seeking a diagnostic assessment for your child, you may see one of many health professionals, whether a clinical psychologist, a child psychiatrist or a paediatrician. You may be referred to a multidisciplinary team of professionals who will have expertise in different areas. They will work together to understand the reasons behind your child's difficulties.

Diagnoses for adults

If you're an adult and think you may have AS, the first person to talk to is probably your GP. Book an appointment to talk through your concerns and the reasons why you think you may have AS. Your GP should then refer you to a specialist psychologist or psychiatrist who will be able to make a diagnosis.

Due to a lack of awareness, some GPs may not know much about AS. If this is the case, take some information with you (for example from this book) that describes AS, and a list of things that make you think you may have the condition.

You may be seeing a psychologist or psychiatrist already for another difficulty (such as depression or anxiety). If this is the case, you can talk to that person first about your concerns regarding AS, instead of your GP.

Fewer specialist teams are available in the UK for adult ASC diagnosis than for children, which means it may be more difficult and take longer to get an appointment for a diagnosis if you're seeking one in adulthood.

Going private

You may prefer to seek a diagnosis privately, because the waiting lists are shorter for private assessment. The cost of private assessments varies, as do the services and post-diagnostic support offered, so make sure you get quotes and find out what's offered by a few different services before you decide. You can expect to pay more than £700, though.

Make sure the individual or team you go to for diagnosis is experienced in ASCs.

Discovering what to expect from a diagnostic assessment

Going for an assessment to see whether you have an ASC can be daunting. Here we explain what the assessment process is like for children and adults.

Diagnostic assessments with children and young people

Different areas of the country use different procedures in diagnostic assessments. If your child is assessed by a multidisciplinary team, the child may have several individual assessments with different professionals. These professionals range from psychologists and psychiatrists to speech and language therapists, occupational therapists, doctors and nurses. The results of these individual assessments are then brought together and a decision is made about diagnosis based on all the results. If the child is assessed by one professional rather than a team, he or she may have only one assessment session or several assessments with the same professional before getting a decision about diagnosis.

During the assessment, the professionals will spend a lot of time talking to the parents or carers to find out about the child's difficulties and early development. You may have an informal chat or a more formal interview with specific questions. You may be asked to fill in checklists or questionnaires about your child. It's also important that the professional spends time assessing your child's abilities and difficulties. This assessment can be done through specific tests, observations and talking, or by playing or interacting with your child. Some professionals may also want to observe a child at school.

Diagnostic assessments can take a whole day, so be prepared. Ask the professionals how long the diagnostic assessment process will take. Be prepared to answer a lot of questions, and try to remember as much as you can about your child's early development.

After all the assessments, you should be given a written report with the findings and details of any diagnoses that have been made. The report will also include recommendations for support that your child needs. You may be given this report straight after the assessments or it may be posted to you later on. When you receive the report, make sure you understand any jargon that may be unclear and ask for clarification of any terms about which you're uncertain. In the glossary at the end of this book we've tried to include all of the terms you may find in a diagnostic report.

Just because you went along for a diagnosis of AS, that doesn't mean you'll get a diagnosis of AS or even a diagnosis of any ASC. You'll still get a report, though, detailing your signs and symptoms along with any diagnosis that the diagnostician has made.

Diagnostic assessments in adulthood

An important part of developing an understanding of a person to see whether they have an ASC is talking to someone who's known the person since childhood. This person is usually a parent or carer, though it can sometimes be a sibling. Obviously, talking to a parent about an adult son or daughter is more difficult, and may not be possible if the parents of the individual in question have died. The information that professionals seek to find out from parents (or someone who's known that person since early childhood) is necessary to get a picture of how the individual developed as a child. For example, did the child start talking in single words and phrases on time? Did the child have any problems joining in with childhood social games?

Because AS is a developmental condition, professionals need to find out as much as they can about how the person developed as a child. Take someone with you who knew you then (ideally your parent or whoever cared for you as a small child). If this isn't possible, try to remember as much as you can about your childhood, and if you have any videos (for example, you at a birthday party), bring them with you because they could help.

Understanding what should happen after getting a diagnosis

Getting a diagnosis of an ASC is just the start! A diagnosis should act as a key to open the door to suitable services and support. Unfortunately, this process isn't always as easy as it should be. Many parents and individuals on the spectrum feel left alone after getting a diagnosis, with nowhere to go for help. Different areas also have different services, so whether something is provided in your area is a matter of luck. This section should help. We can point you in the right direction, but you may still need to fight and be persistent to access the services you need.

For children

If your child has recently been diagnosed with an ASC, you may want to look for support or help in the following areas:

- ✓ Coming to terms with a diagnosis
- ✓ Accessing parent training to help with communication and behaviour
- ✓ Getting appropriate assistance for your child at school
- ✓ Caring for your child
- ✓ Dealing with financial matters
- ✓ Knowing what therapies and interventions may be appropriate
- ✓ Meeting other parents and families or attending support groups

Many of these issues are covered in Chapters 9, 10, 13, 14 and 15 of this book. To find out what's available in your area, get in touch with your local authority, ask the person who diagnosed your child what help and support can be provided, and contact local autism charities or national charities such as the National Autistic Society (NAS).

 The NAS Helpline (0845 070 4004) can point you in the right direction for services in your area and can listen to and support you with any concerns or queries you may have. The Signpost service can also show you what's available in your area based on your individual requirements (www.autism.org.uk/signpost).

For adults

If you're an adult who's just received a diagnosis of an ASC, the post-diagnostic support is even more variable than it is for children who've just been diagnosed. Support you may want to seek (and fight for) includes help with the following:

- ✓ Coming to terms with your diagnosis
- ✓ Dealing with higher education or employment (including access to a disability employment adviser)
- ✓ Managing relationships
- ✓ Gaining financial assistance
- ✓ Sorting out housing issues
- ✓ Accessing social services
- ✓ Meeting other adults who have an ASC
- ✓ Finding someone who can act as an advocate on your behalf

For further information about these areas, see Chapters 7, 8 and 11. You can also get information from the same sources as those listed for children in the preceding section.

Looking at the pros and cons of diagnosis

Some people feel very relieved when they or their child receives an accurate diagnosis of an ASC. Other people feel that a label stigmatises them and aren't happy using the label to describe themselves. Thinking about the pros and cons of diagnosis and what it means for you, your child and family is worthwhile. We list some of the pros and cons that you may want to consider here.

First, the pros:

- ✔ An accurate diagnosis gives people with ASCs and their families access to the right specialist support and services.
- ✔ An early diagnosis for children provides access to early intervention, which may increase opportunity and quality of life later on.
- ✔ A diagnosis acts as a signpost to professionals, family and friends to help them know how best to support the individual.
- ✔ A diagnosis may help you to understand yourself and the struggles or successes you have faced in your life.
- ✔ A diagnosis may bring a sense of relief.
- ✔ A diagnosis may give access to appropriate financial help.

Now the cons:

- ✔ You may feel that having a label is demeaning.
- ✔ A diagnosis emphasises disability and makes people see a label rather than an individual person.
- ✔ A diagnosis may make you feel upset, guilty or angry.
- ✔ A diagnosis may be difficult to come to terms with.

Whatever your thoughts, thinking things through and working out what a diagnosis means for you and your family is important.

The National Autistic Society has produced a DVD and CD-ROM resource called *Being Me*. It's aimed at young people and adults who've recently been diagnosed as being on the autism spectrum and covers many common questions to do with:

- ✔ Your feelings about your diagnosis
- ✔ The positives and negatives of being on the autism spectrum
- ✔ Whether to tell people about your diagnosis
- ✔ The support you may need

Being Me includes recordings of people on the spectrum talking about their feelings about their diagnoses, and has worksheets and ideas for group discussion. You can get it from `www.autism.org.uk` at the online store.

Without a diagnosis, you'll be unlikely to get access to the correct specialist services, support and financial assistance. Research has shown that the right support and services have a positive impact and improve quality of life considerably.

Discussing self-diagnosis

After reading about AS in the media, in books and on the Internet, some adults recognise features of AS in themselves. You may want to "diagnose" yourself as having an ASC. If all you're looking for is an explanation of the way you are, then diagnosing yourself may be enough for you. However, only diagnoses from professionals can get you access to services, support and financial aid.

You can access Internet questionnaires and iPhone applications to work out how many autistic traits you have. Although filling in a questionnaire to see whether you have certain traits that are characteristic of ASCs is interesting, these questionnaires aren't diagnostic (despite what some of them claim). ASCs are a lot more complex than a list of traits that you have or don't have. Take care not to trivialise diagnosis by taking the results of these surveys and questionnaires to be more than just an indication. Every single person will have some autistic traits. Whether a person should get a diagnosis of an ASC can only be determined by qualified, experienced professionals who collect a lot of details about a person and his or her life and development.

Most people who have a lot of autistic traits don't have an ASC. Instead, they're nearly on the spectrum, in what's called the broader autism phenotype.

Coming to Terms with a Diagnosis

Getting a diagnosis on the spectrum may be a relief or a great shock. Either way, it will change the way you view your life and is bound to take some getting used to. Some feelings you may have and some challenges you face in coming to terms with a diagnosis are covered in this section.

For parents

You may have always wondered why your child was different to other children, and a diagnosis on the autism spectrum may help explain all of that. This section details some of the common feelings you may have after a diagnosis for your child, and some tips about telling your child about the diagnosis.

Your feelings

You may feel reassured that the way in which your child behaves isn't your fault or anything to do with your parenting skills. On the other hand, you may feel great shock. You're unlikely to know much about ASCs when you receive the diagnosis, so you may feel lost and worried, with no idea of what to do now or what this means for your family.

You may feel sadness or anger that your child may not achieve the things you'd imagined and live the life you'd wanted for him or her.

All of these feelings are completely normal. Feeling sad, relieved, happy, worried, angry, guilty or any other emotion when your child is diagnosed with an ASC is okay.

Remember that having an ASC doesn't mean your child has to suffer throughout his or her whole life. People on the spectrum can and do achieve their potential and have enjoyable, fulfilling lives. With the right support, love and guidance, people on the spectrum can achieve many things and be happy with their lives.

Getting a diagnosis doesn't change your child. He or she is still exactly the same person as before the diagnosis. You may need time to adapt to things and to begin to accept your child and the diagnosis. Remember that the label doesn't define your child; it just helps you to understand your child and gives you, your child and your family access to the support you need.

Make sure you talk to people about your feelings. Be open with your loved ones about how you feel, try to meet other parents who've been through the same things, and share your thoughts and emotions. Don't be shy or embarrassed about talking to a professional if you feel really down, depressed or anxious. Doing so can really help.

As you come to terms with the diagnosis and find out more about ASCs, you'll begin to adjust to the situation. Of course, you'll have days when you can't cope, feel frustrated or believe that life isn't fair. Have a good cry or shout and let it out of your system with your friends. Sometimes staying positive is very difficult, and when you feel really low, make sure you have someone you can turn to for help.

You need to look after yourself as well as the rest of your family. Take time off to do things you enjoy, refresh yourself and chill out. You'll be helping everyone in the long run if you look after yourself from time to time. See Chapters 9 and 10 (on parenting) for more information.

Look out for local support groups and charities that you can turn to for information, advice and support. To see what's available in your area, go to www.autism.org.uk/signpost.

When should I tell my child?

Many parents worry about when and how to tell their child about his or her diagnosis. Only you can decide when to tell your child, and your decision will depend on your personal family circumstances.

You may decide that it's best to tell your child straight away. Doing so may help a child understand all the assessments he or she may have been having and any extra support given subsequently. Knowing about the diagnosis may help your child understand his or her differences and difficulties.

On the other hand, you may decide to wait until your child is a bit older before you tell him or her about the diagnosis. If your child is older, he or she may be able to understand it better. You may also feel that you want your child to have as "normal" a childhood as possible without the knowledge of a diagnosis making him or her feel different. Think about whether you've decided not to tell your child because you're putting off a difficult conversation. If you are, then the longer you leave it, the more difficult it may become to tell your child. Once your child hits puberty, he or she will have enough going on without finding out that you've been concealing something. If you decide to leave telling your child until he or she is 11 or more, have some very good reasons for doing so.

When you do decide to tell your child, make sure you are both calm, you are not interrupted and you leave plenty of time for your child to ask questions.

Some books that may help you tell your child about his or her diagnosis are *Talking Together about an Autism Diagnosis: A Guide for Parents and Carers of Children with an Autism Spectrum Disorder* by Rachel Pike (National Autistic Society). The NAS also has some useful tips and factsheets (www.autism.org.uk).

For adults

No matter how old you are when you get a diagnosis in adulthood, you're bound to re-evaluate your whole life history. You may have stumbled through life, struggling on and just about managing, unsure of why your relationships or career have had limited success. A diagnosis may put a lot of your life into perspective and help you understand things better.

You may feel angry that you weren't diagnosed when you were younger. Until recently, lack of awareness and recognition of ASCs, particularly AS, meant that many adults with the condition went undiagnosed for most if not all of their lives. You may feel that your lack of access to all the specialist services and support that young people diagnosed nowadays get is unfair. This may make you feel bitter and angry.

If you've been misdiagnosed with a different disorder such as depression, schizophrenia or something else, then getting the correct, accurate diagnosis can be a real help. The diagnosis will help you gain understanding from others and help you understand yourself.

The picture for support and services for adults with AS is still very patchy. Some areas have relatively good services to support adults, others have virtually nothing. You may wonder what the point of getting a diagnosis is if nothing in your area is available to help you afterwards.

You may have a partner and children of your own to tell about your diagnosis. They may feel upset, relieved or worried. You may be concerned about telling them and about how this may affect your family life. You may want to ask the professional who made your diagnosis to help you tell your partner and family about what ASCs are and how it affects you and your life. Telling your loved ones at a quiet time, with no distractions and plenty of time for them to ask questions may help.

Telling other people such as friends and colleagues about your recent diagnosis can be a worry. You may be scared that they won't want to be friends with you any more or may behave differently towards you at work. Who you tell about your diagnosis and when is up to you. You may find it helpful to tell some people but not others. You may want to ask someone else to tell people on your behalf. Whatever you decide, it's your personal decision, so don't feel pressured into telling people if you don't want to.

Receiving a diagnosis of AS or any ASC isn't easy. You may feel a mixture of different emotions from relief to anger to frustration. Try to talk about your feelings with people who know you. Talking to a professional such as your GP or a psychologist may also help.

You could talk to other people who were diagnosed in adulthood — some people find doing so helps. You can join an online community or a social group. More information on linking up with other people is provided in Chapters 6 and 11.

Chapter 4

Discovering Additional Diagnoses in Asperger's Syndrome

*I*f you have Asperger's syndrome (AS), you may have found ways to manage life. On the other hand, you may find yourself in the group of people who aren't coping well. Studies show that up to 65 per cent of those who have AS also have a mental health disorder. A mental health disorder is any disorder or disability of mind which affects how you think and/or feel. In AS, the social communication difficulties experienced can cause disorders like anxiety and clinical depression. You can learn to manage these, and it's not necessary for you to think that suffering is inevitable. In this chapter you'll learn about mental disorders and how to deal with them.

In some cases you or a family member may have been given an alternative diagnosis to Asperger's and you are left trying to figure out why that is and what to do about it. You don't want to question the "experts" and may be uncertain as to what to do with this information. We'll look at how other conditions which occasionally confuse even the experts can look like AS, but are separate and quite different.

Psychological Conditions Found with AS

Having AS can be challenging, but when it's missed or confused it makes things just that bit harder. For a start, you may never have received a diagnosis in childhood. Quiet children who happen to have AS can be seen as "shy" and are conveniently ignored, while children having a meltdown or temper tantrums may be seen as behaving badly and diagnosed with conduct disorder. You feel you can't win.

At other times, professionals only notice the difficulties that happen alongside the AS, for example anxiety or depression, and miss the AS completely. Some studies have shown that up to 65 per cent of people who have AS have an additional mental health condition. This is a really high number, and in this chapter you'll learn about why additional mental health problems may happen, how they're diagnosed and how they can be managed. We start with the more common conditions such as a number of anxiety disorders and depression, and then move on to less common but sometimes difficult-to-manage issues such as drinking too much alcohol.

Uncovering anxiety disorders

The challenges you face if you have AS can cause huge amounts of anxiety. Some studies suggest that 80 per cent of all children on the autism spectrum have anxiety. You may have to think much harder than the average person in social situations, for example. You may be tempted to avoid these situations altogether. Avoidance is one way to reduce the stress of social interaction but, oddly, isolating yourself will only lead to an increase, not decrease, in anxiety and stress in the long run.

Try not always avoiding situations that make you anxious. Challenge yourself to do the thing you are worried about, even if it's for a very short time. That way, you are controlling the anxiety and it is not controlling you.

Several types of anxiety exist. *Social phobia* is anxiety that is specific to social situations. Anxiety about going out at all is called *agoraphobia* (which literally means "fear of the marketplace", although obviously it's not just the marketplace that people are anxious about). Some people never leave the house because of agoraphobia, and it can be quite debilitating. Anxiety may also gradually work its way into every aspect of daily life and become generalised, in which case it is termed *generalised anxiety disorder.*

By reading the previous paragraph, you've probably thought, "Well I definitely get anxious in social situations, and sometimes I don't want to leave the house because I'm worried about what may happen." But having some anxiety isn't the same as having a diagnosable anxiety disorder. Clearly everyone gets anxious at various points in their life — it is totally *normal* to be worried sometimes. In fact, it can be positively beneficial because it is a vital response to danger (known as the "fright, flight, fight response"). Anxiety in such situations is normal. Common triggers of anxiety in all of us include:

✔ Dangerous situations (Gina is currently remembering the time she was lucky enough to be on safari in Africa, but unlucky enough to be stared at by a hungry young lion who was far too close.)

✔ Public performance (needing to go to the loo before giving a presentation)

✔ Meeting new people (this will be worse for people on the spectrum, but most people get a bit worried when they're meeting someone new)

✔ Doing something you've never done before (you worry how to do it and whether you'll do it wrong)

✔ Travelling and going somewhere new (many people are scared of flying, but also people get nervous about travelling to a new place, moving house and so on)

✔ Competition causes anxiety in many people (in fact, so much so for some that they never enter competitions or things where they are compared with others)

We're sure you can add your own things to this list of common situations that make us anxious. The important thing to learn is the difference between this normal anxiety and anxiety that is too high. Anxiety can become an anxiety disorder when it's so bad you stop being able to do things you normally would (for example, go shopping, get to sleep, go to work or school). If you carry on despite the anxiety and it's not too bad, then you're probably fine. If the anxiety takes over your thoughts and actions, then it's time to get some help. However, when anxiety becomes so severe that it interferes with your ability to do things like go shopping, get to sleep or see friends, then experts call this "interference with functioning" and they'll diagnose an anxiety disorder.

When anxiety becomes so overwhelming that you can't get on with your everyday life, then seek help from a GP, psychologist or psychiatrist, because you may have an anxiety disorder that can be treated.

Here is a general principle in mental health: if a disorder is severe enough to be causing "significant" problems in life then you can usually find a diagnosis for it. This way you get the attention you need to be helped and treated.

Anxiety in autism spectrum conditions

Anxiety is common in people on the spectrum. On top of the common triggers for all of us, additional anxiety triggers for people with an autism spectrum condition (ASC) include sensory overload (see Chapter 11), difficulties processing certain types of information (metaphors, requests to summarise information) or anything to do with change. If you are on the spectrum, you'll want to know what to expect before any planned changes take place. "Surprises", lovely as they may be to others, can be disturbing in AS.

If you feel anxious, the sensations you feel in your body can include the following:

✔ An increase in heart rate or palpitations

✔ Shortness of breath and fast breathing

✔ Sweating (maybe sweaty palms in particular)

✔ Going to the loo more often

✔ Shaking

 ✔ Feeling a sense of mild constriction in the chest

 ✔ Feelings of "butterflies" in the stomach

 ✔ Pins and needles

You can also experience a number of thoughts associated with anxiety, which can be frightening. These include a fear of losing consciousness, of falling over or even a fear of suddenly dying.

If you're feeling anxious, try taking slow, deep breaths. This will help trick your body into thinking that you're not anxious after all, and will help slow your heart rate and make you feel more calm.

If you think your anxiety is more than you can cope with, get help from a health professional. You mustn't accept it as simply "part of AS" and something you just have to deal with on your own.

Discovering other types of anxiety

As well as general anxiety disorder, other specific anxiety disorders are common in ASC. We describe these in the following sections.

Panic disorder

When anxiety is severe, this may be experienced as an intense paralysing panic, known as a panic attack. Fortunately, these attacks rarely last longer than three to four minutes, because the body runs out of the chemicals required to support such an attack for long. If panic attacks occur several times a week, then you may receive a separate diagnosis of *panic disorder*.

Obsessive–compulsive disorder

Obsessive–compulsive disorder (OCD) is an anxiety disorder in which you have unpleasant obsessional thoughts, for example thinking that someone you love may die. These thoughts can be accompanied by compulsions, which are intense behaviours that you have to do over and over again (for example, washing your hands or touching things in a certain order). You can have just obsessional thoughts or just compulsions or both in OCD.

OCD is common in people who also have ASCs. Studies have estimated that up to 10 per cent of children with AS also have OCD. When you have OCD, then a) the rituals, compulsions or obsessions are different in nature to those in AS (see tip below) and b) they are much more severe and stop you getting on in life. So for example you might try to resist the ritual and not actually like the repeated rituals or compulsions any more. They become a bit of a pain!

A general rule is that if you have an ASC and find yourself complaining about your obsessions or compulsions, then you are almost certainly dealing with OCD in addition and separately to your ASC.

OCD is characterised by themes. In ASCs these tend to involve compulsions like collecting things (hoarding), repetitive checking, lining things up and touching certain things in a particular order. Obsessional thoughts are less common in ASCs but can revolve around themes such as how things work. Compulsions or obsessional thoughts in people with OCD who are not on the spectrum are commonly about hygiene, religion, aggression or sex.

If you happen to be unlucky enough to also have depression, then you may find your OCD (or any anxiety) getting worse. This is no different for people on the spectrum. So when you spot that your compulsions or obsessions are becoming more intense, it's worth checking whether something is causing this or whether you are getting down. Look at the section on depression (next) for a list of depressive symptoms to look out for.

Post-traumatic stress disorder

Post-traumatic stress disorder (PTSD) is an anxiety disorder that follows an initial traumatic event such as a life-threatening road traffic accident, or abuse. This is then followed by a set of symptoms such as avoidance of situations similar to the initial trauma, flashbacks of the event in the form of seeing lifelike images in one's mind, nightmares, difficulties getting to sleep, irritability and a heightened response to small noises or other perceptual stimuli (the "startle response").

You may also experience *hypervigilance* — being constantly on the lookout for perceived threats. There are some similarities with characteristics found in ASCs, in that hypervigilance and the startle response are similar to heightened sensory sensitivity in ASCs. If you're on the spectrum, you may also have suffered a traumatic event, in which case PTSD can be a co-occurring diagnosis.

John's story

John spent much of his childhood on his own. He recalls not being interested in other children at school and spending time on his own in the playground. By the age of 16 he was given a diagnosis of AS. He recalls having rituals such as folding his clothes at exactly the same time, in the same order and in the same manner on a daily basis, which gave him a "sense of security, much like a baby's security blanket".

By the age of 23, however, he'd experienced disappointment in a succession of failed relationships which he'd previously expected would "sort out" his life. His anxiety levels rose and suddenly his obsessions became unpleasant, interfered with his everyday life, and he was diagnosed with OCD. He had begun experiencing obsessional fears that he might run someone over while driving. He explained that he had no intention of doing so. He realised the thoughts were unreasonable but found himself driving really slowly and becoming low in mood as a result. A course of cognitive behavioural therapy (CBT) and taking anti-depressants helped him recover from his OCD.

Not everyone who has been through trauma suffers from PTSD or other disorders. Indeed the majority of people seem to pick themselves up and get on with life. However, if you do have a problem, then it does need treating.

If you have met someone with the characteristics of PTSD, then:

- ✔ Do urge the person to get help, because these symptoms don't necessarily go away and can sometimes weave themselves into someone's emotional and personality make-up, with long-term problems.

- ✔ Don't urge the person to start talking about the traumatic event, because studies have shown that post-trauma debriefing can lead to a worsening of the condition rather than an improvement.

Treatments for anxiety disorders

Treatments for anxiety disorders tend to involve a mixture of psychological therapy and sometimes medication (see Chapter 15 for more on this). Anxiety on its own is best dealt with through CBT but, if severe, an anti-depressant such as an SSRI (selective serotonin reuptake inhibitor) can help as well. Panic attacks can involve hyperventilating (breathing too fast), and so the best way to stop those is through controlled breathing exercises. Phobias and OCD are best dealt with through behaviour-treatment programmes such as "exposure and response prevention". The exposure bit refers to confronting the situation you fear, and the response prevention refers to doing this without the compulsion that you usually use to reduce anxiety. CBT can be accessed online through a brilliant website run by the therapist Chris Williams at www.livinglifetothefull.com. The best treatments for PTSD are probably CBT and eye movement desensitisation and reprocessing (EMDR) — a set of visual exercises. Medications such as anti-depressants also sometimes help.

Note that doctors can sometimes resort to using a group of medicines called benzodiazepines for anxiety. This group includes drugs such as diazepam or clonazepam. These do reduce anxiety during a crisis but must not be used for longer than three weeks. Used longer than this they will cause dependency, which means you need higher doses for them to work because your body becomes *tolerant* (used to the medication). In the long run, benzodiazepines will cause an increase in aggression, irritability and paradoxically even anxiety. Best to avoid them!

Discovering mood disorders

Mood disorders are a group of psychological disorders that affect your mood. Your moods can be either excessively happy (manic) or extremely sad (depressive). In this section we'll cover the common mood disorders that often accompany ASCs.

Depression

Although we all commonly say we're "feeling depressed" when we just feel a bit sad and down, real depression is a very serious condition. Depression is really common in ASCs. At least a third of people who have an ASC suffer from depression in the course of their lifetime.

Causes of depression are many, but in AS a common thread is difficulties making friends and fitting in socially. Not having friends when you really want to make friends, being bullied and not fitting in with the people around you can all make you feel awful. Over time, feelings can turn from confusion, anger and being upset to depression. In adulthood, relationship difficulties at work or at home can lead to isolation, to unemployment and debts, which in themselves can cause depression.

If you have AS, you will often have the added difficulty of being unable to describe your emotions. This is known as *alexithymia*, which literally means "without words for emotions". However, more accurately it means an inability to *recognise* or *describe* your emotions.

Being completely without emotions is a good description of a robot but *not* of someone who has an ASC. All human beings have emotions but may not always feel them. People on the spectrum may have to deal with some very strong emotions, especially if they've frequently felt left out. Sometimes the best defence in dealing with these is to push them deep into the subconscious (known as "repression"). The problem is that once emotions are sitting this deep, they can be difficult to find, but it doesn't mean they're not there. You will find that this is similar to people who when deeply depressed will tell you they are feeling nothing.

Recognising the key symptoms of clinical depression

You need at least five symptoms to be clinically depressed rather than just "sad", with at least two from the "core symptoms" category. These include:

- **Core symptoms:** Feelings of low mood, or loss of pleasure or interest in things, or fatigue or low energy levels, for longer than usual and in a way that is more than just sad or a bit down.

- **Other feelings:** Excessive or inappropriate guilt, worse mood in the mornings, reduced self-esteem and confidence, reduced emotional reactions (compared to normally), like intense apathy.

- **Biological symptoms:** Increased difficulties with sleep, change in appetite, weight loss, reduced interest in sex, feeling slowed down or agitated. Loss of pleasure and reduced emotional reactivity (degree to which your emotions react to the world) may be included here.

- **Changes seen in AS:** More than the usual social withdrawal, exhaustion, anger, isolation. Obsessional ideas can become more intense and change from positive interests to negative fears such as worries about dying.

✔ **Mental (cognitive) symptoms:** Loss of concentration, increased critical thoughts directed towards yourself, the world and the future, such as worthlessness, nihilism (a sense that all is meaningless). People of faith may lose their faith during depression, but this returns on recovery. You may experience hopelessness and suicidal thoughts.

If you have suicidal thoughts, go to the doctor immediately for help, because cures are available and people can and do get well again regularly. You need to know that there is hope.

So how does the brain get depressed? There are many genetic, chemical, psychological and social triggers for depression, such as a family history, alcohol, stress and unemployment, which we could regard as the answers to why we get depressed. The answer to "How did I get depressed?" is more complicated (like most things to do with the brain). We think that chemicals in the brain like serotonin and noradrenaline (in the USA this is called norepinephrine) are reduced in people with depression compared with people with no depression. But when you talk to scientists currently looking at this, they will show you complicated diagrams with arrows pointing this way and that and involving dozens more chemicals and brain pathways that we never knew 20 years ago. Scientists will tell even doctors not to bother trying to understand, because they are currently all theories they are working to prove! But we do know that anti-depressants like SSRIs work to increase serotonin, and other drugs — serotonin–noradrenaline reuptake inhibitors (SNRIs) — can increase both serotonin and noradrenaline.

Michael's story

Michael was bullied severely at school because he didn't fit in. By the age of 15 he thought he was not normal, felt inadequate and felt trapped in social situations he could not just walk out of. He had a poor relationship with his father, whom he felt was very distant. His mother had depression. Michael was full of self-loathing and developed the idea that his social difficulties would mean he would never lead a "normal" life. He had some suicidal thoughts, although he didn't act on them. He was given a diagnosis of AS and depression. Anti-depressants were prescribed and his mood lifted, although self-esteem remained chronically low for many years.

He remained free of depression until ten years later when work became overwhelmingly busy, his father died and Michael was sacked. He developed symptoms of fatigue, worthlessness, poor appetite and motivation, waking up in the early hours with low mood. He sought help from his local doctor and was diagnosed with recurrent depression, which responded to anti-depressants. This helped him cope better and he was eventually able to find another job.

Depressive psychosis

In some cases of severe depression, worries may go from being reasonable concerns to fixed, incorrect beliefs, known as delusions, such as believing you're dead, which may reflect feelings of low self-worth. A person with severe depression may begin to hear a voice outside his or her head saying that he or she is "no good" (when no one is there). This is known as an auditory hallucination.

Delusions and hallucinations are what psychiatrists call psychotic symptoms, which essentially mean you have lost touch with reality. When this is driven by depression, you may be diagnosed with a "psychotic depression". This is the most common form of psychosis in AS. If you want an idea of how psychosis is produced, read the section "Psychosis" towards the end of this chapter.

Bipolar disorder

If you do have depression, then a well trained doctor should ask whether you have ever felt a high as opposed to low mood. You may have had lots of energy, a reduced need for sleep and food, and a sense of euphoria. You may have spent money excessively and felt more sexually attracted to people. Your rate of talking may have increased, and people may have complained that they could not keep up with you. If you had these symptoms for at least three or four days, you may have had either a "hypomanic" or "manic" episode. The "hypo" means "slightly less" than mania.

In cases where there have been manic or hypomanic episodes, a diagnosis of *bipolar disorder* is made. This used to be called "manic depression". A link has been suggested between AS and bipolar disorder, although it's unclear whether bipolar disorder is more common in people with AS. Note that a family history of bipolar disorder increases the risk that you have it too.

In order to have *mania* you will need to have at least two added symptoms from the following:

- ✔ A heightened sense of self-importance, in some cases leading to grandiose ideas about your identity or powers (like believing you're the president or prime minister when you aren't). You may also find that you have several hundred plans to complete during the day and believe that you will, of course, do so. Realistically, you can't.

- ✔ "Flight of ideas", which essentially means that you experience your thoughts as racing and everyone around you as going at a snail's pace. People around you will notice a pressure of speech and that your thoughts are jumping very quickly from one theme to the next. There is a connection between themes, but this connection may be as slight as a rhyme. Imagine someone saying this at high speed: "I am a pilot flying through the air, hair is a good thing to have on your head, although bald people aren't as cold as you may think, pink, sink — the sink is really filled with water . . ." It's difficult to follow this train of thought, and this person will find it impossible to get on with ordinary tasks in life.

> ✔ Seriously irresponsible behaviours such as really excessive spending or going into bars to pick people up for repeated sexual encounters, where that is inconsistent with how the person normally behaves. In one case a student bought a total of seven very fast cars on credit. When he emerged from his manic state, he realised he had been unwell. He then had a major panic attack, thinking he would never be able to pay back the massive debt! Fortunately, a psychiatrist was able to write a letter explaining that the student had been suffering from a serious mental illness. The student was then able to return the cars to the car salesmen (who were not too pleased!).

As you will have noticed in the example of someone believing they are, say, the prime minister, it's possible to lose touch with reality in mania. In this case, you may be dealing with a manic psychosis. But don't worry, treatment is available. See the next section on treatments.

Treatments for mood disorders

The main treatment for depression in adults is an anti-depressant such as an SSRI. Due to sensitivity to medicines, people on the autism spectrum tend to be given lower doses than other people. In psychosis, an anti-psychotic should be used (see Chapter 11), and in bipolar disorder, a mood stabiliser. In severe mania, an anti-psychotic may be used first because these act more quickly than mood stabilisers. Psychological treatments are useful once the disorder is less severe, and include CBT (see Chapter 12).

The psychiatrist or psychologist treating a person on the spectrum who has an affective disorder should address the social reasons for the person's depression or illness. In schoolchildren, this may involve getting teachers and parents to provide the child with guidance and encouragement to be more socially involved. Depression tends to reduce the motivation to get involved, so a person may need to try extra hard to get over this. For adults, local autism societies, groups and employment agencies can offer support.

Alexander's story

Alexander grew up with no friends. When he had problems with memory, social interaction and being unable to focus in class he received a diagnosis of ADD (attention deficit disorder) and was statemented at an early age in school. This statutory assessment provided a "statement" on the fact that Alexander had special educational needs and what services would meet those needs. He was treated with Ritalin and his attention improved. However, in middle school Alexander was referred for temper tantrums, and found to be depressed because of social isolation; by his early teens, he was diagnosed as having AS. When he was reassessed in his early twenties, whilst at university, his attention had improved significantly and he no longer needed medication. However, his underlying AS continued to cause significant social communication difficulties, and he received help from the university disability department for this.

Attending to attention deficit hyperactivity disorder

Attention deficit hyperactivity disorder (ADHD) is a condition in which there is an abnormal degree of overactive behaviour and there are difficulties in sustaining attention. In one study, up to a third of people who had AS also suffered from ADHD. Some genetic differences are found in both people with ASCs and those with ADHD, suggesting that a common cause may be involved with both conditions. A cluster of symptoms known as the DAMP syndrome — Deficits in Attention, Motor coordination, and Perception — also exists, which suggests a subgroup of people who have both an ASC and ADHD. If you know someone who has been given this diagnosis they will be clumsy, inattentive and have difficulties with social communication. ADHD is particularly common before the age of puberty in children who have AS.

Classification systems in psychiatry can be rigid and make some diagnoses mutually exclusive. For example, if you have ADHD, then technically you aren't "allowed" to have an ASC. Difficulties in attention and activity levels may be due to the ASC alone. However, if a disorder is severe enough that it *cannot* be explained by the main diagnosis — such as being on the spectrum — then an added diagnosis should be made. For an account of the problem with classification, the chapter on ADHD in Ghaziuddin's book *Mental Health Aspects of Autism and Asperger Syndrome* is excellent.

You may have heard of Ritalin, a medication commonly used to treat childhood ADHD. Be aware that ADHD tends to get better over time — like childhood asthma — so medication is rarely needed for adults who have ADHD. The doctor or psychologist may also use behavioural approaches, and teachers should provide a supportive teaching environment for children with ADHD.

Touching on Tourette's syndrome and tic disorders

Between 20 and 60 per cent of children who have AS develop tics. These are involuntary, repeated and non-rhythmic contractions of groups of muscles, and so can involve the vocal cords as well. Tics are worsened by stress, disappear during sleep, and can be simple or complex (see Table 4-1).

Table 4-1	Motor and Vocal Tics Associated with Tourette's Syndrome
Simple Motor/Vocal Tics	*Complex Motor/Vocal Tics*
Eye blinking	Hitting oneself
Facial grimacing	Jumping
Arm jerking	Hopping
Head nodding	Twirling
Tongue protruding	Licking
Barking	Using obscene words
Hissing	Repeating one's own sounds, words
Sniffing	Animal noises and muttering

Tics tend to worsen up to the age of 10–12 years and then reduce so that two-fifths of adolescents aged 18 become free of tics. Sometimes tics are the main problem and the ASC is discovered as an incidental finding. You may find that sometimes tics appear when depression sets in or there has been a withdrawal of anti-psychotic medication.

Gilles de la Tourette syndrome (Tourette's syndrome) simply refers to a tic disorder in which there has been a mixture of at least two motor and one set of vocal tics in a lifetime, with frequent tics on an almost daily basis for at least a year. If you have AS and are showing signs of Tourette's syndrome, then you also need to be on the lookout for ADHD *and* OCD, because these are *both* more common in this case. The sooner these are noticed, the sooner treatment can begin.

People do not have tics on purpose. Children who have tics need more time, and teachers need to be role models and be accepting of the child in front of the class.

Treatment for tics includes anti-psychotic medications and medications used to lower the blood pressure.

We think that tics are due to an excess of a chemical called dopamine in the brain. However, some stimulant medicines that treat ADHD (dexamphetamines) can increase dopamine, worsen tics, and are best avoided. Check with your psychiatrist if you are in doubt.

Eating disorders

You will find two kinds of eating problems associated with ASCs. *Sensory hypersensitivity* will make a person with an ASC dislike foods with a certain texture, smell or taste. Chapter 14 discusses diet in ASCs. *Anorexia nervosa* is a much more serious eating disorder, involving strict control over what you eat and eating as little as possible. Some studies found up to 23 per cent of adolescent girls who had anorexia nervosa also had signs of AS.

Signs of anorexia nervosa include:

- ✔ Self-induced weight loss through fasting, self-induced vomiting, taking laxatives or diuretics (drugs to make you pass water)

- ✔ Seeing yourself as too fat (when in fact you are very thin) — a body mass index (BMI) less than 17.5 is not healthy (BMI is weight in kilograms divided by height (in metres) squared)

- ✔ A body weight that is below the accepted minimum healthy weight for your height

- ✔ Loss of periods (menstrual disturbance, unless you're taking the pill) in women, or in men a loss of libido and sexual interest

Bulimia nervosa is a separate eating disorder in which people repeatedly binge on excessive amounts of food and then vomit to enable the bingeing. People with bulimia still have a distorted body image although their weight is within the normal or higher than normal range.

Anorexia nervosa carries the highest mortality rate in psychiatric disorders. There are many causes of the high death rate, but one reason is that the heart is a muscle, and when you've run out of fat stores, muscles get used up next. People with anorexia can die from heart attacks. They can also die from imbalances in body salts like potassium; potassium is key to the survival of body cells, including in the heart. If you suspect anorexia in someone with an ASC, please seek help immediately.

Treatment is by a specialist eating disorders team, who should check whether there are also signs of OCD and provide a range of therapies. No proven medication works for anorexia nervosa, although fluoxetine can help in bulimia nervosa. CBT is also very useful.

Sussing out substance misuse

Misusing either illicit drugs or alcohol is known as substance misuse. People on the spectrum are no more likely to take drugs or alcohol than anyone else. Problems may occur when a teenager on the spectrum finds that consuming illicit substances helps with feeling more accepted among a local group of "friends". Like others, people on the spectrum may find that alcohol gives them "Dutch courage" and makes them feel more confident in situations that otherwise make them nervous. Other people on the spectrum find that both alcohol and drugs have unpleasant effects and are poorly tolerated by their bodies, so avoid them altogether.

If you have AS and have discovered that alcohol allows you to worry less about social inhibitions, there is a risk of dependency. Increasing consumption of alcohol can cause depression. It also wakes you up after a couple of hours of drowsiness (so causing sleep problems), worsens irritability, anxiety and social withdrawal, and causes serious medical problems.

Understanding catatonia

Catatonia is a mental health condition which affects how you move, how you speak and how you behave. Some people with an ASC also have catatonia. This is particularly true when a person is under stress or their environment is inappropriate for their sensory needs.

Symptoms of catatonia in autism can be very distressing for the person involved and include:

- Slower movements
- Slower verbal responses or mutism
- Problems initiating actions, finishing an action or stopping an action that has started
- An increased reliance on others to prompt movement and speech
- Being very passive and appearing to lack motivation
- Freezing to the spot and not being able to move
- Maintaining a rigid posture for long periods
- Increased repetitive behaviours
- Agitation

Catatonia can be managed if it's caught in the early stages, but so far we don't know what causes it, nor how it can best be treated in autism. If you have catatonia, you should be referred to a neurologist or neuro-psychiatrist.

Uncovering Common Misdiagnoses

You may know someone who has received a diagnosis which you think is quite different to ASCs, yet you feel strongly that you "know" that an ASC is the correct diagnosis and that the person who made the diagnosis cannot possibly be right. You may be a person who suspects you may be on the spectrum, but have been given a different psychiatric diagnosis. This section will help you decide whether you need to look for a second opinion about your diagnosis. After all, an expert's opinion is just that: an opinion.

As you've probably gathered by now, psychology and psychiatry are complicated, and getting the right diagnosis can be difficult, particularly if a person has several co-occurring conditions. That's not to say that it's acceptable to be given an incorrect diagnosis. Sadly, many people go for years with the wrong diagnosis without realising. Here are some common conditions that are diagnosed when an ASC is really the correct one.

Conditions diagnosed in children

We'll start by looking at alternative diagnoses in childhood, like Rett's syndrome, disintegrative disorder, oppositional defiant disorder and conduct disorder, and move on to conditions you may come across in adults, like psychosis and personality disorder.

Rett's syndrome

Occasionally you see a child (usually a girl) who starts having:

- Deceleration (a slowing down) of head growth between 5 months and 4 years old
- Loss of hand skills and development of repetitive hand movements like hand wringing, hand washing, clapping and patting which begin around the age of 2
- Difficulties in coordination when walking and moving
- Problems with social engagement, including eye contact and difficulties with talking, between the ages of 6 months and 1½ years
- Fits or seizures, breathing difficulties like hyperventilation or holding his or her breath, and general slowing down of mind and movement

If you have noticed some or all of the above things, your child may have a genetic condition called Rett's syndrome. It looks similar to an ASC, and because of some autistic traits (verbal and non-verbal communication), it used to be classified as a pervasive developmental disorder. The key feature you will notice is that development is pretty much normal for the first year of life (unlike in ASCs) and then gradually slows down and stops when the child is 3 or 4, after which a deteriorating neurological condition takes over, with all of the problems mentioned above.

Childhood disintegrative disorder

You may come across another disorder of "disintegration" in which development is normal until 2, 3 or 4 years of age. After this age, a child will show regression (loss of skills and abilities) in social, communication, play, bladder or bowel control, and general motor (purposeful movement) skills. You need to know that this condition is extremely rare — only 100 cases have been reported in the world.

Once again, the key thing is that development is normal during the first 3–4 years of life, at a time when someone on the spectrum would be showing autistic traits already.

Oppositional defiant disorder

If, before the age of 10, you had frequent arguments with caregivers or teachers and found yourself repeatedly refusing to do as you were told (for whatever reason), you may have been sent to someone who then gave you the diagnosis of *oppositional defiant disorder* (ODD). The key thing is that your behaviour needs to have been persistently provocative, defiant, negative, disruptive and hostile, and you need to have actively started confrontations for a diagnosis of ODD to be accurate.

Conduct disorder

If your behaviour as a child was very serious, for example involving violating the rights of others through stealing, physically assaulting, repeatedly lying, being cruel to others or destroying property, repeatedly running away from home and school, and starting fires, then you probably met the criteria for *conduct disorder*. Such behaviour can be confined to the home, it can be "socialised" — that is, done in a gang with others — or "unsocialised" — where the child does not belong to any peer group.

In cases of conduct disorder, you need to check whether your child does not also have ADHD. With this combination, you may find him or her hyperactive, impulsive and at times aggressive towards others.

Pathological demand avoidance syndrome

If your behaviour wasn't as serious as that in conduct disorder and you *didn't* actively start confrontations with other people, yet your behaviour was very reactive in confrontation situations, then you may have received a diagnosis of *pathological demand avoidance syndrome* (PDA). People with PDA react to people asking them to do things. They seldom start trouble, although something makes it difficult for them to comply or join in, and they often avoid doing things they enjoy just because someone asked them to participate. Like people on the spectrum, people with PDA are often accused of misbehaving. No one really understands why people with PDA often find it impossible to go along with what they are asked to do, but it's not something they can control. More than a third of those with PDA are also diagnosed with an ASC.

Unless you have a history of rituals, routines, intense focused interests or sensory difficulties, it is unlikely that you sit on the autistic spectrum. On the other hand, if you feel that you're having temper outbursts because some change in your life is happening (new class, change in furniture at home, and so on), and if you've always had all-absorbing interests, rituals and routines, then your defiance or aggression could be due to an ASC. Look at the features of ASCs in Chapter 1 to see which diagnosis fits better.

There are cases where life has been very disruptive to a child. If the criteria are met for both conduct disorder and an ASC, then both may be diagnosed.

School refusal

You may be wondering what to do with a child who's on the spectrum and refusing to go to school. How strange it is, you may think, that school refusal is found in psychiatric classification systems! We don't have "refusal to brush our teeth" or "non-compliance with eating Brussels sprouts" as diagnoses! This is because children are quite frequently referred with school refusal to child guidance clinics. You will then find that professionals usually recognise only two groups of children who refuse school: those who are anxious and those who are defiant of authority.

For children on the spectrum, anxiety can play a big role, but do check for other reasons for not wanting to go to school. Reasons may include that the child is being bullied or that the school isn't fully meeting the educational or social needs of a child on the spectrum. For example, the child may find lessons too fast or too slow. In this case, it's probably worth trying to obtain an educational statement for your child.

Selective mutism

Here's a diagnosis (how doctors love to classify!) for someone who chooses, for example, to speak at home but not at school. A giveaway that you may be dealing with a child on the autism spectrum is that the child may start talking, even at school, about his or her favourite subject. The key for the teacher is therefore to check with the parents what the favourite subject is and then ask the child about it. An educational assessment to decide on a good teaching programme would be the next step if your child does have an ASC.

Conditions diagnosed in adults

In this section we discuss diagnoses more commonly found in adults rather than children. These are diagnoses which may be given instead of an ASC, sometimes in spectacular ways, such as in Hannah's story.

Psychosis

We've already talked about the possibility of depression causing psychosis, but other reasons for psychosis also exist. These could include schizophrenia, which may run in families and appears in your late teens or early twenties. In this type of psychosis, people are thought to be particularly sensitive to stress, so that relatively small triggers like facing exams or extra work at university lead to what's effectively a mental breakdown. A person may experience paranoia, voices and disordered thoughts.

Drugs such as cannabis, cocaine and amphetamines can produce a paranoid psychosis in those who are prone.

Hannah's story

At the age of 23, Hannah saw a psychiatrist when she was suffering from visual and occasional auditory hallucinations (seeing and hearing things that aren't there). She was given a diagnosis of schizophrenia because her symptoms had a "paranoid flavour" to them. Her high alcohol consumption was noted, and she was admitted for a trial of anti-psychotic medication and a detoxification programme (to reduce the problems of withdrawing from alcohol). She made a good recovery but repeatedly became unwell again over a number of years. Eventually a discerning nurse noticed Hannah's lack of eye contact and isolative behaviour. She was referred for a diagnostic assessment and given a "formulation" (or diagnostic description) which said that she had turned to alcohol to deal with social difficulties from being isolated and bullied due to her ASC. Once these difficulties were addressed through support, she was able to permanently give up the alcohol, the hallucinations disappeared and her diagnosis was redefined.

In people in their middle to old age, severe anxiety can sometimes lead to an "anxiety psychosis". Indeed, psychosis may be a normal reaction if you have been sleep deprived or kept in solitary confinement like hostages are.

Symptoms of psychosis can include:

- ✔ Paranoid delusions (false beliefs): for example, that someone's out to harm you in some way.

- ✔ Hallucinations (false sensory perceptions): for example, hearing a voice discussing you with another voice when you're alone. This also includes seeing or smelling things that aren't there.

- ✔ Thought disorder: having thoughts that seem to flow in a disordered way. If you are on the spectrum and like making up new words, you could wrongly be diagnosed as having a psychosis (assuming you have no other symptoms).

- ✔ Other kinds of symptoms including losing control of your thoughts, such as hearing them being echoed or feeling that they are being taken out of your mind or put in there. Some people have severe apathy, little speech, and may have *catatonia*.

About 50 years ago, the word autism was used to denote social withdrawal, and so people who suffered from schizophrenia were also said to have autism. Several studies seemed to confirm a relationship between schizophrenia and autism. However, these studies were poorly designed. In better, later studies, we found that where there was psychosis in AS, it was usually a depressive psychosis. Now, we don't think there is any overall increase in psychosis in people on the autistic spectrum compared with other people.

If you're on the spectrum, other people may think it's strange that you like to spend most of your time on your own. Professionals may misinterpret this as social withdrawal, which is sometimes seen in psychosis. Try to seek a definite diagnosis, to notice whether you have any additional worries you haven't had before that cause risks to your health, and whether you're depressed.. For example, one person on the spectrum became so severely depressed he started believing that all his food was poisoned.

The main treatment for psychosis is anti-psychotic medication. The newer medications (called atypical medications) are less likely to cause side effects in people with ASCs, although they have some problems in the long run. See Chapter 11 for a discussion of these.

CBT is also used to treat psychosis and look at people's underlying assumptions for delusional beliefs, for example.

Remember that CBT is best done by a professional in psychosis, because it can be difficult for a person to have his or her beliefs challenged, and it needs to be done sensitively.

Personality disorders

You may find yourself at the receiving end of a diagnosis of personality disorder rather than AS, and wonder whether this can be right. Here are three possible scenarios:

- ✔ You are sent to an autism clinic, where a personality problem is confirmed and AS is ruled out.

- ✔ You may have had difficulties in relationships throughout childhood so that personality development has suffered, and you may have both AS and a disorder of personality.

- ✔ You are clearly on the autistic spectrum but the experts fail to notice this and decide that relationship difficulties indicate a problem in your personality. They are wrong! You seek another opinion, which you get from a specialist autism centre.

How do we approach the complex area of personality? For a start, if you have AS, you will find that you may have typical characteristics such as perfectionism, obsessionality and sometimes anxious-avoidant traits. You may have very strict standards which sometimes make it difficult to complete projects, or be preoccupied with lists, order and details, and sometimes forget the main point of the task you were involved in.

The point at which these character traits become a problem for you is the point at which your personality may be causing disorder. If there are sufficient numbers of personality traits (a minimum of three) that make your life quite impossible to manage, then you may have a personality disorder.

Josie's story

At 17, Josie was referred to the Early Intervention in Psychosis (EIP) service when she was complaining that others in her class were making fun of her. She felt that people in the street were also laughing at her and that they did not mean well. Josie had difficulties in coordination that led to a slightly awkward gait, which drew attention. When her mother was interviewed with regard to Josie's concerns, it turned out that her classmates and teenagers in her local village were indeed making fun of her. Josie had become increasingly isolated, depressed and ostracised in her own community. She was referred to a diagnostic service for people who have AS, and after in-depth investigations and interviews, received a diagnosis of AS with some depression but no evidence of psychosis. This diagnosis was accepted by the EIP service, who thought that the initial referral for psychosis had been made inappropriately. Josie received support from the local autism society groups in how to handle bullying and regained her confidence. The bullying stopped as her confidence grew and she learnt strategies for dealing with her situation.

Types of personality disorder

You will find many types of personality disorder. Among the most disruptive kinds needing outside help are the "emotionally unstable personality — borderline type". If you have been given this label, then you should be suffering from a core problem of emotions going up and down like a rollercoaster ride on a daily if not hourly basis. During a sudden low, you may harm yourself in an effort to relieve anxious tension, and just as quickly you suddenly feel better again. You may have fears of abandonment, chronic feelings of emptiness, find it easy to form relationships but then lose them just as quickly through arguments and fights.

The usual cause for emotional instability of this severe kind is that of childhood abuse or early trauma. It's as if someone has thrown a large boulder (the trauma) into your emotional pool that was previously calm and is now full of large waves going up and down. Over time, these tend to reduce, but it can take years, depending on how severe the abuse was. A number of mainstream therapies are available to specifically treat this personality disorder, including "coping with emotions" groups, dialectical behaviour therapy and cognitive analytical therapy. New therapies such as mentalising behaviour therapy are also currently being developed.

So where do you stand in relation to an emotionally unstable/borderline personality disorder if you have an ASC? You need to consider at least two things. The first is that in ASCs you may find it tricky to make friends, whereas people with borderline personalities find making friends the easy bit but keeping friends tricky. However, the second consideration is that in some cases you may have had disturbing experiences such as severe bullying or abuse because of being on the autism spectrum.

Disorders resulting from trauma

If you have suffered from bullying, the abuse you have suffered may have left scars on your emotional development. You may be engaging in self-injurious behaviour such as banging your head against the wall. Sometimes this is simply an extension of temper, but sometimes you may find that you have enough borderline symptoms to receive a diagnosis of personality disorder. This can be useful so that you can get the help needed, like emotional coping skills therapy or other forms of therapy.

In most cases, you may have been incorrectly diagnosed with a personality problem if you have an ASC. This is because your social communication difficulties may be misinterpreted as being due to personality issues rather than an ASC.

Unfortunately, we cannot go through all the other personality disorders, nor is it appropriate to because other personality difficulties are seen less frequently. If you're interested in finding out about the characteristics that make a specific personality disorder, look up this most up-to-date website: www.dsm5.org/ProposedRevisions/Pages/PersonalityandPersonalityDisorders.aspx which gives you the latest views on personality disorders in the proposed *DSM-5: Diagnostic and Statistical Manual of Mental Disorders (version 5)*.

Chapter 5

Understanding Asperger's Syndrome in Women

*E*veryone who's involved in working with autism has spent many years wondering whether women really are rarer than men on the autism spectrum. Estimates of the ratios of women to men with a diagnosis on the autism spectrum range from 1:4 to 1:10 (female:male), meaning that women have diagnoses much less often than men. So far experts are uncertain about why this may be the case, or even whether those numbers are a true reflection of the relative gender mix. Genetics are likely to be a part of the reason why fewer women than men are diagnoses, but a lack of recognition of women and girls on the spectrum could also contribute to the relative numbers.

We aren't going to keep saying "women and girls", and "females" sounds too technical and unnatural, so when we say women, remember we're including girls (except for the adult issues, of course!).

Understanding women and autism spectrum conditions (ASCs) is where a lot of progress is likely to be made over the next few years, so here's a chapter that collects much of what's known about women and ASCs. Our particular thanks go to Beth for her help with this chapter.

Diagnosing Women Who May Have Asperger's Syndrome

Researchers have been wondering for some time why women are less likely to be identified and diagnosed as having Asperger's syndrome (AS). In this section we look at some of the reasons why women with autistic traits are either overlooked by professionals who should be putting them forward for diagnosis or not considered to be on the spectrum.

Accurate diagnosis is extremely important for anybody. It offers the ability to understand yourself and therefore to have realistic expectations of yourself. It also enables you to explain yourself to others so that you can be understood. Importantly, a diagnosis opens doors to enable you to access services and support. Women on the autism spectrum may miss out on the opportunity to be diagnosed and the benefits that go with this for several reasons. First, women on the spectrum may have a subtler, less severe or simply different presentation of autism symptoms, meaning that the symptoms are not picked up by teachers, GPs and other professionals. Parents of girls may be reluctant to refer their children for a diagnosis if they seem to be coping reasonably well, even if underneath the external appearance, a girl is struggling. Girls seem to be able to conceal their difficulties more often than boys, so they're not your typical aggressive, disruptive character in the classroom, but simply may not draw any attention to themselves. So they're far less likely to be picked up by appropriate professionals, even those who think they know about ASCs.

Masculinising diagnosis

A possible reason for the difficulties in diagnosing women on the spectrum could be the historical fact that initial descriptions of ASCs were of boys. Because more males have a diagnosis than females, researchers and diagnostic experts have had more experience observing boys and men on the autism spectrum. Diagnosticians may therefore be biased towards male characteristics because they've had most experience of these. Questionnaires called *screening tools* that have been developed to help diagnosticians spot ASCs concentrate on culturally "male" interests such as computers, trains and cars, and take no account of the more social focus of culturally "female" interests such as animals, soap operas, fashion or cleaning. So if you're a woman (or girl), getting a diagnosis is difficult because the diagnostician is looking for "male" characteristics.

When we write "male", "female" and "girly" we're highlighting the *cultural perception* that something is male, female or girly. We aren't saying that something actually *is* male, female or girly.

With more experience of women on the spectrum, diagnosticians will begin to recognise how AS appears in women. Understanding of women on the spectrum is certainly improving, albeit slowly. In future, all diagnosticians, not just specialists, should be able to look at a girl on the spectrum and realise that her obsession with, say, fairies is abnormal in its intensity, despite an interest in fairies being pretty normal in young girls.

Although we'd like to say that men and women (and boys and girls) no longer have to conform to sexual stereotypes in the twenty-first century, that's not true. For example, women are still more heavily criticised for culturally "male" behaviour such as anger than men are. So we put "male" in quotes in that sentence, to show that we don't agree that anger is male behaviour, but that's the cultural bias. We'll be using quotes a lot more in this chapter to highlight terms that have a cultural bias, such as in the phrase "'girly' subjects like hairstyling". Obviously, plenty of men are obsessed with their hair, but our culture still insists that this is a subject for women and talks about men "expressing their feminine side" when they fuss over their hair!

Recognising AS in women

To get a diagnosis of AS, you have to meet enough of the diagnostic criteria and also be really struggling to get by with day-to-day life because of your autistic traits. Diagnosis requires that the person's life, termed "how well you function', is compromised by your autistic traits, which means that diagnosis is based on people's behaviour — how well you're able to wash, shop, work and form relationships, for example — rather than on how hard you have to work in order to achieve that behaviour.

Concealing the problems

Women on the spectrum are much more capable than men (in general) of concealing difficulties and covering up struggles. Women often work hard to appear "normal" and can be excellent mimics of typical social behaviour, even though they may not naturally want to behave in that way. So all the behaviour necessary for a diagnosis is there, all the struggles to cope with life are there, but you may be so good at masking all of this that diagnosticians have to be very experienced and knowledgeable about women on the spectrum to pick up the AS. Unfortunately, most professionals are not sufficiently expert and may miss the AS altogether or diagnose something else (see Chapter 4 for more on misdiagnosis).

If a person appears to be getting by in life without too much struggle, they won't get a diagnosis despite the fact that their success is due to all the effort they're putting in. Such a social mask may fool most people and even some professionals, but it's not really coping. Living with such a mask is an exhausting experience. Unless diagnosis is able to pick up on the struggles behind the mask, many people who need a diagnosis won't get one. The diagnostic criteria for ASCs are currently being reviewed (see Chapter 3), so hopefully this will help the situation.

Recognising ASCs in women is different to recognising them in men. The same diagnostic criteria apply, but subtle differences in how a woman on the spectrum appears, and how she copes with the more difficult autistic traits, mean that teachers, GPs and even diagnosticians may not recognise a woman on the high-functioning end of the autism spectrum. Diagnosis may be even more difficult for adults because they've had more years to develop coping strategies and social skills to mask their difficulties (see the nearby sidebar "Diagnosis — Beth's story").

Differences between how boys and girls learn social rules mean that even a girl with very marked AS is years ahead in social learning compared with most boys with AS. A girl's extra social skills make life easier to cope with, even if she copes by "faking" social competence (see the nearby sidebar "Behind the veil"). And this means she's less likely to be spotted by teachers or doctors as having problems with socialising. However, if she's on the spectrum, she certainly will be having problems.

Adopting the passive female role

A further obstacle to being recognised as on the autism spectrum is the "passive female" role. The passive female is quiet, shy, undemanding, co-opera-tive, friendly, encouraging and compliant. Quiet, undemanding people don't say or do much that reveals their own personality. Many girls and women on the spectrum adopt the passive female role in order to avoid being picked on, to avoid making social gaffes and to avoid upsetting others in their social group. The trouble is, this approach can mask their problems with social skills and lead to people thinking lack of confidence is the reason behind the person's passivity, rather than a possible ASC.

Diagnosis — Beth's story

Beth, aged 37, has AS.

The diagnostic criteria for AS were devised by observing boys with the condition, so AS is often missed in women. Women manifest the characteristics of AS differently as a result both of having female characteristics and having spent years learning to hide their differences.

As Beth says, "Diagnosis matters; no one had heard of Asperger's syndrome when I was a child and, like others of my generation, I wasn't diagnosed until I was in my thirties. By this time, I had struggled with education and employment without support in the dark days before

the Disability Discrimination Act became law. I knew I was different and blamed myself for failure in every aspect of my life: making friends, finding a partner, coping at work; communication affects everything we do."

"Being diagnosed helped me accept who I am, but as women are under-diagnosed, support services for people with AS generally don't cater for women's needs. The issue is further complicated because people with AS often have other disabilities alongside AS, and I am no exception."

Behind the veil

AS is hidden; there are no tell-tale missing limbs. It's frustrating when no one can see there's a problem.

Beth says, "I've learnt to fake social behaviour to avoid making gaffes, but I can't make social functions work for me. They're not fun. I don't remember people's names and faces, let alone make connections or friendships, and as I don't shout about my loneliness (how off-putting), the issue is hidden. Someone who can't get their wheelchair up the steps to their friend's house is obviously left out of the party. The guest with AS is blamed for not wanting to join in the noisy superficial chat. They say that people with AS can't lie, but my whole life is a pretence at normality, and I am a victim of my success. I dread to think what would happen if I looked odd (visibly different), because I lack the social skills to stand up to bullies."

It's different for girls (and women)

All of the problems in this section are more common in people on the autism spectrum than in the general population, and may be more common in women than men on the spectrum. The research hasn't been done yet, so we don't know whether the following are really more common in women who have ASCs, or just anecdotally more common. However, you may want to look out for the following difficulties:

- ✔ **Anorexia nervosa:** This disorder is usually shortened to just "anorexia", a medical term meaning simply "weight loss". Weight loss is a common sign in various forms of ill health, but anorexia, as the term's usually used, meaning anorexia nervosa, is experienced more commonly by women on the spectrum. You can find out more about anorexia in Chapter 4.

- ✔ **Isolation:** Unable to play the social game with other women (or even with men), many women on the spectrum end up lonely and isolated. Unlike autistic men, who may never have been very socially successful, continue to lack social skills and so have less experience of social life, women on the spectrum may have some social success in early life and so may be less able to deal with loneliness. Once playground games are over and adult life begins, it's harder to fake normality. Peers marry and become parents, and the women on the spectrum are left behind.

- ✔ **Post-traumatic stress disorder:** Picked out by the more "predatory" boys and men as submissive and docile, or lacking in common sense and supportive friends, some women on the spectrum suffer bad and sometimes terrible experiences, resulting in post-traumatic stress disorder (PTSD). The results of such trauma are often prolonged and unpredictable, making the PTSD complex and difficult to treat. See Chapter 4 for more about PTSD.

✔ **Borderline personality disorder:** People on the spectrum find others unpredictable, because they have a weakness in their ability to consider other people's thoughts. This weakness makes some people on the spectrum prone to developing borderline personality disorder, which is likely to be more common in women than men. See Chapter 4 for more information.

✔ **Agoraphobia:** Most people think of agoraphobia as a fear of open spaces, but it can also be a fear of what may happen in those open spaces — the outside world. At home, you're safe. You can lock your doors and don't have to deal with anyone you don't want to. Women may be more vulnerable to developing agoraphobia than men. For more information, see Chapter 4.

✔ **Obsessive–compulsive disorder:** This disorder is particularly associated with ASCs, and with women more than men; if men learn train time-tables obsessively, women obsess over cleaning. More women than men have OCD, and on the autism spectrum this gender divide may be even more pronounced. Again, see Chapter 4.

Taking clear-cut cases

Here we describe three common "types" of woman on the autism spectrum to draw your attention to some of the behaviours and the social skills that they've learnt. Those skills actually hide a lack of more advanced social skills and difficulties with socialising and fitting in with society. These are just examples, however — don't take them as comprehensive descriptions of women on the spectrum. Also, although the descriptions are based on real people, they're composite characters, and each one takes features from several different people.

The female mathematician

She's very into her subject and doesn't pay much attention to "girly" subjects such as soaps (of either kind), clothes, hair, make-up or gossip. Like most people on the spectrum, she doesn't see much point in small talk, but gets really into discussions of Gödel's theorem (who wouldn't?). You'd think that such a woman (whether her subject was maths or something else) would be easy to identify, but just because she's not really into fashion doesn't mean she dresses badly — she learnt the importance of how you dress and other social niceties while she was still at school. Only those women on the spectrum who are struggling very badly with socialising and *mentalising* (thinking about their own thoughts and emotions and the thoughts and emotions of others) will display any tell-tale signs of an ASC, like not washing, having unkempt hair or maintaining very odd eye contact (though having unkempt hair is not in itself a sign of ASC — it's often associated with having small children!).

The Asperger's fashionista

She's got all the clothes; her make-up is perfect. She demurely ignores all approaches by the many men who notice her, and scares quite a few of them off just by her presence. An appearance of aloofness may be the result of panic about what to do or say. A subsequent freeze looks, because no outward signs of panic are visible, like an icy and dismissive stare to most people. She may also have a grasp of small talk, which allows her to cope well in the early stages of conversation — another skill that girls are often able to learn from others at school. Talking to other women, the conversation may then slide easily into a discussion of their hair or outfits. Or she may get stuck at the small-talk stage and the conversation then fizzles out. She's learnt to be more aware of when she's dominating the conversation, so she's less likely to talk incessantly and more likely to become the passive partner in the conversation.

The truth is, she's probably studied other women, their fashion, make-up and hair styles in much the same way that an anthropologist studies a remote tribe in the rainforest. Her attempts to fit in may well be slightly wrong and her fashion sense a little bit too idiosyncratic. She probably suffers some subtle bullying from her peers as a result, and the harder she tries, the easier she is for the bullies to target.

The Asperger's cook

This woman is most people's idea of a domestic goddess. Her kitchen is clean and organised; she has dozens of cookbooks on the shelves. When she has a dinner party, she leaves everyone else in the sitting room, and later around the dining table, while she nurses her cooking to perfection (and avoids having to make conversation). The "female" skill may not be cooking, but someone like this will focus all their efforts on getting that part right while avoiding the areas of their life that they find difficult. The combination of focusing on some skills while avoiding having to use others is the key pattern of behaviour here.

The Asperger's model school pupil

In secondary school, she dashes about in a chaotic fashion, often arriving late to lessons and not having done her homework. She's a bit of a loner, and always has her head in a book. She takes a passionate interest in lessons, particularly in English literature when they study Shakespeare, which she loves. In response to class questions, she often shouts out her interpretations of Shakespeare's words, and her teacher finds it difficult to stop her interrupting. But her answers show a lack of understanding of the complex relationships between characters, and her classmates laugh at her simplistic interpretations. She has a few friends who share her interest in Shakespeare, but she's not into make-up, boyfriends and the ins and outs of school social life. Her clothes aren't fashionable, and she tries her best not to draw attention to herself.

Knowing the signs

The previous section covers examples of how women with AS may behave. In this section we look at what specific signs may show that a woman is on the autism spectrum. We don't intend for these signs to be diagnostic (that's what the diagnostic criteria are for) but they may help you to see how being on the autism spectrum can affect a woman's life.

An inability to deal with conflict

A woman on the spectrum may find coping with conflict in a manner appropriate for her age very difficult. People on the spectrum have difficulty mentalising (considering their own and others' thoughts and emotions). Particularly in stressful situations such as those involving conflict, people with poor mentalising skills stop trying to mentalise and fall back on more basic, less sophisticated and less mature forms of reasoning — sometimes giving up on reasoning altogether and just punching someone. Unfortunately, conflict resolution is one of the most complex areas of human interaction, so this is a particularly bad time to stop using this most advanced tool in the human thought cupboard. A situation dealing with conflict will show up the person on the spectrum as being more childish than people expect, and thus more exploitable and teasable.

Gauche socialising

Despite having learnt social coping strategies to conceal any social difficulties, women on the spectrum can come across as socially naive and gauche in their social interactions.

Being a bookworm

Often, women on the spectrum are avid readers. They can be extremely knowledgeable about literature, and literature is a common interest in women on the spectrum. As well as the interest factor, being a bookworm allows you to hide from social interactions and social demands. Reading a book will be far more pleasurable than being with others.

Being a tomboy

A lack of interest in feminine things such as looks, clothes and the opposite sex can be common in women on the spectrum. The socially accepted ways of "being a woman" aren't important or valued by some women on the spectrum, so they may come across as more masculine in their interests, behaviour and appearance.

Poor multi-tasking

Women on the spectrum, although better than men on the spectrum, are generally not as good at multi-tasking as most men. Women are expected to multi-task in many situations, and those on the spectrum don't fit the roles society has handed them. If you're a woman on the spectrum, you're likely to find juggling a number of tasks difficult.

Strong systemising

One of the great strengths of people on the spectrum is their ability to systemise: to make lists, to break things down into components and understand the functions of each component (including ideas), and to arrange and catalogue things. The average woman is less able to systemise than the average man, so spotting a girl or woman with strong systemising skills may make you wonder about the possibility of her being on the spectrum.

Emotional outbursts

Feeling emotional is one thing; understanding why you're emotional is another. Identifying the real reason you're feeling emotional is something many people struggle with. For people on the autism spectrum, knowing how they're feeling can be further confused because they may not notice they're emotional until they're very emotional — ready to shout, cry or hit something. Suddenly feeling overwhelmed by an emotion that you didn't realise you were feeling is quite a common experience for people on the spectrum. In boys and men, this tendency is put down to childishness, a lack of self-control and occasionally to being "sensitive". For women on the spectrum, this sort of behaviour can easily be dismissed as a "typical" female over-emotional reaction.

But Asperger's-style emotional behaviour isn't just what's culturally perceived as "female". Having emotions bursting into your consciousness with no warning is an experience distinctive to the autism spectrum; it doesn't mean just getting overwrought or not showing enough self-control. If you're a woman on the spectrum, you may consistently find controlling your emotions really hard because of the difficulties resulting from ASC.

People on the spectrum often don't show outward signs of stress. Add poor negotiating skills and you have no warning to offer others that an outburst is coming. No stages exist between calm and chaos, and the typical cultural explanations like hormones don't fit, so women on the spectrum can be left misunderstood and without feedback to develop different skills and approaches.

Examining the Role of Culture in Behaviour

Women have more social coping strategies than men, in general, and are able to use them more effectively than most men on the spectrum. As a result, if you're a woman with an ASC you may not come across as being on the spectrum, because your difficulties are so hidden beneath the coping strategies. The reasons why women have more coping strategies than men may include some of the different cultural pressures which we explore below.

As we (meaning everyone) discover more about the way people learn, we're surprised by how much our culture affects how well we learn. For example, most people believe that boys are better than girls at maths. But in Finland and Sweden, girls in secondary school do just as well as boys in maths (in some studies, slightly better). In the UK, where it's part of our culture to believe that certain jobs and tasks are men's, we expect girls not to do as well as boys in maths, and so they don't. Scientists currently reckon, although the area is being studied further at the moment, that this situation arises mostly because girls have been taught by their culture to expect to be bad at maths.

These cultural expectations around gender may make life tricky for women on the autism spectrum. Here we explore the aspects of gender culture that can be particularly problematic.

Playing with the girls

While small boys run around the playground making machine-gun noises, girls play much more social games, and a lot more talking goes on. To fit in to this style of play you need to be sufficiently good at socialising. Due to the social style of female play, girls on the spectrum have more social learning opportunities than boys, but the playground and the social expectations of female peers can make life very difficult for those girls. Girls are expected to have social interests and skills and to play socially complex games, meaning that a girl with an ASC will be disadvantaged on many levels. Girls also play games involving social imagination, such as role-playing being a mother or a fairy. Even if a girl on the spectrum is given a role in a game, she needs to know what to do to fulfil the role and may fail due to a lack of interest or poor social imagination.

Playground politics are more complicated for girls because they tend to fall out over tiny arguments for weeks on end. If you're a girl on the spectrum, you're likely to find this behaviour incomprehensible and bewildering. Boys tend to have a fight, get it out of their system, and carry on, which is easier to deal with for children on the autism spectrum.

"Girly" playground games may seem pointless to you if you're a girl on the spectrum (see the nearby sidebar "Playground games"), and you may avoid the complicated social scenarios of female play by becoming a "swot" and concentrating on your school work by yourself.

Playground games

Beth says, "When I was growing up, the point of many games was something I could not grasp. I once watched some younger children pretending to be horses; I could not understand why they wanted to do this. They were putting filthy skipping ropes into their mouths, which their playmates then tugged on to pull the "horses" along. The idea of someone putting something that dirty into my mouth and have it tugging hard against my teeth terrified me. Even when games were being played that I did want to join in with, such as skipping, the playground was a noisy chaotic place in which to judge when and how to move towards a moving skipping rope to take my turn without being hit in the face by the rope — take too long and others would be fed up; misjudge it and I'd end up with rope burn. Why we were all jumping over the rope as that year's trendy game is still a mystery."

A further important difference for girls on the spectrum at school, compared with boys on the spectrum, is the way that male and female peers behave towards their autistic classmate. Other girls in the class may take a protective role towards their friend on the spectrum. They may help out with things their autistic friend finds difficult and ask her to join in with games. While the quality of the friendship may be different for girls on the spectrum, the fact that the child has a friendship group further masks a girl on the spectrum from teachers and professionals who are looking for the stereotypical "socially isolated" individual.

Girls can also bully a classmate who's on the autism spectrum, and aren't always as inclusive. For more on bullying, see Chapters 9 and 10.

Establishing the social order

Boys mostly determine their social hierarchy by being good at physical things. One boy may be the strongest, another the best at keepy uppy. Competitions and showing off what you can do tend to determine popularity at school.

Girls, in contrast, establish the pecking order in a very social way. More so than boys, girls pair up as friends and spend a lot of time talking and doing things as "best mates'. For girls on the spectrum, this often means you're selected by a girl to "be her friend', sometimes with the feeling that you're not being given any choice about whether you want to pair up with the other girl or not. Sometimes the other girl forces the friendship because she's also an outsider and doesn't want to feel lonely or look like a "loner'. She may not be interested in being friends because she likes you, but more for social acceptance. She may move on and find another girl to pair up with when it suits her social climbing.

Other girls want to be friends with less popular classmates because they want someone they can lead, someone who'll do what they suggest. The apparently shy, compliant girl on the spectrum appears to be a good choice in this situation, and the leader can become very bossy and order her "friend" about. Often these girls get a bit of a shock when the girl on the spectrum simply refuses to go along with anything she don't actually want to do, not caring about the social consequences or what's the "right thing to do". Unfortunately, this situation can mean the girl on the spectrum gains a reputation for being difficult and unfriendly, not to mention "weird".

Finally, some girls who are confident will choose the girl on the spectrum to pair with because they want to bring the outsider into the group. Again, however, because of the passivity of the girl on the spectrum, this motherliness can become very bossy because she doesn't communicate how she feels back to the other in a way that the motherly girl can understand (through emotions and body language).

Girls on the spectrum can feel trapped in any of these "friendships", doing things they don't want to do but unsure of how to change the situation without becoming an outcast.

Society's expectations for adult women

Society places demands on everyone, but its expectations of women may be very difficult to meet for women with ASCs.

Women face the expectation that they'll want to talk and be good conversationalists. Through much exposure, some females on the spectrum learn to fake it, but not having these skills is a bar to being accepted socially as a woman.

Beyond being chatty and good conversationalists, women on the spectrum are affected by the expectation that they'll be very empathetic and show a natural concern for and interest in other people. Not having such empathy or not having much of it can be really frowned upon, and the lack of emotionality can be interpreted by others as a sign the person is cold, mean or odd, rather than on the autism spectrum.

How you look is somehow more important for women than men, yet many on the spectrum don't value such trivial things. Society is quick to judge people who look a bit different.

Issues for Women on the Spectrum

If you're a woman on the spectrum, you have a difficult time of things. Not only may your issues not be recognised or diagnosed, but also some of society's expectations of women make your ASC even more of a problem. This section covers some issues that are particularly challenging for women on the spectrum.

Gauging girls and teenagers

The teenage years are tricky for everyone, but they may be especially troubling for girls on the spectrum. From fitting in with peers, to the interest of everyone in your boyfriend or girlfriend or who you hang out with at weekends, to the physical changes occurring at puberty, this time can be very trying for girls who have an ASC.

Fitting in at school

Often, girls on the spectrum see no importance in wearing the right clothes, listening to the right music or hanging out with the right crowd, meaning that they're often "outsiders" at school. But just because you don't value the social aspects of fitting in doesn't mean that you don't want to have friends. Having meaningful friendships, or a lack of them, can be a source of real anxiety for girls on the spectrum.

Puberty

Having an ASC means that you may not like change. Puberty is a time of massive emotional and physical change for young women, and so may be particularly difficult or worrying if you're a girl on the spectrum. Some girls would prefer to maintain their childlike appearance rather than develop physically into women. This fear of change can go so far as to cause some girls to develop anorexia.

For tips related to puberty and girls with AS, check out *Asperger's and Girls* by Tony Attwood *et al.* (Future Horizons Incorporated). Books and resources about sex education can also be found at www.autism.org.uk.

Girls compete to change or maintain their social status in a different way to boys, and social status becomes particularly relevant at puberty. Boyfriends and girlfriends are part of teenage life, but girls on the spectrum will get left out of all the intricate nuances of who's going out with whom, and the often manipulative, "two-faced" nature of teenage girls. Friendships also become much more complex at this age. For example, friendship can be a sort of negotiation, which may go something like this: "If I'm going to be friends with you, then you can't be friends with her," and "I'm not going to her party, so if you want to be my friend, you can't go to her party either," both of which seek to control someone else's social connections and popularity. All of this jostling for social status can make friendships during the teenage years particularly difficult if you're a girl with an ASC.

School work

Girls on the spectrum may struggle academically, but this may be put down to reasons other than an ASC. For example, if a boy on the spectrum's bad at maths, teachers may attribute that to the diagnosis, whereas girls on the spectrum who are bad at maths will be labelled as "just girls", because girls don't do well at maths generally anyway (so society tells us).

Self-esteem can be damaged in girls (and boys too) if they don't do well at school. Girls on the spectrum are much less likely to ask for help, tell anyone what they're struggling with or draw attention to any academic challenges.

Asperger's and Girls (see the previous Tip) offers advice on helping girls who have AS with their schooling.

Addressing adult women

Adults on the autism spectrum face different issues to younger people. In this section we outline the issues that may be especially difficult for women.

For a personal account of life as a woman on the autism spectrum, check out *Pretending to be Normal* by Liane Holliday Willey (Jessica Kingsley).

Finding fulfilment (by Anne)

Anne says, "Growing up undiagnosed meant there were expectations that I would be participating in various activities, be heading towards a career and want to start going out with boys. I wish I'd been diagnosed earlier in life and been able to set more realistic goals, because I was so good at subjects that required structure and memory that it was possible to get good grades in chosen subjects, and the struggling side was overlooked. Really I was unravelling with mental health problems, which came out when I went to college and found I couldn't cope with student life and all it required. There's always been an expectation that I would want to be in a relationship, especially as I come from a religious family which has a firm view of marriage. From teenage years, however, when someone said 'I want to go out with you,' I had no concept what that meant, other than going somewhere specific as an outing. Being diagnosed meant that I received an explanation as to why I wasn't fulfilling these expectations, and it's been a long path to finding a way of understanding the combination of abilities and disabilities that autism brings, in order to try to live a fulfilled life."

"My idea of fulfilment is more about work than relationships. I don't think of being in a relationship, but working life has always felt like walking around a glass tower looking for the door. The few jobs which went well needed large volumes of detail to be processed and meant working on my own rather than in a team. Each job ended as the project was completed, and it is still work in progress to find an ongoing job, but I am confident it will happen."

Meeting men

Beth says, "A typical female friend once asked me how come typical men weren't snapping me up. I have no explanations for this situation. While flirting confuses me, I have been able to use technological methods of meeting men such as Internet dating. This has resulted in me having scores of first dates but not being able to connect enough to ever practise the more advanced forms of dating. My dates clearly think something is missing."

Work

People on the spectrum are far more likely to be unemployed than other groups. This situation is despite many autistic people having amazing skills. If you're an autistic women, the glass ceiling is double-glazed (you're even less likely than other women to get promoted). Women on the spectrum face the issues other women face at work plus all the issues people on the autism spectrum face.

For women who're on the spectrum, the workplace can be even more problematic. Even if you accept your interest in areas traditionally seen as male, such as engineering, the men in those industries may not welcome you. You could be vulnerable to sexist bullying and you won't have the social skills to cope. Often, women are given work involving typical "female" talents such as multi-tasking, without an appreciation that women on the spectrum are different. This scenario sets you up to fail and will reduce your self-esteem and enjoyment of work.

Love and marriage

An expectation exists that, as a women, you'll need and desire relationships and actively seek them. The need to spend time alone isn't well understood by others, and people think women on the spectrum must be lonely if they do so or are odd for not joining in.

Women on the spectrum will often have to explain themselves if they're not interested in having a relationship. Solo travel on holidays, not needing the opinion of two friends in order to decide to buy a new pair of shoes, and a dislike of parties are poorly understood if you're a woman. This isn't to say that women on the spectrum desire isolation, but being alone as a woman in society isn't the norm. The fact is, if you're a women on the spectrum you may have different values that others may not relate to; see the nearby sidebar "Finding fulfilment (by Anne)".

Some women on the spectrum do like being with other people, though, and do want to have a relationship with a significant other. However, social difficulties may make this tricky, and some women can become sad as a result of not having a romantic partner (see the nearby sidebar "Meeting men').

Sexual relationships

Sex education works on the assumption that teenagers are far too ready to hop into bed with each other and need to be told about the consequences of their actions. For girls on the spectrum, educators need to make the opposite assumption. If you're to have any chance of experiencing positive relationships, romantic or sexual, you need to be told how to relate to boys and have practice doing so. The reality of talking to boys and dealing with their hidden motives, implied meanings, and the social consequences of your own choices come as a surprise if sex education doesn't also include relationship education (see the nearby sidebar "Personal safety").

Some girls take to heart the prescription that "all nice girls are virgins until their wedding night", especially if they're good at following rules and can't see the context in which the rule was made, or aren't motivated to have relationships anyway so are hiding behind such rules. But for some women on the autism spectrum, the "wedding night" never actually comes because they don't learn how to relate to men. Others allow themselves to be persuaded by boys and men into sexual behaviour because it's one of their few sources of social contact and makes them feel wanted. Such women may have fun saying yes to anybody, but do so from a lack of social awareness rather than choice and then bitterly regret the attitude they find others have towards them.

Some girls end up in abusive relationships because they lack the skills to have any other sort of relationship and don't want the loneliness or stigma of not being in a couple. Also, some women may not recognise that abuse isn't okay in a relationship, because of a lack of experience, education and understanding. So some women on the spectrum will be vulnerable to entering into relationships that may be harmful. In turn, a minority may get drawn into the sex industry. A surprising number of women in the sex industry are on the spectrum, where they're further isolated and vulnerable to finding themselves in dangerous situations.

Personal safety

Beth says, "Here again we have the double-whammy effect: being female compounded by being autistic adding up to something more complex than either issue alone. In my early thirties, I was naive enough to go back to the flat of a man who'd said 'let's go back to my place for dessert,' and wondered when we got there why he wasn't making any effort to cook."

Being a mum

Beth says, "If I inherit my autism from my family then I, as an autistic person, may be being parented by autistic people. I will learn atypical social skills from these role models. As an adult in my turn, I must deal with the challenges of parenthood as an autistic parent possibly parenting autistic children. I must cope with changes of plan, because babies never fill their nappies on schedule, and I must try to think when the baby is crying and I can't filter out this 'background' noise, and I must do this having had very little sleep. I must respond with touch to a crying child. I must operate an executive function, not just for myself but also for my children, planning their day as well as mine. Before I begin this, I must ask myself whether being autistic is a good thing, and whether those in my very limited support network will agree that it is and aid me as a parent."

"The degree to which having children provides someone with social glue shouldn't be overestimated — the conversations at the school gates provide a social network which non-parents don't access."

Motherhood

Motherhood was blamed for causing autism in the past (see Chapter 2), but thankfully no one sensible believes that any more. However, motherhood for women on the spectrum is often carefully considered. Some women on the spectrum are extremely maternal, whereas others may not want to have children. Autism does have a genetic basis (see Chapter 2), so if you as a mother have an ASC, a chance exists that your child will too. Many women on the spectrum think very carefully about this possible outcome (see the nearby sidebar "Being a mum").

Part II
Living with Asperger's Syndrome

"I suppose having AS makes you see things differently to other artists which must explain your incredible popularity."

In this part . . .

*I*f you're not on the autism spectrum, chances are you don't really know what it must be like to have AS. If you are on the spectrum, you may be wondering how to cope with your diagnosis and with life in general. In this Part, you'll discover what life is like from the point of view of people on the autism spectrum.

We talk about making friends, coping with family, marriage, sex and relationships. We give you lots of tips for how to live independently, cope at college or university, get a job and survive the workplace. We also explain the complicated world of autism rights and how you can get involved with different autism groups.

Chapter 6

Enjoying Life with Asperger's Syndrome

In This Chapter

▶ Discovering yourself

▶ Overcoming life's obstacles

▶ Embracing life's joys

Most people who are looking for information about their Asperger's syndrome (AS) or other autism spectrum condition (ASC) are looking for help with their problems, but it's not all doom and gloom. It may take a bit of work and a period of years rather than weeks, but big improvements can be made in anybody's life.

In this chapter you'll learn about some of the common difficulties faced by people on the autism spectrum (which includes AS) and some tips to try and help yourself overcome the difficulties as much as possible. Once you've overcome some of the problems, you can then think about what things you may start doing to enjoy yourself.

Understanding Yourself

The first thing to do when you're trying to enjoy life more is to get to know yourself. Understanding your likes and dislikes, what motivates you and what deflates you, will give you a good starting point for making things better.

You hear over and over again that AS *presents differently*, which means that when you meet two people with the diagnosis they're not necessarily going to show the same reactions or have the same personality. Well, of course, different people present differently: They're different people.

People with AS have different interests, backgrounds, skills and abilities just like everyone. It's worth spending time thinking about what you consider to be important in life, what you enjoy and feel comfortable with, and what you'd like to change and improve. In this section you'll find out some of the typical things that may affect enjoyment of life for people with an ASC, such as managing routine, coping with sensory sensitivities, mental health problems and relationships. Some of these may be relevant to you, others may not be. As we've said, everyone's an individual, so use the information here as it suits you best.

The DVD *Being Me* (see Appendix A) includes short films of six people talking about their lives as people on the autism spectrum. It also has a programme you can follow to help you get to know yourself, what a diagnosis on the autism spectrum means for you, and what skills you may want to develop.

Managing routine and change

Individuals who have a diagnosis of an ASC such as Asperger's find routine a very important aspect of life. Getting your life into a routine where you can cope with day-to-day tasks and not become too anxious is extremely important, but sometimes sticking to routines too rigidly can stop you from doing things you enjoy. Routine can be reassuring, but it can get in the way of your hopes and desires, too. For example, the need to be home and eating dinner by seven each evening will cause problems if you're also trying to find a partner. Going on a date usually happens in the evening, and prospective partners are likely to find it self-centred of you to stick to your plans instead of being flexible.

Routines are there to make your life easier. If a routine interferes with another part of your life that is really important to you, then you'll have to come to terms with the need to change that routine.

Changing your routines can be difficult, but can be done. First, you need to really want to change. Next, you need to take one small thing at a time. Trying to change too much at once is very hard, and if you don't succeed you'll feel discouraged from trying again in the future. For example, if you spend the first couple of hours of your day lying in bed reading, you could try changing this routine every Monday; get up straight away, do some chores or go for a walk, then you can read. Notice that this change is quite specific (it happens on a Monday) and doesn't prevent the activity you enjoy (reading), so it isn't going to be too difficult.

Make a list of things you would like to change in order to enjoy your life more. Check whether any of your routines interfere with making these changes. If they do, prioritise which is more important, the routine or the thing you'd like to change. Remember to try to change only one thing at a time.

Handling sensory issues

An important part of understanding yourself and what makes you happy or unhappy in life is to know your sensory sensitivities. Many people with an ASC have strong dislikes of certain noises, textures, smells and tastes. Avoiding these can become a major goal in your day-to-day life. For example, you may never go into your local pub because the lights at the bar flicker in a way you can't stand. To learn more about sensory sensitivities, see Chapter 9.

While avoiding things that aggravate your senses may be the only option sometimes, it's also important to realise that completely avoiding particular sensory input is impossible, especially if you want to lead a full, independent life. Experimenting with different ways of managing your difficulties with sensory information is therefore worthwhile. First, always look for a way around the situation that causes difficulty with your senses. For example, if you want to go out and meet people, but your local pub has flickering lights, explore your local area to find other pubs that don't. If you can't stand going on the bus because it smells unpleasant, investigate other ways of getting to where you want to go. Try and manage life with your sensory difficulties to allow yourself as much freedom and enjoyment as possible.

You can also try and teach yourself coping skills to deal with sensory overload. For example, if you find coping with loud sounds difficult, you could try spending time each day with background music or other sounds of your choice in a safe environment where you can easily get away from the noise (for example at home). See whether you can cope with the loud music, and experiment with ways that help you deal with it (such as deep breathing, twiddling your thumbs, writing something down). If you get used to loud sounds in situations where you can easily escape, then you may be able to cope better when you come across them in new situations. Your senses get used to the level of input, and you can practise useful ways of coping. You can try this with all senses, not just sound.

Overcoming anxiety and depression

Unfortunately, lots of people on the autism spectrum suffer from mental health difficulties (see Chapter 4). Experiencing anxiety and depression or any other mental health difficulty will certainly affect your ability to enjoy life.

Getting to know yourself and what things contribute to your anxiety or feelings of depression can be important in turning things around. You may have learnt to become anxious in many everyday situations. You may feel lonely or a sense that your life needs to be better in some way. People suffering from depression often just describe it as a feeling of failure. You could be unemployed and feel that you need to be employed, or single and feel that you're a failure unless you're married — these are just two examples. You may not have anything you can identify as the cause. Alternatively, the exact cause of the feeling may be very specific to you, such as never having managed to clock up a thousand miles in your car without having an accident. We cannot list every possible cause of a feeling of failure; you need to give this idea some thought yourself. Consider talking things over with at least one good friend or a parent, because they'll be able to provide a different perspective and allow you to form a balanced opinion.

When you know what may be contributing to your feelings of anxiety or depression, try and do something about it. If it's a minor problem in your life, talking to family or friends can help. If it's more serious, go to your GP and ask for a referral to a psychologist or psychiatrist. You can learn more about this in Chapter 4.

Talking about what's going on in your head can help to put your thoughts and feelings into perspective. Just by articulating what you're thinking, and hearing it spoken aloud, you can often make more sense of it and lessen the fears that have built up.

Getting your head down

A good night's sleep helps put worries and sad feelings into perspective. However, sleep disturbance is common in people with an ASC. To help get the best quality sleep, try some of the following:

- ✔ **Close your eyes and let yourself sleep as soon as you start to feel tired:** We realise that this is easier said than done, but the more often you can manage to just let yourself drift off, the better your sleep will be.

- ✔ **Make the room dark:** Your body produces more melatonin when it's dark, which is probably why sleeping for more than 90 minutes in the afternoon is so difficult. If you're having problems with your sleep, try making the room darker. Consider fitting blackout blinds or curtains which stop almost all light from coming through the window (although they are quite expensive). A sleep mask — which resembles a blindfold — is a much cheaper alternative but it does take getting used to, and some people hate the feeling of wearing one.

- ✔ **Avoid stimulants:** Alcohol and caffeine are the obvious suspects. Avoid both to ensure a good night's sleep. See the nearby sidebar "Sussing out stimulants".

- ✔ **Keep your hands and feet warm but don't overheat:** No one's quite sure why this is true, but experiments have proven that staying toasty is important. However, overheating disrupts quality sleep too. Based just on people we know, many people on the autism spectrum say that they wake up sweaty during the night. This is the principal indication of overheating. To avoid overheating, keep the bedroom temperature cool (no more than 20 degrees centigrade) and use a thinner duvet or fewer blankets.

- ✔ **Relax and don't let thinking or worrying dominate your desire for sleep:** Again, this can be tricky to achieve. If you're having difficulty relaxing, consider learning some simple meditation. Lots of colleges offer evening classes in relaxation meditation. If your mind is wandering, try jotting your thoughts down in a notebook so you can forget about them until the morning.

- ✔ **Avoid diuretics:** The main *diuretics* — substances which increase the flow of urine to your bladder — (apart from prescription drugs) are alcohol and caffeine. Alcohol is a significantly stronger diuretic than caffeine and may wake you in the night for the toilet. Such disruptions will affect the quality of your sleep. Avoid diuretics for at least three hours before going to bed.

- ✔ **Drink just enough:** Don't drink too much liquid in the evening. Again, as with diuretics, the problem with being over-hydrated is that you'll wake up in the middle of the night needing the toilet. If you haven't drunk enough, you may wake up thirsty. You may need some practice in getting this balance right.

Exercise can help your mood and your sleep. If you do no other exercise, try to go out for a walk for at least half an hour every day. If you liked a particular sport at school, consider taking it up again, because the more you enjoy the exercise the better it is for you.

Making the most of your melatonin

Twice during each day your body produces a hormone called melatonin. About 90 minutes after you start releasing melatonin, you'll be tired and able to go to sleep. If you fight through this period of tiredness, your body will react in accordance and you'll feel awake again. After an hour or two, the effects of the melatonin will resurface and you'll experience another period of tiredness. During the afternoon, this second period of tiredness is the final one, and most people are fully alert again by five o'clock, whether or not they took a nap. During the night, the periods of tiredness will repeat for about nine or ten hours before you become fully alert again or until you go to sleep.

Sussing out stimulants

Not everyone is affected by caffeine, although its stimulant effect lasts several hours. That of alcohol lasts less than an hour, which is the main reason why most people who drink find it so tempting to have just one more. The brain likes being stimulated, and as the effect wears off, signalling centres in the brain demand more stimulation. Fortunately, alcohol also has a sedative effect which lasts several hours, so after several drinks the desire to rest overcomes the desire for another drink (unless you've become addicted, of course). The quality of sleep you get after drinking is not as good as alcohol free sleep, though.

Many other stimulants exist, for example chilli, pepper (especially black) and ginger. In general, the effects of herbs and spices are much more variable from person to person than the effect of alcohol; a herb may have a sedative effect on one person and act as a stimulant on another. Mint tea is widely advertised as a calming drink, for example, but a few mouthfuls will keep the Goth awake for hours, no matter how tired he is. As an experiment, try to avoid alcohol, caffeine and all strong herbs and spices for at least four hours before bedtime for a month. If your sleep improves, try avoiding just alcohol, caffeine, chilli, pepper and ginger. If your sleep is still better, then you know that none of the other herbs and spices is a problem for you. Carry on with the experiment until you've worked out which substances disturb your sleep. How much of something you eat or drink will also have an effect: small doses probably won't do anything. This is true even for alcohol, which is the only substance (apart from prescription and illegal drugs) that is guaranteed to disturb your sleep.

Using cognitive behavioural therapy

Cognitive behavioural therapy (CBT) has an excellent record for treating anxiety and depression. CBT involves thinking about your behaviour and then trying to change certain bits of it that you identify as problems. (See Chapter 4 and *Cognitive Behavioural Therapy For Dummies* (Wiley) for more information.) CBT is most effective as a short course with a therapist, because the therapist will have experience of using the technique effectively and so will be able to correct you when you make mistakes. You can see a therapist privately, which will cost between £300 and about £600 per course, or you can get a referral to an NHS therapist from your GP. The website of the British Association for Behavioural and Cognitive Psychotherapies (BABCP) is www. babcp.com, where you can find information and therapists local to you. The BABCP website allows you to search for therapists who are specialists in one or two areas, so you can search for one with experience of, for example, both AS and anxiety or both AS and depression.

Finding a therapist with experience of ASCs is crucial, because the approaches used need to be adapted to meet the specific needs of people on the autism spectrum.

Being positive

Using *positive psychology* can be another worthwhile approach. Here, the emphasis is on changing your outlook and not dwelling on the negatives. And if you like a bit of a challenge, or are interested in psychology, there's *Neuro-Linguistic Programming For Dummies by.* Neuro-linguistic programming (NLP) is a fancy name which means understanding and influencing yourself and others through language. Neuro-linguistic programmes are things we all have: they are our characteristic thought patterns and the way we reveal these patterns to others through our choice of words. NLP is not easy, but for those of us on the spectrum, everyday social skills aren't easy either, so NLP can help for some people.

Getting to know your limits

To have a more enjoyable and less stressful life, it's important to know your limits. Anyone can become *overloaded*, though people on the autism spectrum are more prone to feeling overloaded by things that other people seem to cope with. You may feel overloaded with work commitments, overloaded by too many people, too many demands or too much sensory input. The causes of overload are many, and getting to know where your limits are is important to prevent overload or, worse, meltdown.

Recognising overload and meltdown

A *meltdown* is one step on from *overload.* When you are overloaded (or stressed, anxious, overwhelmed) and nothing is done to reduce your stress levels, you may respond by having a meltdown, which is a state in which you can no longer cope, no matter how hard you try. You respond instinctively to get away from the overload, often shouting, screaming, crying, flapping your hands, spinning in circles, or some combination of these. A meltdown feels like a huge burst of emotion coming out of you, and leaves you breathless after a few minutes. Once you've got your breath back, you can take in your surroundings again, all of your previous thoughts banished from your consciousness. The Goth likens it to turning yourself off and on again, like you would with a computer.

A meltdown is similar to a tantrum in some ways, but the word "tantrum" isn't appropriate to use about meltdowns, because "tantrum" has connotations of spoiled children having a strop. A meltdown is more serious, and is an instinctive response to overwhelming levels of stress. Meltdowns cannot be controlled by the person having them. Having a meltdown is completely different to a frustrated toddler trying to get its own way.

There's nothing fake about a meltdown and nothing the person can do about it until it has run its course.

Meltdowns can build slowly or they can catch you by surprise. We suspect this difference is to do with how relaxed you are before the stress that causes the meltdown starts: the less relaxed you are, the less you notice the build-up. Most people, when they can feel a meltdown building up, try to resist it and cope; doing so isn't usually a good strategy, because you miss the opportunity to plan your exit. Using your energy to find a quick, polite way out of the situation is a far better approach.

Coping with overload and meltdown

Once you know what overwhelms you and overloads you, you can do your best to avoid those situations. Sharing workload with colleagues, avoiding certain situations that you know make you very stressed, and coming up with strategies to minimise the demands placed on you can really help.

You don't have many choices when you start to become overloaded. You can spend time thinking about your previous experiences of overload, maybe talk some of them through with someone else, and identify the signs that will let you know it's happening. Your best choice is then to leave the situation that's overloading you before things get worse.

You may be able to change things so that they're less overloading, such as turning out lights, turning down music or closing windows to block out noise. This strategy is good but it requires extra effort on your part, which adds to the overload and so may cause the problem you're trying to avoid.

If you don't spot the signs, or if leaving isn't an option, then you can start ignoring things, maybe by putting your hands over your ears and closing your eyes. Breathe through your mouth if smells are a problem. Don't worry about how you look to other people, you'll look a lot stranger if you have a meltdown. You may have developed this strategy into the ability to shut out the outside world without having to cover your ears or close your eyes. This strategy is called *shutting down* or a *shut down* (some people call it a meltdown: don't confuse it with the meltdown we described earlier in the section). At this stage leaving is still an option, although you may have to do it abruptly and without explaining what's going on to those around you.

Your last hope is that you're lucky and the situation changes so that your overload dissipates. Trust us — this is not a reliable method of avoiding a meltdown.

Talk to people you're comfortable with about your potential for overload. Explain how you feel, what makes you feel like that, and what you do when it happens. For example, you may shake, look at the ground or find it impossible to speak in sentences. Together, you can create a plan of action for when you feel overloaded. The simplest plan is that the other person asks you to leave with them and you both go somewhere that isn't stressful to relax and recover. Overload is another area where CBT can be effective.

Finding hobbies you enjoy

Hobbies are a great way to enjoy life. Sometimes you may feel that having a diagnosis such as AS affects your ability to take up particular hobbies, but it needn't, although you need to allow for all of your difficulties if you really want to enjoy your time. If you enjoy something that usually involves lots of other people at a distant venue which is inherently noisy (such as dancing), you may think that it's impossible for you to ever enjoy your hobby. You're wrong. You may be able to persuade one person you trust to go with you to a dance class to support you, or you could, for example, arrange for three friends to come around each week for a "dancing party" where you'll be able to control who you have to talk to, where you have to travel to and how loud the music is. The only tricky bit here can be finding three friends!

You can find a lot more to do in the evening than go to the pub, cinema or a restaurant. Hobby groups and classes take place in all sorts of venues: village halls, community halls, churches (and other places of worship), schools and colleges. At colleges, evening classes aren't just about learning and exams; they're also social activities, and many aren't exam-orientated. Your local council office and library should be able to provide you with information about what's going on in your area.

If you receive financial support from the local authority, enquire about getting an individual budget. Having an individual budget means that you can spend your support money how you want to, getting the support, leisure activities and equipment that you need to have an enjoyable life. For more information see Chapter 8.

Coping with Your Family and Friends

Some people who aren't on the autism spectrum may find the title of this section rather odd, because they think of family and friends as people who support them and make their lives easier, not people they have to cope with. But these people have learnt the social skills needed for dealing with family and friends. Many people on the autism spectrum need help learning these skills.

Getting along with your family in the best way you can and having one or two friends can make you feel less isolated and alienated. A sense of alienation is fairly common if you have AS, and it seems to be mostly the result of feeling misunderstood. If you weren't diagnosed while still at school, you probably went through a period in which you grew sick of hearing people tell you that everyone goes through the same as you're experiencing. If everyone went through what you go through, cities would be much quieter places, and small shops and delivery services would put huge, crowded shops out of business. People who've successfully made some friends report feeling a lot less alienated.

In this section you'll learn some tips on developing and maintaining good relationships with family and friends. Hopefully, the better your relationships, the more enjoyable your life will be.

Managing family relationships

Despite the petty annoyances and the all-out rows, getting along with family is usually easier than getting along with friends. This is partly because both you and your family have a lot of experience of each other, and this experience makes the relationship predictable. Your parents and siblings also love you, which usually makes them more accepting, understanding and forgiving of arguments and difficult circumstances.

After you get a diagnosis, your family will have to get used to it and spend some time learning more about AS. They may not get things right all the time while they're learning what helps and what hinders family life when one or more members are on the spectrum. Getting things right may be even more difficult if you were diagnosed as an adult. Your family will probably go through a few years in which they learn to interpret all your past and current behaviour in light of the diagnosis of AS. This can be a difficult period, and some family members may never be able to adjust to this new situation. For more on diagnosis, see Chapter 3.

If you have brothers and sisters, remember that they may have a hard time as a result of your condition. This may be because the child with an ASC may get more attention from its parents, or the other child may get bullied at school because its sibling is "different".

Keep in touch with members of your family whom you don't see often (unless you have reasons for avoiding them, of course). Even if you don't get on very well with them, people learn, and sometimes it takes a few years for a closer relationship to build. You can never predict the future, and you may need help sometimes – hopefully your family will be there for you. Equally, you should be willing to help them when they need it.

Inviting family members around for tea can be a good way of maintaining contact, although if you're like most people on the spectrum, you'll need to spend some time preparing questions in advance. Having questions ready avoids long silences, and if you're the sort of person who just talks and talks, then having questions ready can help you stop talking and give the other person a chance to speak.

Throughout this book we continually stress the importance of talking to people. Even if doing so doesn't come naturally, you'll find that talking things through can really help you tackle problems that have arisen as a result of a misunderstanding or an argument, for example.

Nothing can be solved overnight. Don't feel that you have to make a perfect family relationship straight away or even ever. Build things gradually, and be aware that people, including you, often have a more emotional reaction to family than to others. Small comments that may annoy you if a stranger said them can make you very angry or upset when expressed by a family member.

Many people spend their entire lives living with their parents. You can still build up the relationship in this situation by learning not to react when you're annoyed. Instead, calm down and then try to talk about the problem with them.

Making and keeping friends

Having a friend or a few friends is something many people on the autism spectrum long for, yet find difficult to come by. The fact is that having friends to share experiences with makes life more enjoyable, yet when you find social interactions confusing and difficult, making friends and keeping friends is a real challenge. Many people with an ASC also have experiences of being bullied, which makes finding friends feel even more of a challenge. However, not everyone is a bully, and it is possible to meet people who have a positive influence on your life (see the nearby sidebar "Knowing Jack").

The first step to finding friendship is to realise that most friends are made through common interests. People meet each other at school, university, at work and doing hobbies that get them out and about. Singing in choirs, joining a photography club, a local interest group or anything similar that takes your fancy will help you meet people with similar interests to yours. Having something in common is the first step to finding a friend.

Bear in mind that you aren't the only one who is looking for friends. Many people may be looking for friendship, for all sorts of different reasons. Perhaps the person is a bit shy, finds making friends difficult, or they've just moved to a new area.

You can't get around the need to go out and meet people (although some people are happy to have friends on the Internet only), but that's the nature of friendship — it involves meeting people!

Working on developing your social skills may help you to make friends more easily. Various programmes for developing social awareness and understanding exist. You could find some through your local community centre, school (for younger individuals) or through local autism provision (for example autism charities or autism resource centres).

Keeping friends may be harder than finding friends. To do it, you need to develop an awareness of how other people feel and be prepared to compromise so that you both feel that you're being treated fairly. Again, working on developing your social awareness and learning strategies for different social situations will help. You can find a list of books that may be useful in Appendix A. The *Being Me* DVD may also help you to highlight skills that you need to work on; again the details are in Appendix A.

If you have made friends, bear in mind that however much you may want to keep someone as a friend, sometimes people's lives just change, and they have to take on new responsibilities that take up more of their time. In these circumstances they'll see friends less and make less effort to keep in touch with all their friends. You can't do anything to make someone stay friends — life moves on sometimes, even when you don't want it to.

Friendship can be very fulfilling, and everyone will have different experiences of it. Some people will prefer to have two or three close friends, while others will have a wide circle of them. Some may have the same friends all their lives, whereas others have a succession of different friendships. No fixed pattern of friendship exists.

Mastering the art of conversation

Conversation is key to developing relationships. People talk to each other all the time about all sorts of things (and sometimes about nothing in particular!). People with an ASC may find small talk and social chit chat very difficult to understand, because it can seem pointless. Having reciprocal conversations where both parties talk and listen for roughly the same amount of time may also be difficult to master. So conversation skills may be an area to spend time working on if you're thinking about improving relationships with family and friends.

Listening to other people chatting is a great way to learn how to do it yourself. If you don't get an opportunity to do that usually (on the bus or train, for example), then try taking a magazine to a café and buying yourself a drink. Sit at a table and read a little bit of the magazine, then listen to somebody's conversation. Try not to get too engrossed in their conversation, because if people notice you listening to them they may get annoyed, and you certainly don't want the stress of them ticking you off about it. Start reading your magazine again if you think you've been spotted.

It's not important what people are chatting about, nor whether you find the subject interesting. What you're listening to is how they chat, how they keep the conversation going, and how they start the conversation again when it stops. Most people are so good at restarting a conversation that the gap between one part and the next is barely noticeable, so you'll quite often miss it at first.

See some of the books listed in Appendix A which may help with conversation skills. Speech and language therapists may also be able to help.

Knowing Jack

Jack was already on the verge of thinking everyone bullied him when he changed schools at 11 and started at a comprehensive. Being wary of everyone, making no effort to make friends and being hostile when teased soon convinced him that everyone, teachers included, took pleasure in making his life a misery. In the sixth form, the head of sixth form made him a prefect, thinking that it would do him some good to hold some responsibility. But when 30 children co-operate to make a prefect's life hell, there is nothing the prefect can do. Especially not if the prefect thinks that the head of sixth form will take every opportunity to have a go at the prefect as well.

So convinced was Jack that everyone was against him that even people who were friendly were scowled at, snapped at and treated badly. They soon lost patience with him. The end of his school career couldn't come soon enough.

After leaving school, Jack became a keen hill walker, spending very long days walking and getting the bus home. One day on holiday, he was caught out by the weather while up in the mountains. Exhausted and disorientated, he met several other people with the same idea of looking for shelter. He was not at all happy to join the group, but one of the men, Salvadore, was firm and insistent. He tried being aggressively rude but everyone else, following Salvadore's lead, ignored his churlishness and included him in the plan. Together, they all made it down to a village and begged a night's sleep in the village hall.

It took almost ten hours to get off the mountain, including many slips, falls and scrapes. Jack continued to be nasty and resentful the whole time. Eventually he couldn't cope with the contradiction between how he thought the people should behave towards him and how nice they were being, and he burst into tears. He continued crying on and off until he fell asleep that evening.

They all had breakfast the next morning before catching the bus, but Jack didn't have anything like enough money. One of the others was very reassuring, very relaxed about it, and very happily paid for him, even refusing to take Jack's address, because there was "no question" of paying back the debt. Jack found it very hard not to cry.

When he got off the bus, everyone from the mountain shouted a cheery "goodbye" and waved. Jack waved back. Over the next few days and weeks he did a lot of thinking, and was unable to come up with any explanation for the people's behaviour except that he was wrong and that many people were friendly. All the evidence for friendliness from his childhood kept popping into his mind and tormenting him. All his anger fizzled away, it felt like part of him was evaporating. Most people are good.

Salvadore is his real name, but Jack is a pseudonym. Thank you, Salvadore.

Sorting out your social skills

People talk about social skills as though they're well understood. But social skills are like Einstein's general theory of relativity: the reality is that neither is well understood by specialists in the field, let alone ordinary people. Human social interactions are so complex that it's not just a matter of picking up a few skills here and there. Social signals are subtle but absolutely everywhere in our society. Most people who do not have an ASC would be able to tell you whether a smile is false or real, but they would certainly struggle to tell you how they know (it may be something indescribable in the eyes). This makes learning social understanding extremely difficult for people on the spectrum, because it can be more of a "gut feeling" than anything specific that can be delineated and learnt.

Most people (on the spectrum or not) have at least one social skill which they're bad at, and very few people are expert at more than a couple. You may read the last sentence and think "That's wrong; I know someone who has fantastic social skills." You probably do, but it's still rare for someone to be good at every single social skill. The principal technique that most people use when dealing with situations calling for social skills they're bad at is avoidance, perhaps by letting someone else take the lead at that moment, or by leaving before they reach that point. People on the autism spectrum use the same technique, but because there are more skills that they're bad at, they end up avoiding more situations. Don't worry, because there are ways to help improve social skills. You may never be perfect at social interactions, but few people are.

Not even the world's leading expert on social skills could write a comprehensive list of all those needed to live in the UK. (Although many of the social skills needed in different countries will be the same, different cultures will need some different skills.) So here we present a selection of the most common social skills plus a few others, which you'll find particularly useful to learn:

- **Being a good listener:** Surprisingly few people are good at listening. It involves taking in what someone says and fully understanding it, asking questions to check that you fully understand it, and encouraging the person to elaborate — so it's not just a matter of opening your ears!

- **Taking care of others' needs:** Other people are unlikely to enjoy life just the way you like it, and you need to be aware and take their needs and preferences into account. So take it in turns to do things you prefer and things the other person prefers to get a balance of who gets their own way.

- **Taking your leave of someone (preparing to say goodbye):** This involves mentioning your intention to leave a few minutes before you say goodbye, so that everyone can use their skills to prepare the conversation for the end. This usually involves saying something like, "I have to head off in a minute," after which people may say how pleased they were to have seen you, or wish you a safe journey home or some such social pleasantry.

- **Keeping in touch:** This is an important skill for maintaining friendships. Writing an email or phoning your friends and family every few weeks can help you to keep in touch with what they are doing, and to help them learn what you are doing. When you all know a bit more about each other's lives, you'll have more to talk about and can develop more supportive relationships.

✔ **Showing interest in and concern for others:** This is an important friendship-building skill. Similar to keeping in touch, it helps if you know a bit about what a person likes and dislikes if you are to develop a relationship. Knowing what is happening in the other person's life and showing a genuine interest in this can help your friendships to build. For example, if your neighbours recently told you they were having trouble with rabbits eating all the crops in their garden, the next time you see them you could ask them how their rabbit problem is, and whether they'd managed to solve it. If you've also got a problem with rabbits, you could sympathise with their problem and suggest things you've done to make it better.

✔ **Maintaining a conversation:** Very few people master this, but you don't need to be a master — just find a few techniques for filling an awkward pause. Commenting on what is going on around you is a very helpful way to fill a gap in conversation. The weather is a classic example of this. ("Hasn't it been raining a lot recently?" is a phrase many people use to fill awkward silences in the UK.) If you are in a café or having lunch, you could comment on the quality of the food or drink, or ask the other person something about his or her meal, for example "How's your coffee? My tea's a bit cold." If there's an interesting painting on the wall, start to talk about that.

✔ **Control of body language and tone of voice:** This is probably the hardest skill in this list for people on the autism spectrum to learn; any improvement will make a big difference to how well you get along with other people. Many people on the spectrum speak in a tone of voice which comes across as disinterested. Experiment with modulating the pitch of your voice for different circumstances. Usually, the pitch of the voice gets higher with interest and excitement. Body language can be very tricky to get right, but the book *Body Language and Communication* by Simon Perks (National Autistic Society) may be useful.

We don't have space to provide detailed explanations of these skills, but all you're looking for is the next small improvement in each one. You can start by talking to friends and family about these skills: most people can name at least one thing that they do to achieve the skill, so follow their advice and practise. When you've grasped that much, books such as *Body Language For Dummies* by Elizabeth Kuhnke (Wiley) can show you how the experts do it and give you more things to practise. If you're lucky, there may be social skills training available in your area — check with your GP, the National Autistic Society and other organisations.

Any improvements in these areas will increase your ability to join in socially. Ultimately, after you have had lots and lots of practice, no one except an expert will be able to tell that someone on the autism spectrum is in the group.

Looking at Relationships

Very few people genuinely want to be alone, and people on the autism spectrum are no different. Nevertheless, some people choose to be alone in order to avoid the various problems that being in a relationship entails, which may be the right decision for you.

If you do decide to look for romantic or sexual involvement with somebody, here are some things you need to know.

Meeting someone special

In popular culture, meeting someone special always seems to focus on going to bars, dedicated singles' evenings or taking up Internet dating. This image ignores the real situation, which is that the vast majority of people meet their life partners at school, college, work or through mutual friends. Most people met their partners in the course of their normal day-to-day lives, and they didn't make a special effort to go out and find them. So people you meet while you're enjoying your hobby or attending an evening class, and also their friends, are one group among whom you may meet someone you really like and who really likes you.

You need to understand what's attractive and what isn't, so:

- **Do make an effort to look presentable:** Most important here is being clean. If you smell of sweat and haven't brushed your teeth, you are going to make a bad impression, so make sure you have had a shower and are wearing clean clothes.

- **Do talk about yourself a bit, but not too much:** This is a hard balance to get right, because if someone asks you questions and is interested in what you say, it's really tempting to talk about yourself non-stop. Make sure that for every one thing you disclose about yourself, you ask the other person a question about themselves.

- **Do take an interest in the other person:** This sounds silly; of course you're interested in the other person. But you have to show that you're interested in the person in a conversation, and not just stare at his or her body. Ask the person about his or her hobbies, job, favourite sort of food, or something similar. Don't ask people questions that are too personal, like how many boyfriends (or girlfriends) they have had before or when was the last time they kissed someone.

- **Be upfront about your social problems:** If you have a social problem such as going on and on and not being able to stop yourself, tell the other person about it and ask him or her to stop you before you get boring. The other person may be charmed by your honesty, which is certainly better than boring him or her.

✔ **Don't assume that you have to meet your ideal partner:** Talk to people you like, and if you decide they're not for you, you can still enjoy their company, learn about different people's characteristics and work out which personality traits you like, can tolerate or can't stand. You'll probably find yourself deciding that you do like some characteristics that you thought you hated. Meeting lots of people increases the chance of meeting someone you get on well with and also gives you the opportunity to develop your social skills.

✔ **Don't set your expectations too low:** If your self-esteem is very low, think about waiting until you've made some new friends before trying for a relationship. Friends will boost your self-esteem and give you people to talk to about your prospective partner and his or her behaviour. Listen to your friends' advice (though remember that it may not always be good; ultimately, what you do is your responsibility and advice is only a guide, not a guarantee).

✔ **Learn to compromise:** All relationships involve compromise. If you can't compromise, you can't maintain a relationship. You'll need to compromise on many choices, but initially it may be on things like what to do when you go out together, who pays the bill and so on.

Some people don't want or can't manage a traditional relationship, but still want to experience a sexual relationship. There's nothing wrong with this provided you're clear about your feelings and intentions when talking to prospective partners.

All of the skills you develop to help you with relationships can be applied to any relationships — with friends, managers, colleagues and family members. Master a skill once and you can use it all over the place!

Knowing about sex and sexuality

We're not going to try to repeat sex education lessons here (although if you need information in this area, several books have been written with an AS reader in mind; see the Appendix). We just give you the practical information that people somehow expect you to know without having to be told.

People on the autism spectrum are more likely to be true to themselves and not be influenced by the culture they live in. In matters of sexuality, this tendency is particularly noticeable. Compared with the general population, a larger proportion of people on the autism spectrum who are in relationships are in homosexual relationships. Evidence suggests that this is because people on the autism spectrum are following their hearts and don't feel constrained by the social stigma that's unfortunately still attached to being gay.

The majority of surveys into sexuality find very similar results:

- About 5 per cent of people are asexual and don't find either sex attractive.

- About 5 per cent of people are strictly heterosexual and don't find the same sex at all attractive.

- Around 2 per cent of people (several surveys have found the same figure of 1 in 70, which is a little less than 2 per cent of people) are strictly homosexual and don't find the opposite sex at all attractive.

- Eighty-eight per cent of people show some degree of bisexuality, although many often deny this except in anonymous surveys, because of the social stigma.

People on the autism spectrum, because fewer of them are aware of this social pressure and those who are aware refuse to give in to it, are more likely to allow themselves to love whoever they want.

However, some autistic men receive constant taunts of being 'gay', partly because it's a standard insult in the UK and partly because they've grown up being rejected by other boys and so spent lots of time with girls. As a result, the body language of these autistic men is often feminine (regardless of whether they're gay, straight or bisexual), hence the taunts.

Thinking about marriage and long-term relationships

When you have fallen in love with someone and they have fallen in love with you, you may begin to think about sharing a house together, marriage and even children. These are extremely important decisions and ones not to be rushed into.

Especially if you're not good at judging other people's characters, really getting to know someone well takes about three years. And while we don't suggest you should wait this long before getting married to someone you're in love with, bear in mind that the less time you've known someone, the less well you know them and the more surprises they still have to show you in the future.

If you're planning on marriage or buying a house together, consider having some experience of living in the same house as your partner before you make long-term commitments. You could rent together before you buy, or just go on holiday a few times where you share accommodation and household chores.

All long-term relationships are built on communication, so talk to your partner about both your and their expectations. You may need to discuss things like:

- Money
- Children
- Where to live
- Sharing the chores
- The need for some time alone
- Dealing with each other's family and friends

People with an ASC may need their partner to make unusual adjustments to make living with an ASC easier. For example, a person with AS may find touch uncomfortable, and only want a cuddle once a day. The person's partner may need a kiss each morning to feel loved. Communicating all these issues is of vital importance for a long-term relationship to work. You can read more tips and information in Chapter 11. A number of books have been written by people on the autism spectrum, their partners or both, which give guidance on forging a strong relationship and overcoming the inevitable difficulties. See Appendix A for a selection of them.

Once you're in a committed relationship, you may want to consider marriage. The advantages of marriage are:

- It provides a legal framework for your possessions, children and health.
- It makes you each other's legal next of kin in case of accident or incident.
- It's a demonstration of your commitment to each other.
- It's a celebration of your relationship with family and friends. (You can do this without getting married, too.)

On the downside, there's divorce. If you don't have lots of money or possessions, or if you live in rented accommodation, separating can be quite simple unless you're married. If you marry without careful consideration and then regret it, or if things just don't work out between you, splitting up is usually more complicated.

Chapter 7

Getting the Most Out of Education and the Workplace

*E*ven if they don't seem like the most important things to you, education and employment (used in its fullest sense, which we define in the following paragraph) are essential to getting what you want in life, because one or the other, or sometimes both together, give you a purpose in life and self-esteem.

Getting the most out of education or employment is important to everybody, but we're not saying that you need to go to university or slog away the years at the minimum wage. You may have to go to school, but we also look at education at other times of your life, which can be full-time, part-time, provided by professionals or developed by you alone through the books you read and the things you see. Similarly, employment could be through an employer, but we include self-employment, voluntary employment and you simply making use of your time.

We hope you'll gain an understanding of all the options that are open to you and not feel that life is already laid down as a process through school, college, university, full-time work and then retirement. Especially for those of us on the autism spectrum, life's likely to be a lot less planned and much less straightforward than that.

Going to School, College or University

You may assume that school, college and university are very similar apart from the age of the participants. Actually, although they all provide education, the environments are very different and different skills will be needed to get the most out of them. So depending on what skills you already have, you'll probably find that one of them suits you more than the others.

Settling into school

Most of us don't get a great deal of choice about school: the final decision of which one you go to is usually down to your parents or determined by where you live. The environment within the school, as far as it is adaptable, is modified by the teachers as they see fit. Some schools are fantastic at making adaptations for students with an autism spectrum condition (ASC) such as Asperger's syndrome (AS). They consult the individual, talk to the parents and do their absolute best to make school life easier. Other schools are less flexible, and less knowledgeable about ASCs. Obviously, your experience of school will be greatly affected by whether your school is accommodating to you or your child's needs.

Coping in mainstream school

Even in the most accommodating of schools, you'll find some aspects of mainstream education challenging. What you *can* do to help is learn the system and find ways to cope with it. Try to identify the things you find difficult to cope with and tell teachers, parents and tutors about them. Aspects of school you may find difficult could be:

- **The social times at lunch and break.** You could ask to spend time in the library instead of the school playground. A buddy may help you in these times (see the section "Buddies at school" later on).

- **Transitions between lessons.** At secondary school, you're expected to get to and from lessons by yourself. Usually you'll have to navigate busy corridors full of people, noise and chaos. Ask whether you're allowed to leave lessons 5 minutes before the bell rings so that you can travel to your next lesson in peace and quiet.

- **Remembering what you need to take with you.** Organisation can be a challenge if you've got an ASC like AS. You may forget which books to take to lessons, when your homework deadline was, and on what day of the week you need to bring your PE kit. Keeping a diary can really help with organisation. Also, ask your form teacher or peers to check that you have all the homework written correctly in your diary and know what's happening the next day. Having a visual timetable of the week can also really help.

If you find something difficult, tell someone about it. Doing something to change the system may be relatively straightforward, but the organisation won't be able to change unless you make it aware of the need to do so.

A desperately unhappy child is in no fit state to learn. Choose schools carefully and change if you or your child is unhappy and the school fails to make amendments to help make life easier. You can learn more about choosing schools in Chapter 9.

Buddies at school

If you are going to school, one strategy that works well for many people is the *buddy system*. Here, one or more people are nominated as your buddy or buddies. While your buddy may be or may become your friend, his or her purpose within the buddy system is to be your helper. The organisers of the buddy system should agree with you and your parents what parts of the day you find difficult or stressful, and your buddy should be there to help you at these times. In school, this is fairly straightforward, because one of your classmates becomes your buddy; he or she spends a lot of time with you each day anyway, so being your buddy just involves making sure you're okay. Buddies could help you at lunch times, with getting to and from lessons, getting the school bus on time, or making sure you've done your homework by the deadline.

Taking things literally

Children with an ASC such as AS often take everything that's said to them personally, because they don't usually have a good understanding of the intent of other children and the teachers. So, for example, if the form teacher tells the class that they need to be quieter because their noise is disturbing the children in the next classroom, the child with AS will make an effort to be quieter, even if he or she already says almost nothing, and speak in a whisper. Equally, children with AS often treat teasing as bullying, because they can't tell the difference.

You can't solve these problems alone. The solution is talking to people. Teachers are more likely to understand your point of view if you explain things to them calmly. They probably don't realise that you feel angry or upset by something they thought was trivial.

Beating the bullies

People with an ASC such as AS aren't the only school pupils to get bullied, but they are more vulnerable to bullying. Being a "loner" or coming across as "odd" makes bullies target people on the autism spectrum. If you're being bullied, tell someone you trust. This could be a teacher, teaching assistant or your parents. Try and avoid situations where you're vulnerable to bullying, such as empty school corridors and quiet corners of the playground. Staff at the school should be aware of bullying and what to do about it. People who bully should be dealt with and stopped. Sometimes this doesn't happen, but as long as you stand up for yourself and tell as many people as you can about the problem, the bullies should stop. You can read lots of tips to cope with bullying in Chapter 10.

Coping at college or university

If you have decided to go to college or university to study further after you leave school, bear in mind that the lifestyle will be very different to that of secondary school. You're expected to be much more independent, and there are a whole host of new social expectations. Here you can learn about how to cope with some of these. You can also read Chapter 10 for some more tips.

Organising your work

At school, when and where you work is usually determined by the teachers, and parents usually have something to say about when and where you do your homework. At college and university, in contrast, most of your week will be left to you to organise. Depending on who you are, you may find it easy to pursue your subject or you may be easily distracted, but either way you'll have to write your own timetable for when you should be studying during the week.

As well as time to study, you need to realise the importance of regular breaks and of time to relax and take your mind off your studies. Giving your mind time to relax usually improves the amount of learning and problem-solving you can achieve — only a few people don't benefit from this.

Plan leisure time into your timetable as well as study time to ensure you get breaks.

Help from a buddy

Just as it helps at school, having a buddy (someone who can help you with the things you find hard) can be very beneficial at college or university. Arranging a buddy takes a bit more organisation than it would at school. You may be lucky and have a buddy system at your university (usually organised by the disability support team or the pastoral tutors at the university). These buddies will be volunteers who offer their time to help others. If this system isn't available, you may be able to organise your own buddy (or buddies) via your tutor, who may know someone who can help. Alternatively a peer who is on the same course as you could help you out with specific things like finding lectures. Having more than one buddy can be better. At various points during the day, one of your buddies is responsible for accompanying you and making sure that you're okay. Having each buddy only help you a bit means you're able to get more support, because it's unreasonable to expect a student with his or her own workload and life to accompany you all day. Some of the points in the day when a buddy can come in useful are:

- Getting up on time
- Eating communal breakfast (if you have one) in the canteen
- Getting your stuff ready for the morning or day
- Going to your first tutorial or lecture
- Being in your tutorials or lectures
- Time between lectures
- Break times at school
- Lunch (which may be in three stages of getting to, eating and leaving)

> ✔ Going home
>
> ✔ Cooking or attending the evening meal
>
> ✔ Filling your time in the evening

If you have more than one buddy, make sure you have a plan for which buddy helps you at which point in the day. Remember that these points are only examples and you may have fewer or more points where a buddy helps you in your day. You need a buddy only for those points that you find difficult. For an example, see the nearby sidebar "With a little help from your buddies".

Dealing with academic pressures

Academic pressures affect different people at different times. Some struggle at secondary school but then find university a breeze academically, while others never experience pressure *until* they're at university.

One key point about dealing with any pressure is to talk to people about it. Tell people close to you — parents and friends — and at the school, college or university — teachers, tutors and welfare officers. Another key point is to talk about the problem as soon as you notice it — and not to put off doing something in the hope that it will just go away. In the real world the problem, whatever it is, almost never just solves itself.

With a little help from your buddies

Dave doesn't have a problem with living in his hall of residence at university, but he finds it difficult to use the gap between his first lecture (which finishes at 10 o'clock) and his second lecture (which doesn't start until 11 o'clock), because he takes too long to organise himself to do any work in the library during this hour. Therefore he either has to start packing his stuff up after only five minutes' work or he's late for his 11 o'clock lecture. He knows that some people go for a coffee, and he'd like to socialise more, but can't join any of the groups in the coffee shop because he doesn't know anyone. Because of these difficulties, one of the students from Dave's 9 o'clock lecture is his buddy for this hour. Most days they talk about what work to do while they walk to the library, and the buddy does all the difficult social stuff like choosing where to sit and saying hello to

people. The buddy also gets Dave to his next lecture on time. On Thursdays, Dave and his buddy go to the café instead, and now some of the people they regularly talk to will stop Dave and chat to him in the street. Dave is pleased to have these growing friendships, but often wishes people wouldn't disturb him when he's going somewhere.

The only other really difficult time for Dave is in the evening, because he knows others are going out and socialising, and wants to be able to join them. So, two evenings a week, one of the other residents calls on him and takes him to the pub. They go quite early, straight after tea, so that the pub is still quiet. Dave finds the noise gets too much as it gets later and busier, which is handy because it means he doesn't spend or drink too much.

Pressure can take several forms:

- Pressure to get your essay or project done on time
- Pressure that you put on yourself to get very high marks
- Pressure from dealing with multiple deadlines and demands on your time

The first step in dealing with academic pressures is realising that they exist. You may think this sounds silly, but, especially if you've chosen a very demanding subject, getting your degree is not just a matter of going to lectures and learning what the lecturer tells you. You will also have to spend a lot of your own time reading around the subject and developing your skills. If you don't put the work in, the academic pressures will inevitably build up as you approach a deadline for an essay or exam.

Conversely, you may put too much pressure on yourself to work hard (especially if you're a perfectionist). Many people keep going and going until the pressure has built up to nervous-breakdown-inducing levels, and only then realise that they have a problem. To recognise that you've reached this level, you need to talk to people. Particularly, talk to someone who has some understanding of autism, because he or she should know what questions to ask in order to find out how well you're coping. If you don't feel you know anyone you can talk to, your college or university should have a welfare officer who may be able to help (the job title varies, but the job's the same). Others you could talk to include:

- Your tutor
- A lecturer that you like
- A friend or buddy
- A university counsellor
- A non-academic supporter provided by the university or a separate external agency such as the National Autistic Society

Making friends

At school, you may have had a natural peer group of people in your class. At university, you may go to the same lectures as some people, but getting to know others and making friends can be more difficult because you don't see the same people day in, day out. The easiest way to make friends is to join a club based on something you're interested in, or interested in becoming interested in. That way, everyone at the club will already have something in common with you, and you can talk about why you're interested in it and what your previous experience of the subject is. Don't assume that every friend you make is going to be a friend for life or that every friend is going to become a close personal friend. Life is much more varied than that, and really good friendships require a bit of effort by both sides in order to keep them going. See Chapter 6 for more on friendship.

Dealing with bullying

Most people with AS get bullied and, unfortunately, the bullying seldom stops when you move on to sixth form, higher education or even work. A survey by the National Autistic Society found that 64 per cent of people over 18 years old with diagnoses of AS or other higher functioning forms of ASC had been bullied. The bullies target you because you're different and you lack the social skills to defend yourself. Neither of these things is going to change quickly, so to deal with bullies you need help.

Talk to your college or university tutor, a lecturer you trust, or the disability advice service at your university. They can help you to come up with useful strategies to cope with bullies. Having a buddy will put bullies off targeting you, because you're more likely to get bullied if you're on your own.

You've probably been told in relation to bullies, "Ignore them and they'll go away," or words to that effect. This isn't true; it's merely wishful thinking, because the person saying it doesn't want to have to think about or deal with the difficult situation.

To deal with bullies, being confident helps a lot. You can go on self-confidence courses or just practise standing up to the bullies when you're on your own. Prepare phrases you could say in response to nasty comments and practise saying them with conviction to a friend or just to yourself. Bullies like to see you stressed out and upset, so when you rehearse your retorts, practise saying them in a calm voice. That will give the bullies the impression you don't really care about what they say or do to you.

If the bullying is still upsetting and continues after you have stood up for yourself, then tell someone who may be able to help. Tell a friend, colleague, trusted member of staff or your parents.

Having a Job

Most people want to work and find that paid employment gives them a sense of self-worth and builds their self-esteem. People on the autism spectrum often struggle with finding a job and with working effectively once they've found one, until they seek help. And it's perfectly valid to decide that working is too stressful and therefore that you won't make any plans to find a job and instead will employ yourself in other ways. But if you're in work or wanting to work, there are some things you need to know.

Knowing your rights

Your key right under the Disabilities Discrimination Act (DDA) is that your employer is required to make "reasonable adjustments" to your work and to your workplace in order that you can fulfil your work role. (This law also applies to school, college and university.) For example, if you find using the phone stressful, it may be reasonable to change your job description so that you don't have to use the phone; but if your job is as a call-centre operative, then such a change would be unreasonable. No hard-and-fast rules apply here about what's reasonable or unreasonable; mostly, these questions are resolved through discussion or more formal negotiation. A dispute over what's reasonable would possibly have to be settled in a court of law if no resolution could be reached through negotiation, but this is relatively rare. Fortunately, employers very rarely want to go to this expense, and are very likely to agree to changes that:

- Affect only a small part of your role
- Cost little to implement or that a grant is available for
- Maximise the *productivity* of the team as a whole (productivity is the amount of work that gets done)

You also have the right — under the Human Rights Act — to be treated like a human being, so you shouldn't be bullied or otherwise harassed, and you shouldn't be treated differently from other employees, except by prior agreement.

Understanding Asperger's syndrome in the workplace

Compared with most people, you have some extra choices when you're applying for jobs. You may:

- **Decide not to tell your employer about your diagnosis:** Not telling your employer means that you won't be able to ask for any changes to help you do the job, but does allow you to prove to yourself that you can cope, and also can make it easier to fit in. This choice is for the brave few.

- **Declare your diagnosis on your application form or on your CV:** If you declare your diagnosis in advance, you run the risk that the employer will discriminate against you by not calling you to interview. This is a difficult form of discrimination to prove. However, a good employer won't reject such applications out of hand, and larger employers often guarantee an interview to people who declare disabilities under the Government's "two ticks" scheme. (The two-ticks disability symbol is awarded by Jobcentre Plus to employers who've made commitments to employ, keep and develop the abilities of disabled people.)

✔ **Declare your diagnosis after being asked to an interview:** Declaring your diagnosis after you've been asked to go for an interview but before you actually attend is often the best option, because the employer has a responsibility under the DDA to make the recruitment process accessible to you. This may be by rephrasing hypothetical questions, for instance, or by avoiding open questions such as, "How did you find your last job?" (Likely answer: "In the Jobs section of the newspaper".) Providing the information in advance also means the employer has an opportunity to find out about AS before the interview. As a result, you'll have a better chance to make a good first impression, and any wrong assumptions that the employer has about autism will have much less of an effect on his or her opinion of you.

✔ **Declare your diagnosis once you've started work:** Only telling people once you're doing the job can be tricky, because the employer will be concerned that you concealed something important. However, the employer still has the same responsibility to make the reasonable adjustments that the DDA requires — it's just that putting these in place before you start the job rather than afterwards is easier.

If you decide to be completely open about your diagnosis, it'll probably make introducing coping strategies and adaptations easier. People will always wonder why someone is being treated differently, and your diagnosis is all the explanation they need. If people don't know why you're getting special treatment, they can become resentful; but people are very understanding if . . . well . . . they understand. For an example of an adaptation, see the nearby sidebar "Counting up to meltdown".

Having a career

Planning a career is one of the most difficult things for anybody, on or off the autism spectrum. We have friends who are barristers, financiers and executives who say that they never chose to do what they're currently doing, but just sort of fell into it! And if that's the case for these high fliers, the problems that people on the spectrum have with planning — see Chapter 3 for more on this type of thinking, called *executive function* — must make any five-year career plan almost impossible. Nevertheless, if there's something that you really love, like working with numbers, talk to people about it and they may come up with a good idea for a job. You could talk to friends, teachers, tutors, careers advisers, parents or even your parents' friends or other experienced people you know who may have useful advice they can pass on to you.

Try to work out what type of work you want to do (such as administrative work, IT, and so on), even if you're not yet able to be specific. Many people with AS prefer *process-driven* work, which means that it can be broken down into a sequence of smaller tasks.

Counting up to meltdown

When the Goth started working at the National Autistic Society, he was struggling with stress, which surprised his boss because she couldn't see any signs of it. She suggested using a "stress scale" on his desk — a little flipchart of cards marked 1–10. Every hour or so, the Goth considers how stressed he feels and decides whether to adjust the number up, down or leave it as it is. The numbers indicate the following:

- 1 is happy and not at all stressed.

- 2, 3 and 4 are building, but low-level and perfectly normal stress — working can't always be easy.

- 5 is a bad day in the office — the sort of day when things go wrong and the pressure to meet deadlines builds up. Unless you're one of the select few who can calm him, you aren't allowed to talk to the Goth when the scale says 5 or more.

- 6 and 7 are worsening levels of stress. Fewer and fewer people are allowed to speak to the Goth as the numbers go up. People in the office start trying to be quieter, for example by arranging to take phone calls in a different room. Someone will take the Goth for a walk if the scale stays at 6 or more.

- 8 is the sort of stress that you would expect only in exceptional circumstances. It shouldn't happen in an office unless it happens to be struck by an earthquake. Junior doctors in accident and emergency departments suffer this level of stress on a bad day. No one is now allowed to talk to the Goth.

- 9 is critical. The boss is now racking her brains for new strategies.

- 10 on the stress scale has a special rule: if it stays at that level for 20 minutes, the Goth is allowed to quietly get up and leave for the day; no tidying up, no logging out, no questions asked, no goodbyes, no consequences. This has never happened.

A boss has to be quite bold to agree to this adaptation, especially the special rule. Many would fear that the employee would take advantage of it and put the scale up to 10 when he or she wasn't really that stressed. The special rule is essential for stress management, however: without that guarantee of an easy release, the stress would build much more quickly and precipitate a meltdown.

Unless you already have a career in mind, it's best to think about what you enjoy doing rather than to fix on a specific career like "being a doctor", because this allows you to compare various jobs that involve your interests and then make a more informed decision.

Only a tiny fraction of people actually have a career plan that has worked out more or less as they expected, so don't be surprised if you keep having to change yours. And don't worry if, like most people, you never bother to think of one.

Identifying bullying at work

You may think it's obvious when you're being bullied, but if you've suffered a great deal of bullying and aren't very good at spotting humour, you're likely to think that many incidents which are isolated acts of selfishness or mean-ness, or are good-natured teasing, are acts of bullying. This doesn't change the fact that you feel bullied, but it is a different situation from genuine bully-ing. In this situation, it is necessary for all of you to agree that there has been a misunderstanding, and for the others to agree to be more careful in their behaviour when dealing with you. Exactly how they are to be careful will depend on you and your personality. For example, if you value fitting in and becoming part of the team, learning to understand and enjoy being teased is a worthwhile goal.

Sometimes real bullying does happen in the workplace. If a colleague at work is asking you to do unreasonable things or teasing you maliciously in front of colleagues or on your own, then tell your boss.

Dealing with unemployment

In this section, we use the word *unemployed* to mean "not working". We don't mean "claiming unemployment benefits". If you're unemployed, you may be on unemployment benefits or you may be claiming disability benefits, living off your savings or getting by on the goodwill of friends or relatives. The odds are that as an adult, you'll be unemployed if you're not in further or higher education. A recent survey by the National Autistic Society showed that only 42 per cent of people with diagnoses of AS or other higher functioning forms of autism had a job. Of these people, 47 per cent worked full-time, 29 per cent worked part-time, and 14 per cent worked on a voluntary basis. Being unem-ployed often means you have plenty of time to pursue your hobbies; some people succumb to boredom or depression when unemployed, and it's pursu-ing or finding hobbies and interests which prevents this from happening. The majority of people with AS who are out of work want to have a job.

Being unemployed can easily leave you with no particular reason to get up in the morning, or when you do get up, no reason to wash — after all, you're going to be at home and aren't planning to meet anybody, because if you were, you'd have a reason to get up, wash and dress. The lack of a structured day is distressing for some — especially, in our experience, some women with AS. And a lack of purpose to the day, day after day, can also eat away at self-esteem.

A question people often ask in conversation is "What do you do?", which can easily become a dispiriting thing to hear if you're unemployed. Describing your main hobby or interest when replying to this question is absolutely fine. Most people will then get the hint that you don't work, and if you want to, you can then mention the main reason why that's the case. The main reason is unlikely to be AS, because this isn't a reason not to work (if it was, no one with AS would have a job). The real reason may be anxiety, depression or any of several medical complications associated with AS, but it's generally not a good idea to go into detail about your health except with close friends, family and professionals who are treating you. Instead, you could just say that you have long-term health problems. As with hearing that you have AS, some people's reaction to hearing that you have depression can be quite insensitive and dismissive. All such reactions not only hurt but also damage your self-esteem.

Going without a purpose in life for more than a few weeks can not only damage self-esteem and cause depression, but also damage your feelings of identity, and this seems to be a particularly bad effect of unemployment for people on the autism spectrum.

If you are unemployed and looking for a job, make sure you do something other than sit at home writing job applications and waiting to hear back from potential employers. Take up a new hobby or develop your work-related skills by volunteering for something you are interested in.

Getting any job isn't necessarily better than being out of work, because a job that doesn't use your interests and abilities — so-called *underemployment* — can be just as depressing or dispiriting as unemployment. To prevent depression, a job needs to be fulfilling.

Chapter 8

Finding Independence and Advocating for Your Rights

*L*iving independently is by no means impossible if you have an autism spectrum condition (ASC) such as Asperger's syndrome (AS). You may face more challenges, but these can be overcome with the right support and careful planning. Plenty of people with an ASC live in their own premises; they have meaningful activities in their lives and may have jobs. In this chapter, you get to learn about different types of accommodation, pick up tips for getting about by yourself (be it down the shops or to far-flung places in the world), and understand the financial side of being independent. You also find out about having your own identity, and the different autism rights groups that people with an ASC have set up.

Living Independently

Many people on the autism spectrum (for example, people with AS) never move out of their parents' houses, or move back in after a period of living on their own. Others feel that moving out to their own place is a really important goal. Whatever you feel, living independently is likely to be something you and your family think a lot about.

Deciding whether, or how, you're going to live independently is a big decision that's best broken down into lots of little decisions. You may, for example, choose to move out but still get help from your family or professional support workers with shopping, cooking, laundry and cleaning. Moving out doesn't mean having to do everything for yourself, and equally you may come to the conclusion that staying with your parents is the right decision for you. This decision is fine and doesn't mean that you can't develop your independence.

While continuing to live at home, you can take control of shopping for your own food, washing and ironing your own clothes, and maybe even cooking for yourself. Other important skills to master are planning your finances, dealing with utility companies and putting the bins out (which has become more complicated in recent years as a result of recycling). All these skills are needed by everyone who lives independently, and surprisingly, well under 100 per cent of people have mastered them.

You may think that calling a task like laundry a skill is a bit odd, but even though we often don't think of some tasks as skills, these jobs do have to be learnt. And just about everyone has at least one "blind spot", which means they have real difficulty with a skill that the majority of people think of as easy. Typically, people with AS struggle with more of the common skills than most people, so getting a family member or friend to give you a "proper" lesson can be really helpful. Then you can concentrate on what you need to learn, practise in front of someone, and maybe even take notes.

Most people seem to learn something about living independently from their older brothers and sisters or from their friends. Most young people on the autism spectrum, if they have any friends, talk to them only about their common interests. So they miss the opportunity to learn about day-to-day life and all the little tips and tricks people use to make their lives easier. This means more formal ways of learning may be more helpful. You could try cookery classes, or pick up some tips from an occupational therapist. No matter how good the training, some things are just too difficult to learn for some people; see the nearby sidebar "Standing the heat in the kitchen".

Standing the heat in the kitchen

The Goth has a confession to make. He can't cook. Actually, that's a bit of an understatement. For example, one evening last year the mission he'd accepted was to heat a carton of soup in the microwave. Many people struggle with opening these spout-topped cardboard cartons. Not so the Goth: he pushes back the "wings" and squeezes the spout into existence with practised ease. When he was little, everyone in his family turned to him to perform this feat—back then the cartons always contained milk. Some people struggle with operating microwaves. Again, the Goth has no trouble: he stirs, he heats for a few minutes, he stirs again, he finishes heating, he stirs again, and then he waits. The waiting is where the problems start.

It's just about impossible to wait for two minutes without his mind wandering. Twenty minutes later, he comes back to a carton of distinctly cool soup. He reheats it. To stop his mind wandering, he makes a cup of tea. Conveniently, this takes about two minutes before the tea has to be left to brew. Inconveniently, by the time he's poured boiling water on the tea, his mind has wandered and he forgets the soup. He goes back to the telly until the end of the programme. Getting quite hungry now, this break in proceedings reminds him of the soup. He reheats it. Making a real effort this time, summoning all his mental resources, he fails to stop his mind wandering, gives up, and eats the soup cold. What would be nice now is a cup of tea . . .

Finding suitable accommodation

Where to start with finding accommodation will depend to a degree on where you are in your life. If you're a student, the student union will have an accommodation service that can help you find suitable rooms. The college or university may also have an accommodation office that can supply similar information. If you're not a student, then you need to search the local paper's accommodation small ads or use the Internet.

Wherever you're looking, there's no easy place to start; no tip we can give you will help you pick out the right advert for the accommodation that's suitable for you. You'll soon see that renting a whole flat is very expensive, and that bedsits are more expensive than most rooms in shared houses. If you're lucky, you may have a friend with a room to rent, but make sure you know each other well enough to get along as housemates. Agreeing to share with a friend whom you don't know very well is a great way to ruin a friendship — so be warned!

If where you want to live is a long way from places you travel to regularly, like work and your parents' house, travel costs will be more expensive and travelling will use up more of your free time, which can be surprisingly stressful. So you need to consider spending a bit more on rent in order to live somewhere nearer to where you need to be. Because you'll then save money on travel, this shouldn't cost much more overall, and not being stressed is a very valuable thing.

If you rent with complete strangers, they'll expect to chat to you a bit when you view the room, and they'll judge whether they can get along with you on the basis of that chat. If this is very difficult for you, then try renting a place on your own. A bedsit can be reasonably priced and you won't have to share with somebody.

Beyond the basics of bed, fridge and roof, you'll need to consider whether the place will be expensive to heat, how noisy it is and whether there are likely to be strong smells (for example, if the flat's above a takeaway).

People with an ASC often have sensory sensitivities (see Chapter 12), and these need to be taken into account when choosing suitable accommodation. Noise can come from nearby roads, shops, schools and businesses (not to mention airports and railway lines). You may also find other people in the same building noisy (and that doesn't mean just your flat or house; in a flat or a semi-detached or terraced house, sounds can penetrate through the walls, floors and ceilings). You need to discover for yourself how much and what sort of noise you can live with.

Apart from cooking smells from your flatmates and possibly your neighbours, the smells that cause most problems for tenants are those from restaurants, cafés, dry cleaners and farms. Generally, you can't do much about these smells except in unusual circumstances, so if you're particularly sensitive, check that the causes of the smells you hate aren't nearby.

Check the area you're considering moving to at a time when smells are likely — during the day for dry cleaners, lunchtime and evening for restaurants, and so on.

Achieving financial independence

The obvious way to become independent financially is to get a job. This is easier said than done for many people with an ASC such as AS, because although you may want a job and have skills, getting suitable employment in a supportive environment is very hard. Many workplaces require a large degree of social understanding from their employees, which makes life difficult for employees on the autism spectrum. Nevertheless, having some employment improves your self-esteem and feelings of worth enormously, not to mention the fact that you get paid doing a job. You can learn more about employment in Chapter 7.

You may have the view that having a paid job is too stressful for you, or the support required to get a job just isn't available. Being out of work is perfectly okay if it's your choice and you find other valuable ways to spend your time. You may therefore need government support to become financially independent from your parents and family.

Getting financial independence requires money management skills. You can learn skills from your parents, friends and siblings, but courses on this specific issue also exist. You can find information on `www.direct.gov.uk/en/MoneyTaxAndBenefits/ManagingMoney`; also, the National Autistic Society (NAS) has a free managing money resource specifically tailored to people with an ASC, which can be found at `www.managingmoney.org.uk`.

Getting a job

Finding a job you enjoy, that isn't too stressful and where your employer understands AS and is supportive of your needs is sadly a very difficult task. Most people on the autism spectrum need support in finding employment and in maintaining a job once they've got one. If you're looking for a job, think about preparing yourself by doing the following:

  ✔ **Developing interview skills:** To get a job, you'll probably have to go through an interview. Think about whether there's someone who can go with you to the interview who can support you and advocate your skills, because you may find this difficult. Social skills are extremely important in interviews, so you may want to practise interviews with a friend, parent or teacher and focus on the social skills needed. If you disclose your diagnosis to your potential employer, it should be fine for you to bring someone with you to the interview, and the person giving the interview should at least place less emphasis on your social skills and more emphasis on whether you can actually do the job in hand in the knowledge that you have an ASC.

- ✓ **Deciding on part-time or full-time work:** Working part-time may be less stressful for you and may suit your lifestyle. Alternatively, you may love having a full-time job. Think about the pros and cons of each for your individual circumstances. If you currently receive benefits, remember to check whether being employed affects your eligibility for these benefits.

- ✓ **Assessing what support you would need in a job:** Maybe you want to give it a go without asking for special considerations to be made to take into account your AS. Often, it really helps to make a few adjustments to the job, the work environment and your supervision so that the job runs smoothly and you are less exposed to things that are stressful. Under the Disabilities Discrimination Act, your employer is required to make "reasonable adjustments" to your work and the workplace. For example, you may need a quiet workspace away from other people, rather than a desk in an open plan office. Meeting with your boss more often than is usual could help clear up misunderstandings and would give you a chance to express your needs and chat about how things are going.

The NAS Prospects service supports people with AS looking for employment or in employment. Some of their services are UK wide, but the most extensive service runs in the London and Glasgow areas. Prospects also has many tips for employers. Find out more information on www.autism.org.uk/prospects, or phone 020 7704 7450 (London) or 0141 248 1725 (Glasgow).

Being aware of benefits

The benefits system in the UK has changed recently: since October 2008 Incapacity Benefit has been replaced by Employment and Support Allowance (ESA), so anyone making a new claim must now apply for ESA. However, although many small changes in the rules governing the benefit have occurred, it's mostly just a change of name. For people on the autism spectrum, this name change is a good thing, because the title "Incapacity Benefit" feels wholly inappropriate and depressing for people who interpret the word "incapacity" literally — we're not, after all, incapable! Being placed on Incapacity Benefit felt like a judgement.

You may, of course, be unable to claim ESA. The system may deem you fit for work, which only leaves you Jobseekers' Allowance (JSA) as your main benefit, although additional benefits are available:

- ✓ Housing Benefit for paying rent
- ✓ Council Tax Benefit
- ✓ Disability Living Allowance for paying long-term health costs if you're under 65
- ✓ Attendance Allowance for paying long-term health costs if you're 65 or over

- Child Benefit to support your children
- Carer's Allowance to maintain you if you're caring for someone else. Carer's Allowance is paid only if you don't get enough money to live on from other sources, so it should be the last benefit you apply for.

In addition to these benefits, you may also be able to claim:

- Working Tax Credit if you're working more than 16 hours a week
- Child Tax Credit to help support your children.

You may also be claiming benefits which have been discontinued, like Incapacity Benefit. You're entitled to continue claiming these until you are told otherwise by letter from the relevant government or council department, or until you no longer qualify for the benefit (this is true of all benefits, of course).

You need to contact Jobcentre Plus to check your eligibility for benefits and tax credits. You can visit a job centre in person, or go to www.job centreplus.gov.uk or phone 08000 55 66 88.

Applying for a benefit usually involves filling in a long form, especially in the case of Disability Living Allowance. Get help. It may be against your usual habit, but it makes the process a great deal easier and less daunting.

If you need help you can go to your local Citizens Advice Bureau, and they may also be able to help you fill in part of the form. Most Citizens Advice Bureaux have information giving detailed advice about what to put on the forms. The Citizens Advice website www.adviceguide.org.uk can also help.

The NAS Helpline also offers some guidance on claiming benefits, either by email at www.autism.org.uk/enquiry or by phone on 0845 070 4004.

Being a specialist

One Danish company called Specialisterne has woken up to the fact that people on the autism spectrum are highly skilled employees and that given the right support they can produce work to a very high standard. This company exclusively employs people with ASCs for computer programming, software testing and data management. It also trains people with ASCs in skills needed for work in business. Recognising that people on the autism spectrum are reliable, motivated, and have a high level of technical ability, attention to detail, accuracy, a logical approach and an exceptional memory for facts and figures, Thorkil Sonne, a father of a young man with AS, set up this pioneering company. He now aims to create 1 million jobs for "specialist people" (by this he means people with a diagnosis on the autism spectrum) across the world. A branch of Specialisterne has recently opened in Glasgow. In Specialisterne companies, it's "normal" to have an ASC. For more information, see www.specialist people.com.

Taking up travelling

Travelling may sound like a big scary subject or it may be something you've always been desperate to do. And that's before we've even said whether we're talking about travelling to work or travelling to Timbuktu.

But the fundamental similarity between these two extremes (making the journey to work and going backpacking abroad) is that they both involve going out into the world and interacting with people. Travelling is living. The cliché "life is a journey" is true. And travelling away from where you live allows you to make mistakes with total strangers. You can experiment with conversations with people in a distant town and never have to worry that your mistakes will affect your future conversations with them. If you ever see them again, the chances of them remembering you are small and get smaller as the years go by. Then you can use your improved conversational skills with people in your local community.

Getting out and about locally

Even a walk to the shops and back is a challenge for some AS people: it's noisy, which can be a problem for those with sensory sensitivities, there's lots of movement, and you have to be on the lookout and ready to react to circumstances (like avoiding other people on the pavement). A simple trip to buy a paper can turn into a stressful nightmare.

If you find travel stressful because of the crowds, consider changing your plans so that you can travel at quieter times. Also, for longer train journeys, if you book well in advance you can often get a first-class reservation for only a few pounds more than a second-class one. Many first-class carriages have single seats, which some find create a much less stressful environment, as well as the usual double seats. In big cities, some people prefer to allow extra time in order to walk rather than use buses, trams, underground trains and rapid-transit systems.

Most jobs can be adapted so that you start earlier or later, so speak to your employer about changing your start and finish times to avoid the busiest parts of the day. This can apply just as well to changing your lunch time so that you can take your break when there aren't so many people around.

Keep in mind how you feel about travel when looking for accommodation. The ideal flat will be useless if you find the journey to and from it hell. Putting a price on stress, especially if you're on a low income, is difficult, but it's almost always worth spending a little more to reduce it.

Travelling the wider world

At the other extreme from day-to-day travel is going travelling abroad on your own. Many people on the autism spectrum, when holidaying abroad, discover that people are much friendlier and easier to deal with. Curiously, it doesn't matter which country you travel to, although a country that doesn't speak your native language seems to be slightly better. You'll find that most people treat a foreigner who's acting oddly with a lot of patience and tolerance. They put all your unusual behaviour down to being foreign, rather than seeing any of it as wrong. If you also have a good memory (or even if you don't) and learn some of the language, you'll endear yourself to people, which makes them even more accepting. This is true even in another English-speaking country like the USA: put the occasional "automobile" and "elevator" into your conversation and most people will see you as making an effort, and so be well-disposed towards you.

Supporting your local support group

Living independently may be tough sometimes, particularly socially. If you live on your own, you may not see people on a regular basis. Meeting new people can be hard when you move to a new place, but joining in local activities that interest you or going to different support groups specifically for people on the autism spectrum can help.

Various sorts of support group exist for people on the autism spectrum. The NAS and other organisations run many of these, and a growing number take the form of "grass-roots" meetings. Some groups are purely social and usually meet in pubs or cafés; some are discussion groups; some are political or activist groups, which we talk more about later in this chapter; and a few are social skills groups where you can learn the skills that most people are never taught. The NAS is a good source of information about these groups, but other charities also know about some of the groups in their area, especially if the charity has some connection with autism. Charities which do have such a connection include those for epilepsy, youth unemployment and mental health. And if you can't find a group in your area, you can always start one!

Having an Identity

Having a clear identity is important to your self-esteem. Many people on the autism spectrum struggle with having their own identity that is separate from that of other people. Others on the spectrum have a very clear idea about their personal identity. Either way, identity is linked with independence, because if you are sure about who you are and what you want, you will find it easier to live independently. Developing a sense of identity is something that takes most people up until adulthood or even longer.

An important part of your identity is your name. Many people on the autism spectrum insist on their full name being used all the time by everyone, which is unusual because most people have at least a few close relatives or friends who call them by a pet form of their name or sometimes by a nick-name. And many people are known by a *diminutive*, which is a short form of their name (for example, Joe is short for Joseph). Some are even registered with a diminutive as their official name. People on the spectrum sometimes find being called by two different names difficult — responding to two names means thinking a bit more, which adds to the overload.

At the opposite extreme to using your full name, a significant number of people on the autism spectrum use a nick-name or change their name — significant because a larger proportion of people on the spectrum do it than in general. Some people say that those who change their name don't like themselves, which may be true in varying degrees for some individuals, but for others their name has been so abused by bullies that they cannot hear it without feeling the stress of those memories or without feeling like they're being bullied. For the Goth's story, see the nearby sidebar, "Being the Goth by any other name".

Parents and other family members may find it difficult to understand and cope with their child (of whatever age, including adult) deciding to use a different name. They need to be supportive: however unconcerned the person seems, changing names is never an easy decision.

Being the Goth by any other name

For about 30 years, the Goth has been called the Goth by at least some people. This nick-name originated from a character in a role-playing game whom he called Goth. Goth became so successful that the other players in the group got used to calling him "Goth" all the time. That would've been that, a nick-name used by just three people for a period in his youth. But twice more, people coined for him "the Goth", until he decided that this was obviously his right name and adopted it while at university. He feels that the "the" is somehow better than just "Goth", like the Sun and the Moon. An event that happens three times somehow feels more important and significant.

Part of the Goth's reason for adopting his new name is that names have always been a problem for him. He very rarely says anybody's name, and tends to give pets names such as Cat, Dog, Piebald, Four-spot and Nosy. Some people admit to thinking to themselves by name, for example "Come on, Patricia, you can do this." The Goth was in his twenties before he first heard of someone doing this, and it still seems deeply strange to him today.

The Goth was brought up to be proud of his given name, James. He was called this in memory of his grandfather, who was a non-commissioned officer in the infantry and fought in the First World War; he died shortly after the war ended, probably from the effects of poison gas. So the Goth hasn't wanted to change his name completely and instead uses James Mason the Goth, with "Mason the Goth" acting as a fancy surname. The name has the advantage of being a topic of conversation — people are always wanting it explained, especially as he doesn't wear black — so it helps him avoid awkward silences and fretting about what to say.

Learning about Autism Rights

A crucial issue relating to autism rights is whether autism is a disability. As we mention in the Introduction, many people on the spectrum don't consider themselves to be disabled, local NHS mental health teams don't consider autism to be a mental health problem (although anxiety, depression, obsessive–compulsive disorder and many other conditions that are common in autism are dealt with by local NHS mental health teams), and local education authority learning disability teams don't consider autism to be a learning disability, because the problems with learning are non-intellectual. Nevertheless, without help, even more people on the spectrum would be unemployed, and the number of those suffering nervous breakdowns or living in poverty would certainly increase. So at the moment most people on the spectrum have no real choice but to take advantage of disability legislation wherever they can.

Since the creation of the Equality and Human Rights Commission (EHRC) in 2006, this organisation has been wholly responsible for the rights of disabled people in England and Wales. Scotland has the Equality and Human Rights Commission Scotland (EHRCS) together with the Scottish Human Rights Commission (SHRC), and Northern Ireland has the Equality Commission for Northern Ireland (ECNI), which works with the Northern Ireland Human Rights Commission (NIHRC).

This combining of disability rights with equality rights has so far proved to be a problem for people on the spectrum, because it means that a group that already fails to fall strictly within the remit of mental health, physical disability and learning disability now looks to an organisation that tries to pay attention to many more areas in which discrimination occurs. For example, the old organisation (prior to 2006), the Disability Rights Commission, had some autism-specific accessibility features on its website. These features have not reappeared on the EHRC website.

Gaugin was an artist

Some people believe that calling someone "autistic" is wrong. They feel that the person is more important than the diagnosis, so they prefer to use phrases such as "person with autism". Many people on the spectrum, however, cannot see the diagnosis as something separate from themselves, and feel that person-first language is treating their autism like a disease that can be removed. This feeling isn't unique to autism: many deaf people feel the same way — they are deaf people, not people with a disability.

However politically correct they are, no one would suggest that the painter Gaugin, friend of Paul Cézanne (see Chapter 14), was a "person with a desire to paint". Gaugin felt that painting was deep in his soul, that it was not just a vocation but a part of him: Gaugin was an artist in the same way that the Goth is an autist.

Defining degrees of awareness and radicalism

Some people just want other people to treat them the way they want to be treated themselves. Others realise that this isn't going to happen unless they do something to educate people about ASCs. Some decide to harness the power of publicity to get their message to more people. Yet others take this approach further and join an organisation that campaigns to increase the public understanding of autism. Such organisations vary in their approach and purpose.

In terms of rights and self-advocacy, AS is unique. AS people are intelligent, are generally considered able, and are legally considered capable of determining their own lives. However, more than others, people on the spectrum have difficulty understanding how reasonable their decisions seem to other people (including other people on the spectrum). This means that a very radical AS group may demand independence from authority and long-term financial security from the benefit system for all autists, while failing to see that almost nobody has these two things, and that for many autists independence from authority would not be desirable — indeed, many would find being left to make all their decisions on their own deeply distressing.

In many ways, this confusion about the aims of autism rights campaigning is similar to the "anti-capitalist" organisations of the 1980s, who failed to realise that the type of capital they were opposed to didn't include small business people. People running small businesses are certainly capitalists, and campaigners woke up to this fact and changed their terminology to "anti-globalisation", which targeted only international capitalists and international corporations. Given time, autism groups will work out the right words: words that are both precise and easily understood. But at the moment, some campaigners are demanding things that they want and claiming that all autists want them.

People with AS often lack this sensitivity to other people's thoughts and feelings, but fortunately they also have the intelligence to learn it.

Knowing the different autism groups

Several autism groups have been founded by people on the spectrum over the last 20 years or so. The first to get international publicity was the Autistic Liberation Front, though an organisation with that name is no longer in existence as far as we can tell. In the virtual world Second Life, the autistics.org group has set up an organisation called the Autistic Liberation Front, but whether any of the original members are involved in this isn't clear.

Whatever the relationship between the two Autistic Liberation Fronts, what's interesting is the name: the frustration with the way autists are treated in the world is clearly expressed. The other main self-advocacy groups are:

- ✔ Aspies For Freedom (AFF), www.aspiesforfreedom.com
- ✔ Autism Network International (ANI), www.autreat.com
- ✔ Autistic Rights Movement (ARM UK), www.autisticrights movementuk.org
- ✔ Autistic Self Advocacy Network (ASAN), www.autisticadvocacy.org

Getting deeper into autism rights

Society often discriminates against people on the autism spectrum: getting access to employment is full of unnecessary barriers, the education system may not meet the needs of those with an ASC, and adults with ASCs may get overlooked. This makes many individuals on the spectrum and their families feel the need to campaign (locally and nationally) to make the world a better place for those living with an ASC.

If you decide you want to campaign (about anything), you can take several different approaches, either alone or in a group:

- ✔ **A writing campaign:** Write to the organisations you're targeting, to your MP and other relevant officials and, most importantly, to (or appear in) the media in order to get publicity for your campaign. Campaigning letters that are signed by many people are known as petitions (strictly speaking, though, only one person needs to sign a request to an official for it to be called a petition). Generally, the more people who write letters or sign petitions, the better and more successful the campaign.

- ✔ **Lobbying:** If a writing campaign doesn't inspire you, you could try negotiation or lobbying, which are more or less the same thing, but the words are used in different ways. *Lobbying* doesn't refer just to lobbying MPs, but at its most basic level refers to pestering anybody to do what you want. Again, negotiation and lobbying are most effective if you are a group rather than an individual. Negotiations are entered into by both sides: that is, both sides want something. Lobbyists seek meetings so that they can explain their case: the people they're facing generally don't want anything other than to listen to the lobbyists.

- ✔ **Protesting:** Your third option is to ignore the official channels and protest. *Protest* usually takes one of four forms: protest marches, gatherings (marches and gatherings are often called *demonstrations*), sit-ins and publicity stunts. Don't do anything that's illegal, and bear in mind that protest isn't a reliable way of campaigning, because some protests damage your cause instead of helping it.

If you're considering joining a group, spend plenty of time thinking about what you want from it, what skills and ideas you can bring to it, and what types of campaigning you're prepared to be involved in. You need to be aware of the group's values and methods, where it meets, how many members it has, and as much other information about it as you can find. Think carefully about whether it is the right organisation for you to join. If the group allows it, you could try going along to a meeting to see what it's like — going to a meeting doesn't commit you to anything.

Sticking up for your rights

You may need to stick up for yourself in many situations in life, from expressing your opinions to others who disagree through to more serious situations like advocating for your right to work, live where you want to and do the activities you enjoy in life. Having help to do this is always advantageous, and you can get family members, friends or professionals to help fight your corner.

Considering the C-word — cure!

Few things are more likely to make someone with AS angry than to talk about a cure for autism, even if you're only referring to classic autism. Many sociable people on the spectrum know people who have a variety of diagnoses, and they get to see the minds and personalities of these people. A kindred spirit exists and can be felt, along with a feeling that any attempt at a cure would also destroy the person and create a different one. Nobody wants to lose their identity.

What people on the spectrum often do want to lose are those signs and symptoms which affect their lives in ways that they don't like. If they're more severely affected, this is especially true. Exactly what people don't like about their autism is a very individual choice, and it's important to recognise the difference between "curing" autism and helping people to live their lives and be themselves.

Some critics of autism rights say that everyone who is against finding a cure for autism is "high-functioning" and lacks empathy (for a definition of "high functioning" autism see Chapter 3 and the Introduction). While it's true that the majority of rights campaigners are "high-functioning", this criticism is neither fair nor accurate, not least because some people who are against a cure aren't on the spectrum. Many people who are on the spectrum view autism as part of their identity, and talk of curing them is then a personal attack. Many feel they empathise with other people on the spectrum: they only lack empathy for non-autistic people. They look forward to the day when they can recognise themselves in the diagnostic criteria.

For the record, the Goth has long advocated dismantling fences. Doing so would have two advantages: it would stop people sitting on them, and bring the people on either side together.

Because public understanding of ASCs is so poor, learning how to be your own advocate, called *self-advocacy*, is an important skill for people on the spectrum. An advocate is literally someone whom you "call in" to help you (which is why the term is used to describe lawyers, who are called in to help with legal issues). So "self-advocacy" doesn't really make a lot of sense, but a lot of words turn out to be pretty silly when analysed in this way.

Self-advocacy is a tricky skill to learn, so it helps if you can rehearse and get some honest feedback about how you're doing, both during rehearsal and when doing it for real (this means a friend or support worker will need to be with you so that they can listen to you in action).

We can't give you a set of rules about how to be a self-advocate, because exactly how to do it will depend on your personality, where you live and what stage of life you're at. Many organisations and support groups are able to offer advice about self-advocacy, and some can also provide training on it. You can check with the NAS and other support organisations for groups in your area.

Part III
Supporting People with Asperger's Syndrome

"Because I have Aspergers, I have an exceptionally good memory – I remember you teasing me unmercifully as a very young child."

In this part . . .

Many of you reading this book will be parents or professionals working with people on the autism spectrum. Having a good understanding of Asperger's Syndrome and how best to support people is really important, so let us guide you on your way.

In this Part, we'll take you through all the things you need to know as a parent of a child on the autism spectrum. We advise you on managing stress, coping with comments from others, and choosing the right school. You can also learn about the issues facing you as your child gets older like housing, work and what happens when you're no longer around to look after them.

Parent or otherwise, you can also find out about how best to support adults with AS through making environmental adjustments and having an understanding of the sensory difficulties of those on the autism spectrum. You can also pick up lots of tips on how to relate to your siblings, work colleagues or friends who have an ASC.

Chapter 9

Parenting Children Who Have Asperger's Syndrome

A s a parent of a child who has Asperger's syndrome (AS), you're probably an expert on the autism spectrum. If you're not an expert already, you'll inevitably become one as you advocate for your child in various different situations. You're on a steep learning curve: you'll have to navigate through an enormous amount of information and assess the various systems of support. You'll also have to cope with some tough struggles like dealing with nasty comments from members of the public. In this chapter you can find out how to communicate effectively with your child, how to cope with difficult behaviour, how to develop ways to teach social skills and, importantly, what you can do to help yourself stay sane.

You've not got an easy road in front of you, but loving, well-informed parents make a huge difference to their children's lives.

Managing the Early Years

You may be lucky enough to have had a diagnosis for your child when he or she was quite young. If so, you can get started finding out all the information you need to help your child in the early years of development. A lot of evidence these days shows that the earlier you start helping your child, the better. Don't worry if your child was diagnosed later, though. You can still discover new things and try new strategies to help your family. Remember, people can learn new things at any age.

This section covers a few key points about parenting for children on the spectrum. Although we aim this chapter at younger children, all of the suggestions can be used with children of any age. You may also want to consider specific approaches to teaching your child or helping your child's development. Specific therapies and approaches are covered in Chapter 13. If you're interested in trying out a special diet for your child, see Chapter 15.

Look out for courses that help parents of children on the autism spectrum. For example, the National Autistic Society (NAS) runs free courses for parents, called *Help!*, details of which can be found at www.autism.org.uk.

Communicating with your child

The most important thing to sort out early on is how you and your child can communicate effectively with one another. Children with more severe autism spectrum conditions (ASCs) may not communicate using words at all (to find out more about communication with children at this end of the spectrum, see *Understanding Autism For Dummies*, by Stephen Shore and Linda Rastelli (Wiley)). In this section we talk about communication strategies that are useful for children at the higher end of the autism spectrum who have diagnoses such as AS.

Communication is a two-way process. All individuals involved in a conversation need to understand what is being communicated, and need to be able to express what they want to put across. Both you and your child will need to make an effort to communicate effectively with each other.

Communication is complicated and involves many different elements. You've got the speaking part and saying what you want to say, and the understanding part, where you figure out what someone's trying to communicate to you, but on top of all that come body language and emotions, which contribute another layer of complexity. Most people on the spectrum have difficulties with at least one aspect of communication. To help them, they need to learn strategies to communicate effectively, but you and your family will also need to learn techniques to adapt your communication so that your child has the best chance of understanding.

When you've worked out useful ways to help your child communicate, or to help other people communicate with your child, try writing a guide for the key people in your child's life to tell them what you've learnt. That way, whoever comes into your child's life will have some tips and techniques to follow, and your child will benefit from the improved communication. You can give the guide to nursery staff, swimming teachers, grandparents, doctors or anyone in your child's life.

If your child doesn't seem to understand what you say, doesn't follow your instructions, or ignores you, you may find it daunting. You may feel overwhelmed by the difficulty communicating or unsure of what to do.

Lots of children on the spectrum will communicate with someone else only if they need or want something such as food or a favourite toy. Communicating with you about other things that aren't directly related to their needs may seem pointless to them. "Small talk" is very unlikely to happen, but children who have AS will happily chat to you for hours about their special interest, be it a particular computer game, types of dinosaur, or buses.

You may feel upset if your child's communication is very one-sided and he or she doesn't seem interested in you. But don't worry, this lack of interest doesn't mean your child doesn't love you. Children who have AS will show their affection in different ways and when they do, it'll be very special.

Helping your child communicate

Children on the spectrum often struggle to understand what's being said to them. To get around this, you can try several different communication styles.

First, make your instructions, questions or conversation clear. To make sure you're communicating clearly, try the following:

- ✔ **Speak slowly, and give only one instruction at a time:** For example, rather than saying, "Go and brush your teeth then get dressed," ask your child to brush his or her teeth, then wait until that task is finished before you ask your child to get dressed. The same thing goes with questions. One thing at a time is always best.

- ✔ **Avoid sarcasm, metaphors and idioms:** People on the spectrum find these really difficult to understand because they tend to take words and expressions literally. So if you want your child to know that you're keeping an eye on him or her, don't tell your child that (you can't put an eye on someone without doing yourself a lot of damage) or worse, say "I've got eyes in the back of my head" (how scary!). If you remark that it's "raining cats and dogs", expect your child to look outside and be a little confused.

- ✔ **Be clear about what you mean, and be concrete when you talk about abstract concepts:** This applies especially with things like feelings, which children on the spectrum will have even more difficulty understanding.

- ✔ **Be patient and give your child plenty of time to respond to any questions or requests:** It will take your child more time to process verbal information than you may expect, so count to ten before expecting a response or before repeating your question.

As well as changing how you talk to your child, you can also help him or her to communicate by using visual prompts. Pictures, symbols, visual timetables, or cartoons of particular situations will all help your child understand what you're talking about and what's going on in his or her day.

 Stick pictures up around the house to help develop your child's independence. For example, put a cartoon strip or instructions with pictures in the bathroom so your child knows what to do, in what order, when going to the toilet or brushing his or her teeth.

Symbols can be used to help your child make choices, for example between two activities or two things to eat. You can also use visual timetables to help your child know what they're going to be doing each day. By using pictures instead of words, you can help your child to understand what's going on.

For more on using pictures and symbols, see Chapter 13. Also look at www. widgit.com, www.dotolearn.com and www.pecs.org.uk, and *Comic Strip Conversations* by Carol Gray (Future Horizons).

Encouraging conversation

As well as helping your child to communicate his or her needs and understand what you're saying, you also need to try to encourage your child to talk about a wider range of things. Improved conversational skills will help your child to develop social skills, and will let your child know that he or she can talk to you about anything, not just his or her immediate needs or special interest.

Do your best to engineer situations in which your child can strike up conversation with you. Use everyday activities to ask your child questions about what he or she is doing, and encourage conversation whenever you can. For example, if your child is playing with a particular toy, ask him or her a few questions about it. If a plane flies overhead and catches your child's attention, comment on it and use it as a way to talk about planes.

 You can learn more about ways of encouraging conversation and communication from the Hanen programmes "More than Words" and "Talkability", available from www.hanen.org.

Your child may be very chatty but only about certain topics that really interest him or her. Rather than having a conversation, you may feel as though your child is talking at you (rather than with you) in a monologue. Helping your child to understand how to take turns in a conversation is really important. You can introduce rules such as "talk for two minutes, then stop" and use an egg timer or watch to time how long he or she speaks for. A physical signal to show when it's your child's turn to speak is really useful. Try using a small object such as a ball to pass between you in conversations. When you hold the ball, it's your turn to speak. Physical signals for turn-taking can also help if your child interrupts a lot.

Courses for parents of children on the spectrum often focus on communication between parent and child because this is the starting point for so many skills. You may be offered a programme called *Early Bird* by the team who diagnosed your child. This programme focuses on parent–child communication as well as on managing difficult behaviour and is well worth attending. For more information, ask your diagnostic team: see Chapter 13 or look up www.autism.org.uk/earlybird.

Managing behaviour

One thing guaranteed to worry all parents is their children's behaviour. Children who have ASCs may follow odd routines and rituals, they may have meltdowns or tantrums, or they may act aggressively towards others or themselves.

Reasons for difficult behaviour

Children who have an ASC may demonstrate unusual behaviour, but usually for a reason. For example:

- **Getting their point across:** If children find it difficult to communicate what they want or need, they're likely to start communicating through their behaviour. The behaviour could be aggressive, socially inappropriate or embarrassing, but it has a purpose. If you can't communicate your wishes, you're bound to get really frustrated and you'll use behaviour to get attention.

- **Keeping up routines and rituals:** Disruption to routines is a common reason for difficult behaviour. A child may feel severe anxiety when things change or unpredictable things happen. Interrupting rituals or your child's favourite activity is likely to cause distress, which then shows itself in challenging behaviour.

- **Not being aware of others:** Problems picking up on social signals may mean that a child's behaviour can seem insensitive or rude.

- **Having their senses overloaded:** Sensory sensitivities may make a child upset, confused or distressed. These emotions are likely to be shown through behaviour. You may not even realise what your child is sensitive to, and all you see is the resulting difficult behaviour.

If you're trying to tackle a particular behavioural issue, the first step is to figure out whether the behaviour has a purpose and if so, what that purpose is. Is it to communicate? Is it the result of sensory issues? Is it to get attention? Sometimes, behaviours may have more than one function. So the first step in tackling difficult behaviour is to ask yourself "What is achieved by this behaviour?"

Once you've worked out why a behaviour happens, keep a note of when it happens. For example, does it happen every time you stop your child following a particular ritual or routine like flapping his or her hands? What comes before the behaviour and after the behaviour? A detailed record of the context in which the same behaviour has happened over the course of a few weeks can help you to work out why it's going on.

A useful acronym for recording behaviour is ABC, which stands for

- ✔ **A**ntecedents (what comes before the behaviour)
- ✔ **B**ehaviour (what the behaviour is)
- ✔ **C**onsequences (what happens as a result of the behaviour)

You can note these down in an exercise book.

Tackle only one behaviour at a time. Don't expect too much of your child all at once. If you try to change more than one thing at a time, you're setting yourself and your child up for failure.

What to do about difficult behaviour

Coping with your child's behaviour may seem overwhelming and impossible at times, but you can do things to help your child and so prevent or minimise problem behaviours.

Change doesn't happen overnight. Be patient, consistent and keep trying, even though changes may take months or even years.

Some things you may try to help your child's behaviour include the following:

- ✔ **Giving things an order:** For example, say "First you need to get dressed then you can play on your computer." Structuring events in this way will help your child to understand that he or she can do the activity they want, just not now.

- ✔ **Setting some rules:** People on the spectrum like rules, so consider writing a list of them, such as "no hitting", and putting it on the wall, with accompanying visual symbols.

- ✔ **Using images:** If communication difficulties are causing behavioural outbursts, then try using symbols and pictures that your child can point to or show you when he or she wants to communicate something.

- ✔ **Giving your child choices rather than asking him or her to do one thing:** For example, say "Do you want to do your drama or maths homework first?" rather than saying "Do your homework." Choice will give your child some control over what he or she does.

- ✔ **Giving positive rather than negative instructions:** Tell your child what he or she should rather than shouldn't be doing. For example, "Remember to talk in a quiet voice" rather than "Stop shouting."

- ✔ **Using Social Stories to explain behaviour:** See the nearby sidebar "Social Stories" for more on these.

Social Stories

Social Stories describe a particular situation, skill, behaviour or concept to help a child on the spectrum understand the situation and practise appropriate behaviour. Parents, teachers or other professionals can write Social Stories with or without the help of your child. They can be written to teach social skills, to address challenging behaviour, to explain when something new is going to happen and to help with conversational skills.

Stories can use words, pictures or comic strips, depending on their aim and the particular needs of the child.

Personalise the story to the individual and the message that you're trying to get across. Include any social clues involved, common responses to the situation, and what your child should or could do. Once the story's written, your child can read it alone or you can read it to your child. Prompt your child to ask any questions that the story raises for him or her. Your child may then want to keep the written story to refer to when necessary.

Here's an example of a Social Story:

"My name is Ben. Sometimes I get angry. When I get angry, my hands form fists and my face screws up. Sometimes I hit people. One of the things that makes me angry is not being allowed to play on my computer.

I can't play on my computer all the time because sometimes I have to do homework and at 8:30 p.m. I have to go to bed.

Everybody gets angry sometimes.

When I get angry, I will try to tell Mum or Dad that I'm getting angry. I can say something like "That makes me cross!" or "I feel angry." I will try not to hit people.

When I feel angry, I will try to take deep breaths and count to ten. This may help me to calm down. If it doesn't, I can go to my quiet space and spend some time on my own reading my favourite dinosaur book.

When I'm calm, I feel much better."

Social Stories don't have to be just about things your child struggles with. In fact, creating more Social Stories highlighting what your child does well than about what they find difficult is better. For more information about Social Stories, go to www.thegraycenter.org.

In our opinion, praising your child as much as you can is *the* most important tip. If your child has some behaviour issues, he or she is likely to get told off at school, get in trouble at home, and get frowned upon when out and about. Most adult attention is thus negative. So whenever you have a chance to say "well done" or "thanks", do it! Positive attention is far better for your self-esteem than negative attention. You can write a social story to praise your child when he or she has done something brilliant (see the "Social Stories" sidebar).

When you're giving praise for a particular behaviour that you've been working on, be specific. Rather than saying "well done", say "well done for asking your brother for that toy and not just taking it." That way, your child will understand the reason for the praise and may just repeat the good behaviour again to get some more of the lovely positive attention.

Try using a sticker chart to reward good behaviour, and give a prize when your child has received five stickers.

Controlling anger

Many people on the spectrum have anger-management problems and suffer from high levels of anxiety and stress. Your child may have angry outbursts, perhaps shouting and swearing, throwing things or hitting people.

If your child is angry or exhibits challenging behaviour and seems to take it out on you, remember that it's not your fault. You're not a bad parent, and many parents in your situation go through exactly the same things.

Your child can learn certain techniques to help him or her calm down and control angry outbursts. Deep-breathing exercises can be calming, as can any other relaxing activity such as taking a bath or playing relaxing music. Lots of children on the spectrum find bouncing on a trampoline great fun and very calming.

Children with ASCs need to learn to recognise sensations of anger, stress and anxiety so that they can see when they build up and can try to calm themselves down. They also need to learn what being calm feels like, because without understanding that, they won't know what they're aiming for.

Try playing a game in which you and your child (or whole family) role-play feeling angry and feeling calm. Move in an angry way, speak in an angry tone of voice and do things that angry people do (within reason — don't start smashing things!). Then try doing the same things calmly.

See Chapter 13 for some emotion-recognition tools. Also look out for anger-management courses for parents and children at your GP's surgery or community centre.

If you're really concerned about your child's behaviour, consult the professionals who diagnosed your child. They'll be able to look into the reasons for the behaviour and give you some strategies to help.

The Incredible 5-Point Scale: Assisting Children with Autism Spectrum Disorders by Kari Dunn Buron and Mitzi Curtis (Autism Asperger Publishing Company) is an excellent resource for helping your child to identify his or her feelings and come up with ways of dealing with difficult behaviour and controlling strong emotional responses. *The Red Beast: Controlling Anger in Children with Asperger's Syndrome* by K. I. Al-Ghani (Jessica Kingsley) is another good book on learning to deal with anger.

Developing routine and preparing for change

Routine is important for any child, but is especially significant for children with an ASC. Having a clear daily routine will help reduce your child's anxiety about what's happening next and will make for a calmer child. So when you're at home, keep to a routine in your daily life as much as you can.

Visual timetables are a particularly helpful way for the child to know his or her routine. The timetable can use pictures only or pictures and words showing the different steps involved in completing a particular task. Your child can then tick things off as he or she goes through the steps. You can create timetables for getting up, going to bed, eating dinner or whatever suits your family's needs. Figure 9-1 provides an example.

The websites www.widgit.com and www.dotolearn.com provide resources for making visual timetables.

While sorting out routines for home and school is fairly straightforward, changes are bound to happen at some point, and your child will need to prepare for them. Even if the change only involves having a supply teacher at school instead of the usual teacher or the usual brand of biscuits being out of stock, change can be extremely stressful for people on the spectrum.

Try to give your child as much notice as possible of any changes. That way you can prepare your child for what's going to be different, and he or she will be less anxious.

You may have to be quite proactive in finding out the details involved in a change, because your child will want to know as much as possible about what's different. For example, if your child has a different music teacher, you'll need to ask the school who the new teacher is, how long she'll be there for, and what she may do in the lesson that's different. You'll also have to let the new teacher know about your child's ASC and what the teacher can do to make life easier for your child.

Other changes in life are much bigger. Moving house, changing school, going on holiday or getting a divorce, for example, are all big changes in anyone's life and will need particularly careful planning if you have a child on the spectrum. If you're moving house or your child is changing schools, try to visit the new place as much as possible. You can write the date of the change in the family calendar or create a count-down chart to tick off the days until the change will happen.

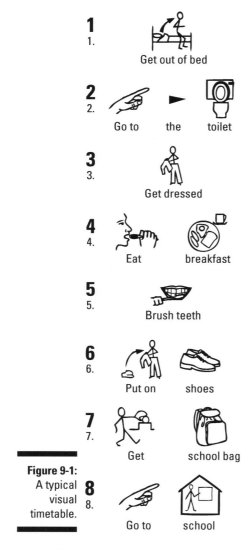

1.
Get out of bed

2.
Go to   the   toilet

3.
Get dressed

4.
Eat   breakfast

5.
Brush teeth

6.
Put on   shoes

7.
Get   school bag

Figure 9-1:
A typical
visual
timetable.

8.
Go to   school

Make a Social Story about changes that are about to happen. Such a story will help your child to understand what the change is, why it's happening and what the consequences are. See the earlier sidebar "Social Stories".

If you're concerned about how a major change is affecting your child's life, don't hesitate to contact professional psychologists who can help. Talk to your child's school or to the professionals who diagnosed your child. They'll be able to support you and point you in the direction of people and resources that can help.

Learning social skills

The earlier your child learns the basics of social interaction, the better. Encouraging conversations is part of this process, but your child also needs to start learning the rules of the society he or she will be living in. Most children learn social skills without the need for direct instruction, but children with an ASC won't pick up on social aspects of life automatically. They'll need some help, guidance and rules to follow in order to feel more able to cope in social situations.

The trouble is, because social interactions are so complex, and because they change depending on the people you're with and the context you're in, teaching naturalistic social interactions is an almost impossible task. Don't worry, though, here we run through some strategies that will help.

Topics to cover when thinking about social skills include:

✔ Conversational skills (starting, maintaining and ending conversations, talking about appropriate topics, avoiding one-sided conversations)

✔ Turn-taking (in games and conversations)

✔ Tone of voice and loudness of voice

✔ Personal space

✔ Emotion recognition and controlling emotions

✔ Body language

✔ Listening skills

✔ Sharing, helping and cooperating

✔ Joining in and playing fairly

This list is far from exhaustive. So many different skills make up social interactions, and the social signals can vary from individual to individual. For each different skill, you can help your child to learn what's expected socially and what's not. We don't have the space to go through each skill here, but you can access some very useful websites:

✔ www.thegraycenter.org has information and resources about Social Stories.

✔ www.dotolearn.com has games, resources and picture symbols to help teach social skills.

✔ www.autism.org.uk has lots of information and links to books and resources.

✔ www.jkp.com lists many books by Jessica Kingsley Publishers on learning social skills.

Don't try to tackle all social skills at once. Try one thing at a time.

Things to do at home

While formal social skills groups are helpful (see Chapter 13 for more on these), you can also do lots to help children on the spectrum learn social skills at home.

Being on the autism spectrum means that your child cannot easily generalise learning from one situation to another. Your child may learn something in a social skills group that he or she may never use in any other context. It helps if you communicate with your child's school, social skills group and other important people in your child's life so you can all work on the same skill at the same time. For example, if you're working on turn-taking at home, ask teachers, friends and professionals to work on turn-taking too. That way, your child will learn the skill in more contexts and is more likely to take his or her learning from one situation to the next.

Rather than teaching social skills formally, you can incorporate them into everyday life. Whenever you see a chance for social learning, take it. For example, if you're out in the park and your child asks a stranger "Why are you so fat?" take the opportunity to talk about what things are okay to say to strangers and what things aren't.

Social Stories are a good way of helping children learn socially appropriate and inappropriate behaviour. See the nearby sidebar "Social Stories".

Try to make learning as much fun as possible. If you can, incorporate your child's special interests. For example, if your child loves a particular character from a TV programme, try to get pictures of that character showing different emotions and then use the pictures to talk about facial expressions, or play emotions "snap" with the pictures.

Magazines and newspapers are full of pictures of people feeling different emotions and demonstrating different relationships. Cut out useful images and use them as discussion points. You can also play games like guessing how the people in the picture feel and deciding what they may be thinking. You can use the pictures to talk about body language or relationships, and you can even make up little stories and scenarios about what may be happening in each picture.

If you're looking at relationships, feelings or body language by using pictures, make sure you explain why you think someone is feeling a particular way. Point out the eyes, the direction the people are looking in, how close together the people are standing or any other body language that gives you a clue to how they may be feeling. If you just say "I think she looks cross" without saying why, your child may not pick up on the subtle signals that help you know the person's cross. Equally, if your child thinks the person in the picture is sad, ask your child why he or she thinks that and get your child to point out any features of the picture that make your child know the person's sad.

Use photos of your child or your family to discuss relationships, facial expressions and body language. Story books can also be useful.

Playing board games as a family is also really helpful. Simple games like snakes and ladders can be lots of fun and are perfect for practising turn-taking. Dice are great visual indicators of when it's your turn, making it easier to understand and practise this skill. Board games also help children learn how to cope with winning and losing.

Look out for the *Socially Speaking Game*, a board game in which you have to think about social skills such as greetings, compliments, listening, expressing emotions, and turn-taking while you play. Praise is super important! Whenever your child does something socially appropriate or remembers not to do something inappropriate, praise your child or give a reward.

Encouraging friendships

Children who have AS often want to make friends and join in games. However, they may misunderstand what real friendship is, and try to dominate games and control their playmates and make them do what they want to do. Their play is less cooperative. Friends can get tired of this, and the lack of reciprocation may mean the friendships fail or don't develop. Other children on the spectrum are less involved with peers and prefer to hang out with adults or younger children.

You can encourage your child to interact with other children the same age. Go to playgroups, parks and small social events so your child gets lots of opportunities to try to make friends and do things with other children. Groups for children with learning disabilities or ASCs and small, well-supervised and well-structured play activities are usually the least stressful for children on the autism spectrum. If you have friends with children or your child likes a particular person at school, invite the child around to play. When the child comes around, make sure you have some structured activities for the children to do together, otherwise your child may simply play alone and ignore his or her playmate. You could do some cooking, watch a film, play a board game or kick a ball. Stay around to encourage social interaction and deal with any problems.

Schools can do a lot to help your child develop friendships with peers. See *The Complete Guide to Asperger's Syndrome* by Tony Attwood (Jessica Kingsley) for some useful tips for teachers and parents.

Sometimes your child may not know how to join in with other children or ask a child to play. You can practise scripts or set phrases with your child to help. For example, encourage your child to approach children and say "Can I play with you?" or "Please may I join in?" Practise what the child should do if the other children say yes or no to the request.

Children who have AS need time on their own. Socialising and being with others can be very stressful, so while practising social interactions and getting as many safe opportunities to play with others is important, remember that children need some time to relax, be how they want to be, and do things they enjoy.

Learning what's socially appropriate

Children on the spectrum won't naturally pick up on what behaviour is appropriate in different situations. For example, they won't know that you talk quietly in a library or don't laugh when someone falls over. You can help your child learn these expectations by modelling what you should do yourself, practising whenever you're in that situation, and writing Social Stories.

Sometimes, children with an ASC have cute habits that are unusual but which may be misinterpreted, for example a fascination with feet or toes, or enjoying sitting on someone's lap. Bear in mind that if your five-year-old child has a habit like this and no one tells your child not to do it, he or she may still behave in this way as they grow up. A small child tickling people's feet may be cute, but this behaviour is odd in a 13-year-old and may make your child vulnerable to bullies and teasing. Even worse, a 20-year-old tickling a stranger's feet may be misconstrued as sexual harassment.

If your child's behaviour is a bit odd, think about the consequences of not stopping that behaviour at a young age. It may seem okay now, but ask yourself how the behaviour will be interpreted when the child is an adult, and what the possible outcomes may be. Behaviour that's new is much more easily stopped than behaviour that the child's been doing all his or her life.

Social skills groups

Social skills programmes in which your child is formally taught appropriate behaviour can be really helpful. Finding the right group is important, though, because your child may experience a great deal of anxiety when attending if he or she does not enjoy social situations and has low self-esteem about his or her social relationships. Children also may not see the point in going to social skills groups if they have no interest in social interactions and don't understand why learning social skills could be useful. The best groups are fun and activity based rather than based on listening to someone talk about what to do and what not to do.

You can get information about social skills groups from your child's school, speech and language therapist, psychologist or local autism group. More information about social skills groups can also be found in Chapter 13.

As well as formal teaching, try to widen your child's social circle by going to different group activities. These needn't have the aim of teaching social skills, but can give your child lots of practice with any new skills you're working on. Community notice-boards at libraries and leisure centres often have information about groups and clubs in your area. Pick a club that focuses on something your child's already interested in, for example chess, Lego, trampolining or model railways. Any group or club at which your child gets to practise interacting with other children helps. And as an added bonus, you may get to meet other parents, expanding your friendships too.

You may find play schemes and after-school clubs that specifically cater for children on the autism spectrum. The NAS website (www.nas.org.uk/signpost) provides information on such provision, and you can seek information from your child's school, on community centre notice-boards and via any professionals working with your family.

Sex education

Talking to your child about sex may be a bit embarrassing, but getting sex education right for people with AS is so important that here we include a whole section on it. And we put it in the "early years" section deliberately, because your child will inevitably grow up, and the skills you teach now will have important consequences for his or her behaviour and understanding of relationships later on.

While sex education is important, what's more important is sex education in the context of relationship education. Without understanding different relationships, sex education can be misunderstood.

Sexual images are constantly portrayed in the media, so trying to protect your child from sex and sexuality isn't an option. Clear, down-to-earth education from a young age is the best way to protect your child and give him or her the best chance of understanding the complexities of adult relationships.

At a young age, teach your child about the difference between public and private. For example, at home you may leave the door open when you go to the loo, but in public this behaviour isn't okay. Consider the different situations in which taking your clothes off is okay: at home in your bedroom (alone, when mum's there, when a friend's there), at school, in the swimming pool changing room. Many different scenarios exist in which undressing is or is not acceptable behaviour, depending on the place and the context. Use photos and pictures to help discuss these different circumstances.

Develop rules about private parts early on. For example, "If it's to do with private parts, then do it in a private place at a private time. If it involves someone else, then I need his or her permission." The earlier a child understands what his or her private parts are and the fact that they're private, the better. A little boy of five fiddling with his willy in a lesson is probably not too socially inappropriate or surprising, but if that boy has AS and he's not told the rules, then when he's 20 he may still touch himself, but this time during lectures. If no one tells you something's wrong, how are you supposed to know?

The age at which your child reaches puberty or becomes interested in sex varies considerably. Many children on the autism spectrum aren't interested in boyfriends and girlfriends at the same age as their peers are, and are behind in their understanding of relationships. This doesn't mean that you can't teach some skills that are relevant to relationships and sex education from a young age. You just need to tailor what you teach to the developmental level of your child.

Like everyone, people on the autism spectrum can be heterosexual, homosexual, bisexual or not interested in sex full stop. All of these preferences are normal and okay.

When talking about sex, relationships and sexuality, use straightforward, matter-of-fact language. Because most of us are embarrassed when talking about sex, we tend to use euphemisms and slang, which can be baffling for people on the spectrum. All of the following can be misunderstood by someone who takes language literally:

- Slang terms for sexual intercourse
- "She's got a bun in the oven."
- "Would you like to come up for coffee?"

You probably know many more of these expressions, and the slang for private parts is even more extensive.

When talking about relationships, sex, puberty and so on, use accurate language, and also actively teach your child the common slang terms, euphemisms and idioms.

If your child's receiving sex education at school, make sure your child is also discussing sex in terms of relationships. School sex education often doesn't cover this subject in enough detail for students who have AS. Topics that should be included are:

- ✔ Body parts (using clear, accurate pictures)
- ✔ Puberty and growing up (including menstruation, wet dreams and masturbation)
- ✔ Hygiene
- ✔ Differences between boys, girls, men and women
- ✔ Sex (same sex and heterosexual), including whom we can and can't have sex with and why, and consent
- ✔ Contraception and sexually transmitted infections
- ✔ Appropriate and inappropriate touching, personal space
- ✔ Relationships (friends, family, romantic partners, sexual relationships, marriage)
- ✔ Keeping safe (including online) and saying no
- ✔ Knowing what behaviour is appropriate in what situation, place and time

You may be able to organise extra tuition for your child, in which your child can learn more about relationships and be given time to ask questions. Providing accurate information, and helping your child develop an understanding of relationships and personal values is really important. If your child doesn't learn these important things from you or another trusted source, he or she may seek the information in other ways such as via the Internet; then you can't sure what information your child is learning and how accurate or safe it is.

See *Making Sense of Sex* by Sarah Attwood (Jessica Kingsley) for more information about sex and relationship education for people on the autism spectrum.

Sorting out sleep

Children on the autism spectrum often have unusual sleep patterns. Some children may not sleep very much at all, going to bed really late and waking up extremely early in the morning. As a parent, your child's sleep pattern can contribute hugely to how you cope, because in all likelihood if your child's awake, so are you. No one copes well when deprived of sleep.

If your child has problems with sleep, ask your GP or social worker to refer you to an expert in sleep problems. Although getting a referral can be difficult, psychologists, psychiatrists and paediatricians who are experts in sleep disorders can offer some excellent advice.

As a first step, if you're worried about your child's sleeping, keep a sleep diary in which you write down when your child is asleep, when your child is awake, and any other circumstances which may affect his or her sleep (for example, if your child's ill, then he or she is not going to sleep as well as usual).

Try these tips for helping your child sleep:

- ✔ Don't give your child any caffeine for at least three hours before going to bed (including Coca–Cola and chocolate, as well as tea and coffee).

- ✔ Keep the bedroom for sleeping and nothing else. Don't ask your child to do homework in his or her room, keep the TV and computer games out, and make the bedroom a quiet, relaxing environment with few distractions.

- ✔ Try some relaxation techniques before bed. Having a warm bath, listening to calming music or reading a book quietly can really help.

- ✔ Keep to the same simple evening routine each day, as far as you possibly can. Eat dinner at the same time then have some quiet or reading time, followed by a snack, a warm bath, brushing teeth and going to bed.

The bedroom environment is very important to people who have AS. If light comes in through the window or sounds wake your child up at night, reviewing where your child sleeps may be worthwhile. The quietest, darkest room may be best, but this depends on your child's sensory issues. Minimising sensory issues will make a big difference to how good a night's sleep you all get. For more information about sensory issues in AS and how to help, see Chapter 12. More information on sleep can be found in Chapter 6.

For more information about sleep, including information about children who sleep too much, call the NAS Helpline on 0845 070 4004.

Getting Support for You

All parents reading this chapter have probably done so to find out what they can do to help their children. While this is obviously really important, we also want to say "Don't forget about yourselves."

Looking after yourself is really important if you're going to feel happy, stay in control, not get over-tired and be able to devote as much time and energy to your child as he or she needs. Look after yourself and you'll be able to look after your child. You're not helping if you take on everything yourself and then become stressed and exhausted.

Being a parent isn't an easy job and can be even harder if your child is on the autism spectrum. You're bound to have good days and bad days but, as a parent on the NAS website says,

> *Everyone is entitled to a bad day here and there where they feel as if they have hit rock bottom. However, the whole point of having a good cry or a moan is to get it out of your system and then get on with your day.*

In this section we run through some tips to bear in mind to help you stay as calm and healthy as possible.

If you need someone to talk to, advice, support or a friendly ear, call the NAS Helpline on 0845 070 4004 (10 a.m. to 4 p.m., Monday to Friday) or the OAASIS helpline on 0800 197 3907 (10:00 a.m. to 4:30p.m., Monday to Friday). If you're feeling sad or distressed and need someone to talk to, call the Samaritans on 08457 909090; this service is available 24 hours a day, seven days a week.

Parenting and stress

Research has shown very high levels of stress among mothers of children who have an ASC, more so than among mothers of children with other disabilities. So you need to look out for the signs of stress, and do your best to build in preventative strategies to stop the stress from building up too much.

We all get stressed sometimes, but you can do things to help. You also need to ask for help when you need it rather than trying to battle on alone.

You have a lot to cope with as a parent of a child on the autism spectrum, so try to do things to make your life easy. Get a cleaner, accept help from friends, do your shopping online and get it delivered, and do anything else that eases the strain of daily life. Doing so doesn't mean you're not coping or not as good a mum as other people. It just means you're sensible and recognise both your priorities and your limitations.

Finding or creating a support network

When you have a child on the spectrum, you can feel very isolated, especially if your friends and wider family don't understand autism. Finding a group of people who are in the same situation as you can be invaluable. You'll have other parents to chat to, and people to share tips with and to help you during the lows and celebrate with you during the highs.

Around the country, many groups of people affected by ASCs have set up parent support groups or informal gatherings. Different charities or proactive parents in a particular area organise coffee mornings, talks, play activities, family days and access to information, among other things.

To find out what's going on in your local area, look on notice-boards in libraries, leisure centres and community centres. You may also find some things going on by using the NAS Signpost service, which you can find at www. autism.org.uk/signpost.

You may live in quite a remote area or there may just be nothing available where you live. If this is the case, try the following:

- ✔ Go online and read Internet articles and blogs, and talk to other parents in chatrooms or on social networking sites (you could even write your own blog).

- ✔ Go to www.togetherforautism.org, a website offering information and forums for parents, siblings and others affected by autism.

- ✔ Talk to the team that diagnosed your child and to staff at school to find out what's available nearby or what they can offer in terms of support.

- ✔ Talk to other parents and ask whether they know anyone whose child has AS.

- ✔ Try setting up your own support group for parents with children who have an ASC in particular or differences and disabilities more widely, by contacting community centres, churches, nurseries or schools. Your group needn't be anything formal or complicated — you could all just meet up for a coffee or a curry every now and again.

See *The OASIS Guide to Asperger Syndrome* by Patricia Romanowski Bashe and Barbara Kirby (Crown Publishers), which has some useful tips, insights and information for parents whose children have been diagnosed with AS.

Recognising the need for respite

No one can carry on at full pace all day, every day. Rest is crucial to help you and your family stay positive and healthy. Make sure you work out ways of getting respite for yourself and for other members of your family on a regular basis, otherwise the stresses and strains of daily life could get on top of you.

Respite can be anything from an hour for yourself to do the shopping, go for a swim or meet up with friends, to several weeks holiday alone or with your partner, without your child.

Don't feel guilty for needing time away from your child. Having a rest is important for both of you, because you'll be much more fun to be around if you're not completely stressed out.

You may have a friend or neighbour who's able and willing to keep an eye on the kids while you have a night out, or perhaps other members of your family are able to help out. You could also look for professional services that offer short breaks, befriending or longer-term respite for families in your situation. The NAS Helpline (0845 070 4004) can help you find services in your area.

If people offer help, accept it. Your friends will feel flattered that you've responded positively, and your wider family will be pleased to help out every now and again.

Looking out for other family members

Your partner and other children may also become very stressed as a result of living with a child on the autism spectrum. Feeling stressed is nobody's fault, but bear in mind that you all may struggle at times.

For your partner, creating time for just the two of you is crucial to maintaining your relationship. Respite, short breaks and getting help every now and again are really important to give you this time. Keep talking, because the best relationships are founded on open communication.

Relate offers useful tips on relationships and runs relationship counselling for couples. Go to www.relate.org.uk for information.

If you have other children who aren't on the spectrum, they need some special attention too. At times, you may not be able to give them the attention they need, because of the demands of raising a child on the autism spectrum, but if you make sure they know that you love them and are there for them when they need you, they'll be fine. Again, encouraging communication and making sure your children feel they can talk to you if they have any problems is really important. See Chapter 11 for information about being a sibling of someone with an ASC.

Often, children who aren't on the spectrum want to talk to someone outside their immediate family about their worries or problems. You may have friends or less immediate family members who can take on this role. If not (or as well), websites catering specifically for siblings of children with an ASC are available:

- ✔ http://groups.yahoo.com/subscribe/autism_sibs is an online discussion group where siblings of children and adults with autism can talk with other siblings in the same situation about their experiences

- ✔ www.sibs.org.uk is a charity for siblings who grow up with a brother or sister who has a disability, chronic illness or other lifelong condition; the website provides information and support

Look out for a sibling group if your area has a local AS support network. Meeting up with others in the same situation could be really helpful for your children.

Feeling jealous or a bit neglected by their parents, because their parents only spend time with their brother or sister on the spectrum, are common experiences for siblings. Try these tips to make sure your other children feel that they get as much attention as their sibling who has AS:

- ✔ Take time out to spend with just your children who aren't on the autism spectrum. Go to the cinema, play their favourite games or just have some time alone with each other.

- ✔ Tell your children you love them, as often as you can.

- ✔ Attend all the important events in their lives, such as parents' evenings, football matches, concerts and so on.

- ✔ Ensure your children have ways of telling you when they're worried or if they have a problem or question about their sibling (or anything, for that matter). They could jot down their thoughts in a worries book or you could set aside time in each day for them to have a chat.

Dealing with other people

Other people can be helpful, supportive, friendly and kind. They can also be mean, judgemental and obstructive. Here, we run through some of the tricky situations relating to the latter sort of person and give you some strategies to cope.

Nasty comments

We've all seen naughty children having tantrums in the supermarket when their mothers refuse to buy them a packet of sweets. Others expect the parent to tell the child off, drag the child out of the supermarket and provide a bit of discipline to sort out the child's behaviour. That's all very well if your child is having a tantrum because he or she can't have a bag of sweets. What most onlookers don't realise when a child on the spectrum is having a tantrum in a supermarket is that the child is shouting and screaming because of the noise, lights, number of people and stress that go along with being in that environment. So when onlookers see you, as a parent, helping your child when he or she is shouting and screaming, and not telling the child off when he or she appears to be being naughty, they judge you as a "weak parent" whose child can't behave. Some may just "tut", others may come up to you and say highly unpleasant things.

If you find yourself in this situation, as a first step try not to get angry with the interfering onlooker. Keep calm, keep doing what you're doing to help your child, and ignore other people's comments. Consider using "autism awareness cards" (also called "autism alert cards"). These resemble credit cards and state that your child has autism, what it is and how it affects your child's behaviour. The cards are really useful, because generally you won't want to or won't have the time to explain to others why your child is behaving the way he or she is. Different varieties of card exist; some are for parents to carry around, while others are for the individual with AS and may look like the one shown in Figure 9-2.

Figure 9-2:
An Asperger's awareness card.

This person has Asperger syndrome

> Asperger syndrome is a lifelong disability that affects social and communication skills.

> People with Asperger syndrome may behave in unpredictable ways as a result of their difficulty in understanding language and social situations.

> People with Asperger syndrome are likely to be extremely anxious in unfamiliar situations.

> Please help by being understanding, patient and tolerant.

For further information, contact our
Autism Helpline on 0845 070 4004
(10am-4pm, Mon-Fri) or go to **www.autism.org.uk**

The National Autistic Society is a registered charity

The National Autistic Society

Other types of cards can be individualised, and your child can carry them around to give to people if he or she gets into a difficult situation. The card will tell police, teachers, bystanders — or anyone, really — that the child has autism, what this means for the child personally, and who to contact in an emergency.

These cards are available from www.autism.org.uk and www.paains.org.uk. If you don't want to buy them, you can make your own on the computer fairly easily.

If a certain situation is particularly stressful for your child, evaluate whether you really need to put your child through it, and what you could do to make it less stressful. For example, you could do your shopping online or carry out lots of preparation to help your child cope in this difficult environment. You could show your child pictures of the shop, read stories about going shopping, gradually build up the amount of time you spend in the shop, and provide a visual timetable of how long you'll be there and what you'll be doing.

The supermarket isn't the only place where you may have to deal with nasty comments from other people. Other parents at school, members of the public at special events or people attending your child's clubs may all come out with some really hurtful remarks. Ignorance about ASCs is usually the reason behind other people's comments and, because ASCs aren't physically obvious, explaining why your child is different, and that your child's behaviour isn't always his or her fault (bearing in mind that kids on the spectrum can be naughty just like anyone else!), can be really difficult.

Talk to other parents if you're feeling upset, or if a particular type of comment leaves you not knowing what to say or do. They may have some good tips, and if they've also got a child on the spectrum, they can empathise with you and provide an understanding shoulder to cry on or an ear to listen to you.

Informing others

Throughout your child's life, you'll often have to explain autism, AS and your child's individual needs to other people. Often it will be up to you to decide who to tell and when to tell them. Some people will need to know about your child's diagnosis, such as your child's teachers and professionals who work with him or her. These individuals will need lots of detail about the diagnosis and how it affects your child to enable them to understand your child and support him or her in the best way possible. Other people may not need to know so much, or even that your child has AS at all. You need to decide whether you want to be open and honest with everyone, or if you think it's best for some people not to know. When deciding who to inform, ask yourself the following questions:

- ✔ How helpful will it be for my child if this person knows about his or her diagnosis?

- ✔ In ten years' time, how will my child feel if this person knows about his or her diagnosis?

- ✔ If this person misunderstands my child as the result of lack of knowledge about autism, will it cause my child distress or embarrassment?

For guidance on telling your child about his or her diagnosis, see Chapter 3.

If you find a good article or leaflet that seems to explain AS well, get several copies or photocopies so that you can hand them out to people who come into contact with your child and need to know about AS. A useful book that may help you or your child when telling others is *Can I Tell You about Asperger Syndrome? A Guide for Friends and Family* by Jude Welton (Jessica Kingsley).

Chapter 10

Parenting During School, College and Adult Life

In This Chapter

▶ Understanding the challenges faced by children who have Asperger's syndrome at school

▶ Discovering how to get support for your child at school, college and work

▶ Planning for life in the future

*P*arenting doesn't stop when your child goes to school. In fact, it probably gets more complicated! Getting the right education is really important so that your child can fulfil his or her potential and have a positive schooling experience. Too often, children on the spectrum find school enormously stressful and get bullied. In this chapter we cover how to get the right support for your child and how to prevent bullying.

As your child grows up, he or she may leave home, go to college or university and try to live more independently. Huge life changes happen which both you and your child will have to get used to. We offer tips on facilitating transitions between schools and between education and adult life. We also provide some ideas on supporting your child if he or she wants to find a job and embark on a career. Beyond that, you also need to think about where your child is going to live when he or she grows up. You child could live at home, but chances are that he or she will want to move out and try to live more independently. Different housing options are thus also considered in this chapter.

Beyond that, you need to prepare your child for life when you're no longer around. Hard though it may seem, the preparation you do now will help your child to live a full and enjoyable life when you're no longer there to look after him or her.

Sussing Out School

School is often the place where children on the spectrum stand out the most. The school environment is full of sensory and social challenges, not to mention the expectations for being organised and flexible. On the other hand, the right school can give your child the chance to meet other people, learn independence and develop interests and talents.

The Autism Education Trust is an organisation set up to help improve educational support for all children on the autism spectrum in England. Its website (www.autismeducationtrust.org.uk) offers information for parents, professionals and children. It also provides a Kids Zone and a Den — interactive resources for young people who have an autism spectrum condition (ASC), where they can ask questions, get advice, watch films about dealing with aspects of their lives, play games and so on.

Getting the right education for your child is really important. Fortunately, you've got many options, ranging from special education, inclusion units within mainstream schools, full inclusion in mainstream settings, and residential schools to home education. Whatever your preference, getting it right for your child will make the difference between a positive schooling experience, in which your child can fulfil his or her academic and social potential, and a negative experience in which your child doesn't learn and gets bullied.

Children on the autism spectrum, including children who have Asperger's syndrome (AS), are entitled to extra support at nursery, primary and secondary schools and college. Transition between these settings may be particularly difficult, and your child is entitled to extra support at these times too.

In this section, we cover the pros and cons of different types of education and how to get the support your child needs at school. We also get to grips with bullying, what it looks like and how best to deal with it.

The National Autistic Society (NAS) runs an autism services directory listing details of schools that cater for children and young people on the autism spectrum. You can search for schools in your area at www.autism.org.uk/directory.

Finding the right sort of schooling

Unfortunately, not all schools have an adequate understanding of ASCs. Lots of children on the spectrum struggle at mainstream school as a result of the nature of the school environment alongside a lack of understanding from staff. Special needs schools may be inappropriate for academically able children on the spectrum, such as those who have AS. Only a limited number of specialist autism schools, placements in resource bases for children who have AS, and inclusion units for people on the spectrum are available, meaning that the only option for some children is home education. Many parents have to fight to get the right support for their children in school, and often have to resort to taking their local authority to a tribunal. Here, we explain what sorts of difficulties children on the spectrum can face at school. We describe how to access adequate support for your child when he or she is in school using terms and rights taken from the education system in England and Wales. Further information about the system in Scotland and Northern Ireland is available on the NAS website www.autism.org.uk. We also discuss the relative benefits of home and school education.

You know your child best, and you should have the final say when it comes to your young child's education. Don't be pushed into situations that you and your child aren't happy with.

Coping at school

Sometimes school is the first place where an undiagnosed child is noticed and referred for a diagnosis of AS. This situation arises because school can be a very difficult place for children who have AS to deal with, so their behaviour sticks out from that of the crowd and is drawn to the attention of professionals. Different children will struggle with different things at school, but some situations tend to be stressful for all children with an autism spectrum condition.

Children who have AS find the social aspects of being at school a real challenge. Going on the school bus, and lunch and break times when the whole school (or a large part of it) is milling about together at the same time can seem like torture for some children who have AS. Large class sizes may also make life more stressful.

> *I don't like registration because people are all running around and they talk too much and sometimes I get really stressed.*
>
> — David, quoted in the NAS's report Make School Make Sense

Any situation in which interacting with peers is the expected behaviour will be a challenge for a student who has an ASC. Often, teachers encourage group work at school. For children who have AS this can prove too stressful and may cause behavioural outbursts. If a child is expected to sit in close proximity to others and work in groups without suitable support, he or she may struggle and get upset. People who have AS need a quiet, calm space to work best. The noise, movement, chaos and social expectations in the school playground can be totally overwhelming for a child who has sensory sensitivities, a preference for structure, and difficulty interacting with peers.

Explaining IEPs and statements

An individual education plan (IEP) is a way to plan, teach and review targets for children with extra needs at school. It outlines what additional interventions and teaching support a child needs that aren't provided through normal school activities. Usually teachers, parents and the student are involved in writing an IEP. In the IEP, your child and the child's teachers are given about three specific targets to achieve within a particular period. These targets could address behaviour, maths, literacy, social skills or whatever else the child needs help with. An IEP target may state, for example, "This term, Eleanor will spend three lunch times per week in the playground playing structured games with her teaching assistant and other children. On the other two days she can choose to spend time on her own in the library or classroom." IEPs and targets are reviewed regularly — at least twice per year.

The Autism Education Trust has useful information about IEPs at www.autismeducationtrust.org.uk.

A statement of special educational needs (generally just called a *statement*) is a document specifying your child's needs and the extra help that he or she should have. This statement is reviewed every year to keep it up to date. If your child isn't doing well at school or needs lots of extra help, the local authority can carry out a detailed assessment of your child to find out what his or her needs are and what extra help is needed. You or your child's school can ask for an assessment. If you want one, talk to the school's special educational needs coordinator (SENCO). After carrying out an assessment, the local authority decides whether your child needs a statement or whether his or her needs can be met with normal schooling. You generally receive an answer within 12 weeks of starting the assessment process. As part of the statement, the local authority will identify a school that should meet your child's needs. If you disagree with the statement, or the school, or if your child doesn't get a statement and you think he or she needs one, you can appeal to the Special Educational Needs and Disability First-tier Tribunal.

The UK Government website www.direct.gov.uk offers lots of information about special educational needs, assessments and statements. You can also download a leaflet called *SEN: A Guide for Parents and Carers*.

Sensory sensitivities may make the whole school environment a difficult place to cope with. For example, most schools use cheap flickering lights that may make some individuals on the spectrum distressed. School bells which ring loudly and suddenly can be awful for those with sensitive hearing. In fact, the school can be a brutal assault on a person's senses, and many behavioural difficulties seen at school could be a result of sensory problems.

The school can be an extremely challenging environment for people who have ASCs. Children need adequate support to help them cope and a suitable environment in which to learn, otherwise school can turn into a negative life experience rather than one which opens up opportunities for them.

Communication differences mean that children who have AS may not understand instructions or lessons that are about abstract concepts. While they
may be very clever at particular subjects (often science, maths and IT, which
have clear structures and are based on fact), children who have AS may
struggle with more conceptual subjects such as English literature. Failure at
particular subjects can have negative consequences for self-esteem.

You may wonder how children on the spectrum manage to get through the
school day when you consider what school can be like from their perspective. However, some schools are sympathetic to children with different
needs, and support is available for children who have AS to help make school
easier to cope with and a fun environment in which to learn.

Your child needs to get an *individual education plan* (IEP) outlining his or her
educational needs. He or she may also get a *statement* of special educational
needs. See the nearby sidebar "Explaining IEPs and statements'.

Choosing a school

You probably feel that finding out about all the different educational options,
systems and support entitlements is overwhelming and you need a lifetime to
get to grips with it. Don't worry — many parents have been in your situation
before and have come through to the other side.

Your first step is to look for a supportive school, preferably one that has suitable expertise in ASCs. When looking around schools, ask them the following
questions:

- ✔ What provision is there for children who have an ASC?
- ✔ How much training have your staff had in ASCs?
- ✔ Who is the SENCO, and can I talk to him or her?
- ✔ How many children on the autism spectrum are there at your school?
  Can I talk to any of their parents?

Have a look around the school, take your child with you to see what he or
she thinks, and talk to the class teachers. Visiting at break and lunch times as
well as during lessons to see what the students and teachers are doing is also
a good idea. A high staff-to-student ratio is a good sign, because it will reduce
opportunities for bullying. Structured playground activities such as games
led by teachers are useful for children on the spectrum who struggle with
interacting with peers in the playground in less structured ways.

Not all schools have specialist autism provision. If that's the case, look for a
school where the staff are supportive, have a good understanding of autism,
and make time to answer your questions and listen to your concerns.

If your child has a statement of special educational needs, your local authority will identify a school in your area that should meet your child's individual educational needs. If you're not happy with the school that the local authority has chosen, you can ask for a review. See the nearby sidebar "Explaining IEPs and statements".

Educating at home

For a whole range of reasons, some parents decide to home-educate their children. You may simply feel that you can best offer what your child needs at home. You're legally entitled to educate your child at home and can choose to home educate for a period and then start your child at school again. You can even choose to mix and match between school education and home education. Some positive and negative aspects of home education to think about are listed in Table 10-1.

Lots of children with AS are excluded from school because of their difficult behaviour. This usually happens when children are at schools that don't understand AS (they just think the child's naughty) and no support is in place to help the student cope with the challenges of school. Often this happens at secondary school, when the expectations are different and the independence and flexibility required are much greater than at primary school.

Table 10-1   Considering the Pros and Cons of Home Education

Pros	Cons
You can provide the right sensory environment for your child's learning, because you know your child best.	Educating your child yourself is a huge responsibility which you may not want to take on.
You can meet all of your child's learning needs; at school some of these needs may never be met.	Your child may miss out on social learning opportunities or extra-curricular activities that take place in school.
You don't need to follow school hours; your child may be very alert in the morning and open to learning, and cranky and need to spend time alone in the afternoon.	You may not get any break from childcare, because you may be with your child for the majority of the day.
You can decide which exams your child takes, if any.	You may not have access to the educational tools, science labs or educational equipment that are available in school.

If you're considering home education, some useful organisations to contact are:

- ✔ **Education Otherwise:** Provides information and advice on home education, including a directory listing other home-educating parents in your area. Tel: 0845 478 6345; www.education-otherwise.org.

- ✔ **Home Education Advisory Service (HEAS):** Provides information on educational materials, resources, GCSE examinations, special educational needs, information technology, legal matters and curriculum design. Tel: 01707 371 854; www.heas.org.uk.

- ✔ **Touch the Sky:** Provides distance learning and therapy for children on the autism spectrum. Tel: 01903 507 744; www.acrosstheworld.eu/.

Fighting for adequate support at school

We wish we could change this heading to "Getting adequate support at school", but sadly we've chosen the word "fighting" because all too often that's what you'll experience. According to the NAS's report *Make School Make Sense*, produced as part of a campaign for adequate education for students who have an ASC, more appeals for educational support are made to the Special Educational Needs and Disability Tribunal for children on the autism spectrum than for children with any other disability. So lots of parents have a fight on their hands. On the positive side, the report also stated that 79 per cent of parents who appealed won their case.

Many children on the spectrum need some form of support at school, or specialist education of some kind. The support or specialist provision should help children cope with the stresses and challenges that school presents, so that they can concentrate on their academic learning and get the most out of social and extra-curricular opportunities.

To access specialist support such as a teaching assistant, or to attend a special school rather than a mainstream school, your child needs a statement of special educational needs — a *statement*. Statements are legally binding documents produced by local authorities which outline the specific educational needs of your child and how the local authority will meet them. To get a statement, your child has to go through an assessment process, which can take around six months or longer. You, your school or other professionals involved with your child can request an assessment from the local authority if you think your child needs a statement. See the "Explaining IEPs and statements" sidebar earlier in this chapter.

A statement is based on a child's need rather than on his or her diagnosis, so even a child who hasn't been diagnosed or is in the process of getting a diagnosis can access the support needed.

Once you've got it, the statement will specify a school for your child to attend. This school may not be the school of your choice, but is one that the local authority thinks will meet your child's needs adequately.

If you're unhappy about the local authority's choice of school, you're entitled to ask for a review of the decision.

Finding a school, getting a statement and so on can seem daunting and very hard work. Keep going and remember that organisations have been set up to help you with this very process. The following can steer you in the right direction:

- **Autism Education Trust:** This organisation has information about a whole range of educational issues for parents, teachers, children and local authorities. Tel: 020 7903 365; www.autismeducationtrust.org.uk.

- **NAS:** The NAS runs its Advocacy for Education Service relating to special educational needs provision and entitlements, including getting extra help at school, statutory assessments, getting a statement, annual reviews, exclusions and admissions. It also runs a telephone support service offering education and tribunal advice (on 0845 070 4002). Tel: 020 7833 2299; www.autism.org.uk.

- **IPSEA (Independent Parental Special Education Advice):** This organisation provides advice on all areas of special educational needs. Tel: 0800 018 4016; www.ipsea.org.uk.

- **Network 81:** This charitable organisation is a national network of parents working towards properly resourced inclusive education for children with special needs. Tel: 0870 770 3306; www.network81.org.

Keep a folder with important information about your child, documents relating to his or her support needs, and information about AS, so that you can readily access it to share with schools or local authorities.

Bullying and AS

Over 40 per cent of children with autism have been bullied at school. Bullies tend to pick on people who are different, unusual and socially isolated, which means that students on the spectrum are particularly vulnerable. Obviously, people on the spectrum are subject to bullying in many areas of life, not just at school. You can find some information about bullying at work in Chapter 7. Here, we focus on bullying at school and how to deal with it, because this is the most likely scenario for parents to have to deal with.

Bullying in different ways

Bullying can be physical, verbal or emotional. It includes hurting someone physically as well as things like name calling and teasing. Bullying is done on purpose and happens more than once. It can make your child feel worried, stressed, sad or angry, and may make them not want to go to school. Bullying is serious and should be treated as such by teachers, staff and parents.

Now that most people have access to the Internet, and virtually everyone has a mobile phone, bullying can take place via email, text message or through social networking sites. Nasty things can also be posted on the Internet in blogs. This sort of bullying — known as *cyberbullying* — is particularly difficult to deal with.

Recognising the signs of bullying

Your child may not tell you directly if he or she is being bullied, but your child's behaviour may reveal that something's wrong. Look out for these signs:

- Fearing going to school
- Being anxious, upset or stressed
- Going to school by a different route or asking you to take him or her to school when your child usually goes alone
- Playing truant
- Doing worse in school work than usual
- Behaving aggressively towards siblings or others with no reasonable explanation
- Having unexplained injuries such as bruises or scratches
- "Losing" pocket money constantly
- Being very hungry when getting home from school (someone may be taking your child's dinner money)
- Sleeping problems and nightmares
- Missing or destroyed possessions
- Avoiding talking about what's wrong

If you notice any of these behaviours or clues, ask your child directly if he or she is being bullied and take steps to deal with the situation.

Preventing bullying

You can't be there to protect your child all the time, so you can't prevent bullying occurring. But you can do things to help prepare your child so that he or she knows what to do if bullying starts.

Your child needs to know what a bully is. You could read some stories together dealing with bullying and discuss the issues they raise. Specifically ask your child what a bully does. If your child knows bullying when he or she sees it, your child is more likely to ask for help.

You can find resources for talking about and dealing with bullying at www. incentiveplus.co.uk.

Sometimes, but not always, children who have AS can misinterpret accidents (for example, another child bumping into them) and normal playground interactions (such as children laughing at them, but with kind intentions) as bullying when they're not. Such misinterpretation is usually down to difficulties interpreting social signals. Making sure your child really understands what bullying is can help. But always investigate whether the bullying is real.

Talk to your child about what to do if he or she gets bullied. Teaching your child how to say "No" to things he or she doesn't want to do is really important. Try to identify a trusted adult at school — such as a teacher or teaching assistant — whom your child can talk to and encourage your child to discuss any problems with this person.

Encourage your child to talk to you about any worries so that he or she is more likely to tell you if getting bullied. Try using a "worries book" in which your child writes down or draws things he or she is anxious about. Writing or drawing saves your child from having to talk about difficult things such as feelings in a conversation which he or she may not know how to have.

Dealing with bullying

If your child is being bullied, be as loving and supportive as you can. If your child hasn't told a teacher at school, you need to go and talk to the teacher. See the nearby sidebar "Bullying: my experience".

If your child feels unable to talk about the bullying, see whether he or she would prefer to write it down on a piece of paper, in an email or in a notebook and show it to you or a teacher. Some schools have a "bully box" in which children can post a note — they don't have to pluck up the courage to speak to the teacher. Teachers then read the note and help to deal with the bullying.

If your child's being bullied, try these useful tips:

✔ **Encourage your child to keep away from the bullies and not to fight back:** Retaliation often makes things worse. What bullies actually hate is to be ignored. Maybe a teaching assistant at school can organise structured play activities at break or lunch times away from the bullies.

✔ **With your child, practise some answers to bullies who tease or call your child names:** Make up some things that the bully may say to your child, such as derogatory comments about his or her looks or the things your child likes doing. Role-play some suitable responses and maybe write them down for your child to refer to.

✔ **Get your child to practise saying "No!" firmly and loudly to the bully:** You pretend to be the bully in a range of scenarios and encourage your child to really raise his or her voice and to stand upright and look as assertive as possible.

✔ **Where possible, encourage your child to frequent places where other people are always around, for example the library:** Adults should then always be present, and bullies are obviously less likely to strike.

Bullying over the Internet or mobile phone is harder to deal with. However, although many cyberbullies think that no one will be able to find out who they are, fortunately that's not true. If your child is being cyberbullied, advise your child to:

✔ Block users that send unpleasant messages.

✔ Not retaliate, because doing so makes things worse.

As the parent, you need to:

✔ Print out or save any messages, pictures or videos that are bullying in nature, keeping a note of when they were sent to your child or posted online.

✔ Find out as much as you can about the sender, for example the sender's user name, ID, website address and so on.

✔ Bear in mind that you can change your child's user ID or profile if he or she is being bothered by cyberbullies.

Tips on staying safe on the Internet can be found at www.cybermentors. org.uk and www.kidscape.org.uk.

Bullying: my experience

Jack is 10 years old and was interviewed about his experiences of bullying for the NAS's report *Make School Make Sense*.

Who do you go to if you need any help at school?

I go to a teacher called Mrs A. I like her better than all the other teachers at the school. She is very nice, she's kind and she never shouts.

What sort of things do you go to her about?

Out in the playground and stuff and when people shout at me. One boy just shouts the F word at me. I just run off. I go to Mrs A or just run off.

When you tell Mrs A, what happens?

Nothing, really. I don't think any of the teachers believe me.

When people don't believe you, do you tell your mum?

Yes, she has written a letter to them and she's been to speak to the teacher as well.

Do they believe her?

Yes.

What happens to the boy when they believe you?

Well, they either put him on the wall, which isn't a punishment, because his friends are still around in the playground. Or they tell him to go inside, but then all his friends go to the window and wave at him.

Do you have many friends at school?

Not many, because they all hate me cos I'm funny. Funny in a happy way and funny in a bad way. They just sort of shout and kick me. I do it back sometimes cos it makes me really angry.

Making Transitions

Change can cause many children (and adults) on the spectrum to feel very anxious and stressed. The transitions from primary to secondary school and then from secondary school to adulthood are particularly difficult times for children on the spectrum. Key transitions in a child's educational life are:

✔ Starting school

✔ Moving from primary school to secondary school

✔ Leaving secondary school (maybe going into further education)

✔ Leaving further education

Planning the changes and transitions is essential to minimise stress for young people who have AS and to enable them to make informed choices about their lives. The earlier planning starts, the better. You, as a parent, and your child should be consulted at all points during transition planning and the actual transition itself.

Moving from primary school to secondary school

Secondary school is very different to primary school. You have different teachers for each lesson, more students moving about all over the place, and large demands placed on your organisational skills. The school may be in a very different area, so transport arrangements may change. The new school will also have different lunch time arrangements, new things to learn and unusual timetables. All these details make for a big change in anyone's life, but are particularly stressful for a student who has AS.

Your child needs to visit the new school at least twice before he or she starts in September. Meeting the new teachers and teaching assistants will help to reduce your child's anxiety about the unknown and give your child a chance to ask questions about the new school. If you can, accompany your child on the first visit so that he or she feels less anxious and more able to focus on the new people and environment. Your child's special educational needs co-ordinator or teaching assistant could also go with your child to talk to the new teachers about him or her.

Communication between the two schools is really important. Your child's current teachers need to tell the new teachers all about your child and his or her particular needs. Make sure the new school has the following information:

- A clear description of AS and how it affects your child personally

- All documentation about your child's educational needs (including statements and IEPs)

- Tips and instructions from your child's current teachers based on their experience of what has and hasn't helped in the past

- An understanding of you and your child's concerns and worries about starting secondary school

You are the expert on your child, so make sure the schools work closely with you during transition.

Leaving secondary school

Setting off from school into the big wide world is a huge life transition. Whether your child wants to go to college or university or try to get a job, or will be going into residential care or a supported living environment, lots of planning and preparation is needed.

When planning your child's future, the most important person's opinion is your child's. Your job is to advocate for your child's wishes, help your child to understand his or her choices, and do your best to support your child.

Planning for the major transition between school and adult life should begin when your child is 14 years old (Year 9 at school). Lots of different organisations are involved, including social services, employment services, education, housing and health. Adult social services, as well as children's, enter the picture and work together with you and other agencies to ensure your child has a smooth transition.

The goal of transition planning is to create a document stating what your child wants to do when he or she leaves school, how this will happen, and how your child will be prepared and supported through the process. Future needs and how they will be met are also described in detail.

If your child has a statement of special educational needs and intends to go on to higher education (university), the local authority must legally assess your child's needs in his or her final year at school.

Transition for children who have AS leaving school is often not as well planned as it ought to be. As a parent, you may have to make a fuss in order to get suitable transition planning started. For information on doing so, go to www.autism.org.uk or phone the NAS Helpline on 0845 070 4004.

Going on to college

Your child will start to grow up faster than you realise, and in adult life new and different challenges arise. You'll have to think about further education, getting a job and letting go of your child so he or she can live as independently as possible. Sadly, we're none of us going to live forever, and you'll have to plan for a time when you're not around to look after your child. In this section we offer advice on how to support your child through further education and getting a job. We also outline the different options available for living arrangements and provide tips on preparing for the future when you may no longer be here.

Figuring out further and higher education

If your child has decided to continue his or her studies after leaving school, you face some new challenges. Often the transition from school to college or university is very difficult, because your child will have to get used to less structure, being more independent, and the social side of being a student. Before your child goes, he or she will have lots of decisions to make:

✔ Which college or university should I go to?

✔ What do I want to study?

✔ What grades or qualifications do I need in order to get in?

✔ How do I apply?

✔ Shall I live at home or on campus?

✔ What support will I get?

✔ Will I have to tell everyone that I've got AS?

Your job is to help your child answer these questions, and that too will involve some difficult decisions.

Visit the colleges and universities your child is interested in studying at. Talk to the staff about the accommodation and the level of support in place for students with an ASC. No matter how academically gifted your child may be, he or she is likely to need a great deal of support to cope in higher education. Suss the support out before you send your child off to fend for themselves.

The website www.users.dircon.co.uk has some useful tips for students on the spectrum, including study skills, surviving the university environment and exam tips.

If possible, organise for your child to make contact with other students doing the same course. Nowadays, students link up with others on Facebook and develop relationships before they even meet at college or university. Also ask staff whether they can arrange for your child to actually meet and chat with other students on the spectrum who are already at the university. Hearing about other students' experiences may alleviate some of your child's anxieties about this big step. While your child is chatting to the students, you can be talking to the staff about your child's likely needs and the support that's on offer. Some supports and adjustments that may help your child are:

✔ Getting a buddy or mentor for your child to help with the organisation and social side of university life

✔ Studying fewer courses at a time, particularly in the first year, so your child has plenty of time to get used to the new routines and expectations

✔ Creating the opportunity to meet course tutors more frequently than usual to help clear up any misunderstandings

✔ Setting up alternative methods of learning; lectures can be overwhelming for students who have AS, because of the sensory overload created by the number of people in the room, background noise, and so on

Some universities have special social groups, support groups or advisers for students who have AS. Look out for these when checking out suitable universities. Most students on the spectrum who drop out of further and higher education do so because they're stressed. The more support you can get for your child, the less stressed your child is likely to be and the more likely your child is to succeed.

Colleges or universities within commutable distance are also worth thinking about. Your child can live at home for the first year while getting used to the lectures and learning side of studying. Once your child has got used to it, he or she can move into halls of residence and start to get more involved in the social side of university. If the place your child has chosen is too far away, make sure you keep an eye on his or her stress levels and try to organise as much support as possible.

Rather than university, your child may want to go on to further education and attend college to learn life skills, practical skills and social skills. Your child can attend college on a full- or part-time basis.

The NAS has a list of colleges and further education establishments for students who have an ASC. Many of these offer residential placements too. See www.autism.org.uk/directory.

Getting a job

Having employment, a vocation or a career is really important for all of us, but may be particularly important for individuals who have AS. Having a job that matches your interests and qualifications gives a person a purpose in life and a sense of self-worth. Sadly, very few people on the spectrum are in this situation, despite the vast majority wishing for a full-time paid job. Lots of barriers to the workplace exist for people on the spectrum (see Chapter 7), most of which could be overcome by an increase in understanding of ASCs and improved support for employees on the spectrum. In this section we offer some pointers to help your child achieve employment. Getting a job will not only give your child some financial independence, but will also mean your child meets new people and improves his or her self-esteem.

People who have an ASC such as AS can work in all sorts of careers and are capable of successful employment. All that's needed is the right support and a degree of understanding from employers.

The areas that most employees on the spectrum struggle with are:

- Time-keeping
- Concentration

✔ Multi-tasking

✔ Communication

✔ Social skills

✔ Anxiety and stress

✔ Coping with change

The more you can help your child to develop these skills before starting to apply for jobs, the better the chances of successful employment.

To help your child learn about the workplace and develop some relevant skills, try to organise some work experience, even if it's just on a voluntary basis. Work experience can start at school or at college, and will also give your child the chance to try out different sorts of jobs and figure out what it is he or she enjoys doing.

Your child may have a really clear idea of what career he or she would like to pursue. Lots of successful careers can develop from special interests, for example in computing, engineering, taxi-driving, translating or equestrian science. If your child's dream career is realistic, then do all you can to support your child in finding out about the job, getting relevant work experience and achieving the necessary qualifications. Sometimes, your child's dream may not be realistic; for example, your child may want to become a fighter pilot but have vision problems. If your child's dream is not realistic, you need to help your child understand why he or she can't pursue this chosen career and help your child look for alternatives.

Alternatively, your child may not have a clue what job he or she wants to do. Gaining lots of work experience is very useful here, because it lets your child try out different types of jobs and see what's good and bad about each one.

Take your child to the Connexions service to get information about different career choices, how to find a job and support in employment. Alternatively, go to the Connexions service websites: for England, www.connexions-direct.com; for Wales, www.careerswales.com; for Scotland, www.careers-scotland.org.uk; for Northern Ireland, www.careersserviceni.com.

Careers advisers may be able to give your child some useful pointers to careers you or your child may not have thought of. An assessment of your child's strengths and weaknesses can be really useful to help identify areas in which he or she could pursue a career and those in which he or she needs extra support or some teaching. The *Asperger Syndrome Employment Workbook* by Roger Meyer (Jessica Kingsley) is a useful resource for helping your child to explore his or her employment strengths and weaknesses and identify potential avenues for employment.

The dreaded job interview is the next hurdle to jump over. A mixture of difficulties with interpersonal skills, anxiety about meeting new people and the pressure of going for a job interview can make this process really tough for people on the spectrum. Nevertheless, they have to go through it. Your child will have to decide whether to tell a potential employer about his or her diagnosis. If the potential employer knows, then he or she is less likely to focus on the interpersonal part of the interview process and will place more importance on the skills and qualifications your child has.

Having a really clear CV that outlines your child's qualifications, skills, interests and work experience will help a lot in the job hunt. By looking at the CV, the employer will be able to read about your child's abilities and not need to rely on your child exhibiting his or her talents during the interview. Sending in some references from prior work experience placements and some examples of previous work can also help take the pressure off the interview.

A part-time job may suit your child better than full-time employment, because working fewer hours may be less stressful.

Once in work, your child may need more support than the average employee, and the employer will legally have to make reasonable adjustments. Chapters 7 and 8 have more on employment and being independent.

The NAS runs an employment service called Prospects, which has lots of tips for employers and people on the spectrum about getting jobs and support at work. Find out more information at `www.autism.org.uk/prospects`.

Moving out

After leaving school or university, your child may need to or want to move out of the family home. If your child has a statement of special educational needs, you'll have discussed housing at the transition review when your child was about 14 years old (see the "Leaving secondary school" section earlier in this chapter). If you haven't already done so, you'll have to start planning and thinking about some of the options yourself. If your child has a social worker, you can discuss the options with him or her.

Different individuals on the spectrum have different needs, and their housing requirements will be completely different. Some people who have AS can live independently, but others may need a bit or a lot of support. Investigate all the options available to you, and consider what suits both your child's and your family's needs.

If your child is capable of living independently, he or she can buy a property or rent privately or through a housing association. Another option is to buy into a shared ownership scheme, whereby the housing authority owns some of the house and the individual owns a certain percentage (the person pays rent to the housing authority on the part that he or she doesn't own).

Most families need extra financial help to meet their children's housing needs. If you're in this position, get an assessment from social services and your local housing authority.

If your child lives at home or lives away from home but still relies on you (a parent) for support with day-to-day tasks like doing the shopping, paying the bills and cooking dinner, then you're entitled to an assessment by your local social services to ascertain your eligibility for a carer's allowance.

Some individuals on the spectrum can live semi-independently but may need a small amount of formal support, usually from social services. Here, the options are supported living or shared housing. In supported living, your child can live mostly independently in his or her own home or in rented accommodation, with support as and when needed. Alternatively your child could live in a self-contained flat with on-site professional support available 24 hours a day. The amount of support your child gets in these settings will depend on his or her individual needs, and can range from a few hours a month for help with bills to several hours each day for help with everyday tasks like cleaning, personal care and cooking.

Other individuals will need specialist round-the-clock support. They may need this level of support because of additional mental health issues, physical health problems or because they're vulnerable. They can live in their own homes, with parents, in rented accommodation or in residential homes, as long as adequate support is provided by social services or the residential home.

Your child will probably be entitled to a community care assessment by social services to assess his or her individual housing and support needs. Contact social services in writing to request an assessment. Once your child's needs have been assessed, he or she will be able to access funding for housing and support.

Funding sources that your child may also be entitled to include the following:

- ✔ **Independent Living Fund:** This is for individuals who live in their own homes but still need full-time support. Go to www.ilf.org.uk for more information.

- ✔ **Direct payments:** The local authority can give individuals their own money within an individualised budget to purchase their own services and support. Ask your child's social worker about this benefit and go to www.direct.gov.uk and follow the links to "Disabled people" and then "Financial support" for a detailed run-down of the application process.

> ✔ **Disability Living Allowance and Housing Benefit:** People living semi-independently can access both of these. For more information, go to www.direct.gov.uk and follow the same links as listed in the bullet point above.

Your child should be as involved as possible in making decisions about housing. He or she is going to be living there after all. For more information on any issue surrounding housing or funding, get in touch with the NAS Helpline on 0845 070 4004.

Planning for the Future

Sadly, you'll have to come to terms with the fact that you may not always be around to care for, advocate for and support your child. Upsetting though it is, planning for all eventualities is really important to make sure your child lives the life he or she deserves when you're no longer there. Things you need to think about are:

✔ Who will advocate for your child when you're not there

✔ What financial support you should put in place

✔ Preparations for bereavement to help your child understand what's happened and to deal with his or her emotions, if you or a person close to your child dies

Siblings, family friends or friends of your child can all act on behalf of your child when you're no longer around. Try to find someone willing to take on the jobs you do. Draw up a list of such jobs (attending review meetings and assessments, keeping in touch with managers at housing placements, sending birthday cards and so on) and, if no one person is able to do all of them, ask a number of people to do one job each.

Hard though it may be, we can never predict the future, so making plans earlier rather than later is advisable.

You need to write a will and think about setting up a trust fund for your child; seek advice from a solicitor. You also need to consider how any money you leave your child may affect eligibility for any benefits his or she currently receives. The NAS (www.autism.org.uk) offers a free guide to wills and trusts.

People who are part of your child's life are likely to be the ones who support your child when you eventually die. If you and your child have special things that you do together, a special way of talking about death and bereavement, or certain wishes about funerals or ceremonies, make sure the people in your child's life are aware of them. Consider writing a document specifically detailing everything, so you know that your and your child's wishes are going to be met when the worst happens. Going through this document when you have died may also help your child to understand what has happened and go through the grieving process.

We don't want to end on such a depressing note, so just remember that life is for living and, as a parent, you can do lots to help your child live a fun, meaningful and enjoyable life!

Chapter 11

Relating to People Who Have Asperger's Syndrome

In This Chapter

▶ Realising how relating differs for people who have Asperger's syndrome

▶ Investigating relationships with siblings, friends and partners

▶ Understanding how to work alongside a person who has Asperger's syndrome

*E*ven if you've read a whole host of books about Asperger's syndrome (AS), relating to people who have AS — or any other autism spectrum condition (ASC) — can be difficult. Knowing that a person's on the autism spectrum and what that means doesn't actually make changing your behaviour in response easy. For example, if someone's tone of voice is flat, he or she may sound bored and uninterested. Feeling upset when someone doesn't seem to take an interest in what you're saying is natural. Unfortunately for the relationship between the two of you, the other person (the autist) in this example isn't bored — the person just can't control his or her tone of voice. If you react because you're upset, the person with AS also becomes distressed because you appear to be cross for no apparent reason.

So relating to people who are on the autism spectrum involves creating some different rules about socialising and expressing how you're feeling. And this chapter offers lots of techniques and tips to help.

Because this chapter is mostly aimed at people who don't have AS, and in order to avoid too much repetition of the phrase "people who have AS", we use the word "they" a bit more than in other chapters. We are definitely not suggesting a "them and us" scenario, however.

People with at least a few autistic traits are everywhere. Most people with only a few traits are nowhere near qualifying for a diagnosis on the autism spectrum. The person who has no autistic traits at all has never been found and may not exist.

Interacting with People Who Have AS

Some general rules exist for engaging in conversation with people who have AS, such as:

- ✔ Use their names when you address them so that they understand you're talking to them.
- ✔ Try to maintain a flat tone of voice, avoiding too much emotional expression.
- ✔ Useg literal language, avoiding similes and metaphors.
- ✔ Speak in short sentences.
- ✔ Get the level of eye contact right. If the person doesn't like eye contact, don't make it. If the person needs you to make eye contact to show you're talking to him or her, then make sure you look at that person.
- ✔ Avoid shaking hands.
- ✔ Ensure that the person is focused on what you're saying before you say anything important.

Obviously, finding out about the individual person is the most important rule of all. No two people who have an ASC such as AS are the same. Like everyone, people with an ASC have their own personalities, likes, dislikes and foibles. Your approach needs to be tailored to the individual.

As a rule, be yourself at first and then adjust your behaviour as you discover more about the person. People on the autism spectrum are used to others behaving normally, even if they find it a bit stressful. Often, people who try to be considerate by immediately adapting their behaviour cause more stress because they act in odd or unpredictable ways.

Understanding Problems with Relating to Others in AS

Whether the person on the spectrum is your friend, colleague, relative or romantic partner, understanding a bit about what he or she often struggles with is helpful. Knowing about these characteristics may help you understand the person and allow you to relate to each other better.

Relationships aren't a one-way process and involve effort from both parties.

Mentalising

Mentalising is the technical term for the ability to think about your thoughts and feelings and the thoughts and feelings of others. People who have AS aren't very good at mentalising — even mentalising their own thoughts and feelings can be extremely difficult. Understanding and coping with this aspect of AS is probably your greatest challenge.

Two techniques are helpful when relating to someone with weak mentalising abilities. First, speak your thoughts. If you feel sad, tell the other person. If you're cross with the other person, explain why. You can't expect a person on the spectrum to guess how you're feeling. You need to state how you feel explicitly, and then you can both have a sensible discussion about how to overcome any problems. Similarly, if you think your friend, colleague, relative or partner looks upset, instead of showing concern and asking what's wrong, say that you think the person looks upset. (Don't say "You look upset." You have to go the whole hog and say "*I think* you look upset.") The person then has to agree or disagree with what you think. If you just say "You look upset" and the person isn't, he or she may become confused about why you think that and withdraw into himself or herself. If the person is feeling happy, being told he or she is upset can come as a bit of a shock.

Second, be sympathetic and not confrontational. Not being able to pick up on your subtle hints about how you feel isn't the fault of the person with AS. You need to be sympathetic to the other person's difficulties rather than tell the person off for not being intuitive about your emotions or his or her own emotions.

When developing relationships with people who have AS, being open and honest about your emotions and thoughts is crucial. Don't expect people with AS to guess what you're thinking or how you're feeling — tell them.

Professionals who work with people with poor mentalising skills use a technique called validation. *Validation* of what someone says means agreeing that what he or she has said is what the person believes or thinks, even if you're strongly opposed to what he or she has said. Validation of someone else's thoughts is important because it prevents anger, fear and confusion and enables the person on the spectrum to carry on the conversation using his or her (possibly limited) mentalising skills. This technique works with anyone: if you're appearing on *Question Time* and you deliberately anger your opponent, you can make the person look silly and "win" the debate emotionally. If you validate what the other person says, you can carry on and have an intelligent debate, hopefully bringing the person around to an understanding of your point of view, even if he or she still refuses to agree. This second possibility doesn't happen on *Question Time* very often!

People on the spectrum often continue using social strategies that don't work, and they aren't good at learning from their mistakes. They often think that their solution is correct and doesn't need to be altered. Always help them in a calm and logical way to see when they're mistaken. Heated debates won't get you anywhere.

Reading faces and emotions

People on the autism spectrum often have difficulty recognising faces and facial expressions. In extreme cases, they may be unable to recognise that a face is a face, and fail to notice when pictures of faces lack key details (like an eye, for example). Most people's brains have a region that specialises in faces and facial expression, but in some people who have an ASC these regions are smaller and less active, so faces seem like any other objects. These people usually focus on the individual features of the face and not the whole. So, for example, they may notice a slight smile, which could be a sign of contentment, amusement, boredom, anger or several other emotions. Then they see an intense look in the eyes, which could be love, anger, amusement, frustration or something else. Then they move on to another part of the face, and then another. Finally, they try to put all this information together to understand what emotion you're expressing. No wonder that they take time to conduct this analysis and then often get it wrong.

 When you're talking with a person on the spectrum, bear in mind that the person may not pick up on what you're feeling from your facial expression. Similarly, the person may not pick up on your body language or tone of voice either. If in doubt, always state what emotion you're feeling: be honest and upfront.

People with an ASC often use the "wrong" facial expression or emotional response for what they're trying to express. So they may laugh or smile when anxious or upset. You can be easily misled by this strange response, but also upset, particularly if the situation is causing both of you distress, or if upsetting personal information or feelings have just been disclosed.

You may sometimes see people on the spectrum physically struggling with facial expressions, taking a long time to "shape their faces" to show the feelings they're trying to express. Or they may appear to be flicking through different facial expressions to decide on the correct one.

 If a person who has AS seems to be struggling with different facial expressions, try checking out how he or she is feeling with a statement, for example "I think you're feeling worried." The person can then tell you whether this is the case.

People on the autism spectrum often dislike public praise, and that includes gestures or words of affection. They're often struggling with very complex situations when in public, so praise and affection add an extra burden which can lead to overload.

Being the Sibling or Friend of a Person Who Has AS

If your brother or sister has Asperger's or another ASC, your life may be very hard at times. You may have to make a lot of allowances and sacrifices for your sibling because of his or her rigid routines, narrow interests and behavioural difficulties. Sometimes your sibling may do hurtful and upsetting things such as interrupting your time with parents or friends, or taking or breaking something that's important to you. You may find it upsetting that your friends can play all kinds of games with their brothers and sisters, but you feel like everything always has to be done in the way the person on the spectrum wants it. The way in which your family spends time together will often be with your sibling in mind rather than you, which may make you feel resentful or jealous sometimes.

Having a sibling who has AS can make you feel a whole range of different emotions. You may feel angry that your sibling seems to get most of your parents' attention. It may be really unfair that your sibling doesn't get into trouble when he or she has done something naughty, when you always get told off. Your sibling may seem not to care about you at all and you may get into lots of arguments. All of these feelings are totally okay and normal. Being angry with or jealous of your sibling doesn't mean you don't love him or her.

Tell your parents if you're feeling left out or neglected, because sometimes they may simply forget that you need lots of attention too.

Your parents love you just as much as they love your brother or sister with AS. It may just be hard for them to give you as much attention when your sibling needs so much just to get through the day.

Living with a sibling with AS isn't all bad. You'll be glad to know that no negative consequences for your own personal development result from having a sibling who has AS. Many siblings value having a sibling on the autism spectrum because people on the spectrum can see the world from a different perspective and are more understanding of people's differences as a result. A sibling with AS may show love in different ways, and when he or she does, it can be very special. If you can establish common interests with your sibling, the relationship can become even more rewarding (see the nearby sidebar "Laura and Scott"). Your sibling may not tire of a particular subject that you can talk about together or game that you two can play. Your sibling may be extremely knowledgeable about something really interesting.

Getting along with your sibling

Finding out about AS will help you get along with your sibling. The more you know, the more you'll be able to understand your sibling.

Get to know your sibling's individual likes and dislikes and how AS impacts on his or her life. This knowledge will help you avoid scenarios that may cause conflict, and you'll know how to help your sibling out when he or she gets into difficulties.

Make sure you tell your parents how you feel about your sibling. If you're upset, tell your parents why. If something great happens, share it. You may not want to tell your parents things that could upset them, but in the long run doing so will help. Your parents can't know how you feel unless you tell them, and they may be able to help you, answer your questions and sort out any problems you are having.

Here are some more helpful tips for getting along with siblings:

- ✔ **Give them space and time to be alone:** Sometimes your sibling will need to be solitary, so don't interrupt them.

- ✔ **Be as calm and as patient as you can with them:** Even if they've just broken your favourite CD; don't lose your temper. Explain why you're upset or cross and then let it go.

- ✔ **Use clear language, and let your sibling know how you feel:** Remember that people with AS can only know that they've upset you or done something you don't like if you actually tell them.

- ✔ **Accept them for who they are:** Having a diagnosis of AS doesn't change a person; he or she is still your sibling.

- ✔ **Use their special interests or skills as a motivator to spend time with you:** Offer to attend a game fair, play chess, do a puzzle or whatever else they particularly enjoy.

- ✔ **Be patient and give them time to talk to you:** Try chatting on car journeys when you don't need to look each other in the eye and you won't be interrupted.

✔ **Try to put yourself in their shoes:** Consider what living in an autism-unfriendly world is like, where most people don't understand you and you find communicating with others very difficult.

✔ **Show them that you care and that they have someone on whom they can depend for help, however they may want it:** Support your sibling in any way you can; at times you may be the closest person to your sibling, and knowing you're there can be hugely important to him or her.

Laura, whose brother has AS, sums the situation up nicely:

"Love them, plain and simple. Generally it's on their terms, in a way that's comfortable for them. My brother allows me a couple of cuddles a year, on special occasions, and I make the most of them!"

Laura and Scott

Laura works with people who have autism spectrum conditions, and thought that her brother, Scott, might also be on the spectrum. Here's her story of referring Scott for diagnosis and the ups and downs of their relationship.

"When I first referred my brother for diagnosis I felt very confident about my decision to raise my concerns with my family; however, sitting through his diagnosis process was horrible, to say to least. To watch my brother ticking all the Asperger's syndrome boxes was very unpleasant: I struggled to think of my brother as having the same disorder as the people I support day after day. Having professional experience of AS, I knew how much support he might need at various points throughout his life.

Having a brother with AS does have its good points, though. When Scott does something nice for me or pays me a compliment, it makes it even more special and I appreciate it more. For example, my favourite thing that he says is that 'we are two halves of a genius', meaning that we are each good at the skills that the other one finds difficult. I love that Scott smashes the stereotypes of AS in that he understands me very well and that we get on so well.

However, things aren't always lovely. Perhaps because we're so close, I often get the backlash of his pent-up emotions. He's also incredibly stubborn and complicated and can be difficult to reason with at times. Although I know him inside out, I worry about him being misunderstood by other people.

One thing I will say is that I'd never change a thing. Having his diagnosis of AS makes him Scott, and I love him just as he is. It's thanks to him that I found my career in psychology at 7 years old, when he was diagnosed with severe dyslexia. I knew that I wanted to get into a line of work in which I could help families like ours. So what I have to say is, 'Thank you, Scott, for being my inspiration, passion, ambition and joy.'"

Making friendships work

The idea that people who have an ASC such as Asperger's can't have friends is a myth. Making friends may be harder and require a bit more effort on both parts, but no reason exists why people who have AS can't have meaningful friendships.

You may find being a friend of someone with AS frustrating at times. Here are some pointers to help you understand where the person is coming from. For many people on the autism spectrum, idle conversation — small talk — makes no sense and often prevents them from thinking about things that they need to say. So if you're their friend, talking about the weather, the latest gossip or other idle chit chat probably won't be appreciated. Silences are not uncomfortable if you're an autist, so just being quiet is usually better than trying to initiate small talk.

Talking about your mutual interests is a good way forward, as is doing something constructive together, for example watching a film, listening to music you both like or going to a museum. Don't expect your friendship to revolve around sharing intimate emotions and relationship details.

You'll have made friends for a reason, probably because you have something in common such as a shared interest or hobby. If you base your friendship on this interest and follow some of the tips offered in the "Understanding problems with relating to others in AS" section at the beginning of this chapter, you can't go far wrong.

Having a Partner on the Autism Spectrum

Many people on the autism spectrum enjoy successful romantic relationships. Having an ASC certainly doesn't mean you're never going to fall in love or that someone else will never fall in love with you!

You may fall for someone with AS because of his or her intellect, a shared interest or any number of things. If you have AS yourself, you may have a partner who's also on the spectrum or who doesn't have an ASC at all. Whichever the case, having AS creates challenges for developing and maintaining a relationship, so both partners will have to work that little bit harder.

Hendrickx Associates (www.asperger-training.com) has information and training for those in a relationship where one or both partners are on the autism spectrum.

Developing understanding

If you don't know about ASCs and your partner has AS, then maintaining a romantic relationship can be extremely difficult. So our first piece of advice to you is to find out as much as you can about AS and how it affects the person you're with. See the nearby sidebar "Let me count the ways".

You won't be surprised to hear that the relationships of people on the spectrum are as atypical as everything else in their lives. Many books have been written about autism and relationships; most are by typical women who've married autistic men; some are about partnerships where both people are autistic; none are about autistic women having relationships with typical men, and none are about homosexual or bisexual relationships.

People who have AS seldom spend time in their teenage years talking to friends about normal teenage preoccupations such as boys, girls, working out if someone's interested in you, kissing and so on. So they come ill-prepared for the world of dating and relationships, and may base their idea of appropriate behaviour on films they've seen or other fictional sources. Men with AS may then seem very romantic, but gauche and awkward. Women with AS may start dating thinking that "playing hard to get" or "treating them mean to keep them keen" are what counts. Any or all fictional clichés may be believed and taken too much to heart. Part of your role as a partner could be educating your other half about usual behaviour in relationships, and explaining that relationships aren't always like those portrayed in films (in fact, they hardly ever are!).

 Be patient when starting a relationship with someone on the spectrum. Learning new things is hard and may take practice, experience and moral support.

Let me count the ways

Tony has always taken great care of his most prized possessions, a collection of antique toy cars. He carefully dusts them and oils the axles and other joints with a tiny brush. At least once a week, he also counts and arranges the cars in perfect formation on a special set of shelves. Tony also cleans and rearranges my [his wife's] dressing table, removing the hairs from my brush, pairing the earrings, standing up the lipsticks, polishing the mirror, and generally creating a display fit for a shop window or a magazine photo-shoot. I could never understand why he interfered with my stuff. Even less could I understand his cold, unloving way of relating to me. Following his AS diagnosis and his burgeoning awareness that he needed to communicate more, I asked him why he still didn't show me that he loved me. He replied that he didn't realise he needed to do anything more to show how much he loved me, because he took such care of my own prized possessions, on the dressing table!

People with AS are likely to be inexperienced at all types of relationships. Being on the autism spectrum, by its very nature, makes developing and maintaining relationships difficult. Past experiences with friends, boyfriends, girlfriends and work colleagues may have been negative, so they have little relationship success to build on. As a result, their self-esteem may be low — treat them gently and kindly.

A romantic relationship with someone with AS is going to be different, and you, as the person's partner, have to be flexible. Here are some adjustments that you may need to make in order to have a successful loving relationship:

- **Communicate clearly with each other:** Be direct rather than insinuating how you're feeling or making hints. Say what your needs are, both emotional and practical, rather than expecting your partner to work them out.

- **Don't feel let down when your partner fails to respond to your moods and feelings:** Difficulty mentalising (see the "Mentalising" section earlier in this chapter) means that your partner may not recognise or even notice how you feel. Rather than being upset, try to explain how you feel and why you feel that particular way. If you react badly in this situation, your partner may feel that you're suddenly having a go at him or her for no reason. Such misunderstanding isn't going to promote positive communication in your relationship!

- **Remember that your partner may not desire the same level of social contact as you:** Instead of insisting that your partner comes to the pub every Friday to meet up with your friends, consider going on your own. Often, if you're autistic, noisy, crowded environments are stressful. Pursuing independent social lives can be good for a relationship.

- **Give your partner plenty of warning before social engagements:** If you're invited to a function and would really like your partner to attend, give him or her lots of information about the venue, how long you'll stay and who'll be there. Always allow your partner to decide whether to accompany you, based on as much information as possible.

In actual fact, all romantic relationships need to be worked at; living together or marriage involves making lots of compromises. You may just have to work harder if your partner has AS.

Showing affection

As a result of poor mentalising skills or sensory problems, a person with an ASC such as Asperger's may enjoy a brief expression of affection but become overloaded by anything more intense. Sometimes, if the environment is well managed and the person feels very safe, the intense, loving overload can be enjoyable in a "so-good-it-hurts" sort of way. The opposite is also possible: someone may need very intense and frequent expressions of affection just to feel loved. In the same way as they may have sensory problems (see Chapter 9), people on the autism spectrum can be over- or under-sensitive to emotions — both their own and those of others. And they can change from over- to under-sensitive or the reverse at different times and in response to different emotions. These intense reactions can create an emotional roller-coaster for those around them. People who have AS often lack the skill to express themselves with variety and nuance. Emotions can feel as though they're either on or off; for instance, happiness may be experienced in only three forms: negativity (intense depression), neutrality or intense elation.

People on the autism spectrum are also more likely to find out about sex from "adult entertainment" than by talking to their peers. Lack of discussion with peers may leave the person with little opportunity to understand the difference between sex in a relationship and sex for entertainment. As a result, men with AS may appear to objectify women and behave in a dominant way, and women with AS may be sexually submissive or overtly sexual with their partners.

Everyone makes mistakes in relationships, but people on the spectrum may make more or different sorts of mistakes as a result of lack of experience or intuition or from gaining their knowledge from inappropriate sources of information.

Sarah and Keith

Sarah has been with her partner, Keith, for six years. Keith has a diagnosis of AS. Here Sarah explains why their relationship is such a success.

"My relationship with Keith is by far the best I've ever had. We're extremely happy together and have very few arguments or problems. How can this be? I put our success down to a number of things. First, we don't live together. I know that's not possible for everyone, and may not even be necessary for most people, but for us it allows Keith the down-time that he needs after a day at work. Keith has never shared a home with anyone, and the fact that he doesn't feel able to do so with me is something I respect. I don't consider it to be a sign of a lack of love or commitment.

Second, I've discovered lots about Asperger's syndrome and met many people who have AS since meeting Keith. Without this knowledge, I doubt we'd be together. The more I learn and the more people I speak to, the more I realise that Keith's way of thinking is real. He's not being awkward, selfish, difficult or lazy (as is often the perception of others); he is being the only way he can, given his way of processing information. I don't always agree with his conclusions about the world, but I respect them as his.

Third, I find accepting exactly the person I have with me today a positive and liberating experience; I'm not constantly hoping for change or looking for potential. I love the quirks and eccentricities that AS brings and have no problem in helping Keith to navigate the bits of life he finds difficult. I think people feel I've had a great impact on his life, but they don't realise how much he's also changed me and my world. His solid support, rational outlook and unshakeable love for me are priceless, and I wouldn't swap him or AS for anything."

Whatever mistakes occur in your relationship, don't blame the person who has AS if the mistakes arise from lack of inexperience or naivity. Explain the mistake as calmly as you can, and discuss ways to behave differently in future.

Although it may be hard work, a relationship with someone with AS can be as rewarding and loving as any other romantic relationship. If you've got lots in common, enjoy similar things and develop productive ways of communicating with each other, no reason exists why the relationship can't be a success. See the nearby sidebar "Sarah and Keith".

Being the Partner on the Autism Spectrum

The world of romantic relationships may be scary, exciting, overwhelming, baffling or downright terrifying for you. Actually, everyone feels like this, not just people who have an ASC! To have a successful romantic relationship you have to take risks, make yourself vulnerable and learn from your mistakes. Relationships are difficult but, when they work, they're extremely rewarding and a fantastic part of life.

As a person on the autism spectrum, you will find relationships a bit more difficult, but having an ASC isn't the only reason that relationships will seem complicated. Everyone struggles with relationships; some give up altogether and many people are single by choice.

If you're struggling with romantic relationships, you're not the only one. Having AS isn't the only reason why a person may find falling in love or finding a partner quite tricky.

Meeting someone is the first hurdle. Most people meet their partners at college, university or through a hobby. Others meet the love of their life via a mutual friend. If you're struggling to meet people, try joining a club related to one of your interests. Club members will obviously share your interest, and enjoying a mutual hobby is always a good starting point in a relationship.

If you meet someone you like, be brave and ask the person if he or she would like to do something with you. The something could be going to a quiet pub for a drink, seeing a film together or having a coffee. You could also do something related to a mutual hobby, if that's what you'd both enjoy. Start off by trying to be friends. The romance may or may not follow, but being friends is a really good start.

We can't give you a magic formula for finding the partner of your dreams (there isn't one!), but here are a few tips that may help you to navigate the world of romantic relationships:

✔ Most people have more than one relationship, which means that relationships often end. A finished relationship doesn't mean you've failed or chosen the wrong person, just that someone wasn't right for you or has changed. This experience is a natural part of life and doesn't mean you'll never meet anyone else.

✔ Your partner will probably need a higher level of emotional support than you if he or she is not also on the spectrum. Find out what these needs are. Maybe your partner needs a hug every morning or a kiss when he or she gets home from work. Perhaps your partner likes you to call every couple of days for a chat about nothing in particular. Meeting these emotional needs (once you've worked out what they are) will really help your relationship.

✔ Your partner can become upset for no obvious or visible reason. You may perceive this distress to be your fault, even though you didn't intend to cause it. Don't be alarmed by this situation; ask your partner why he or she is upset and what it was that you did or didn't do to contribute to this mood. Your partner should talk to you and let you know why he or she feels this way.

✔ If your partner is upset, although you may have no idea what to do, doing nothing is often the worst possible reaction. Doing nothing may make your partner feel as though you don't care or don't love him or her. Just saying, "I can see you're upset but I don't know what to do. I'm afraid of doing the wrong thing. Please can you tell me what you'd like me to do?" will help.

✔ Learn as much as you can about your partner. Work out how your partner reacts to different situations. If you don't understand why your partner is behaving in a certain way, ask. You can find out what your partner expects and enjoys in a relationship; for example, how often does your partner like to be hugged, does your partner like you to ask about his or her day, does your partner like you to say nice things to him or her? Many people who aren't on the autism spectrum find remembering to do these things easy and natural. Doing so may be harder work for someone with AS.

✔ Learn as much as you can about yourself. Recognise when you need to be alone or to behave in a certain way, and tell your partner. For example, don't expect your partner to understand why you don't want to go to the pub to meet his or her best friend if you haven't told your partner that the noise in the pub is overwhelming for you.

All in all, having a relationship can be tricky, but if you're willing to make an effort and to be flexible in meeting your partner's needs, and if you're lucky enough to have a partner who's also willing to work out what you need, then your relationship is likely to be a success. A loving relationship won't happen overnight, or possibly with the first person you meet and like, but there's no reason why it can't happen for you one day.

Having a Parent Who Has AS

If one of your parents has AS, having a "normal" upbringing can appear to be an unattainable dream. But don't despair — people on the spectrum can and do make great parents.

Coping with the difficulties

As a first thing to consider, does your parent have a diagnosis of AS? Receiving a diagnosis late in life may create turmoil in your family as everyone gets used to the idea and you re-interpret your parent's behaviour in the light of this new information.

Be patient at this difficult time. Everyone will need to get used to the diagnosis in the family and to figure out what it means for you all (see Chapter 3). Keep talking to each other about how you feel.

Your parent may do or say things that you find difficult. Your parent also may not do or say things that you want him or her to! Most parents are like this, but certain frustrations are more common if your parent has AS. Consider these behaviour traits:

- ✔ **Not providing warm physical contact:** A lack of cuddles, pats on the back and so on may make you feel unloved.

- ✔ **Not being able to guess how you're feeling without you telling them:** For example, your parent may not realise you need comforting when you're sad. This is especially true if the only clues to your emotions are the look on your face or a story you've just told your parent.

- ✔ **Unusual eye contact:** Common differences in the way that people on the autism spectrum use eye contact can be confusing or disconcerting for someone else, and you may sometimes feel that your parent isn't interested in you.

- ✔ **Not telling you that he or she loves you:** Your parent may assume you know how much he or she loves you and so may not tell you as often as you'd like.

- ✔ **Constant observation of what you're doing:** An obsession with small details and incessant negative feedback on your actions — for example, not using your knife and fork correctly, not observing how many miles a journey has taken and the resulting petrol consumption — may make you feel useless.

- ✔ **Saying or doing odd things:** All parents inadvertently embarrass their children, but this is especially likely if they have AS. Maybe your parent doesn't realise, unless told, that certain things can cause embarrassment or that some things are supposed to be kept private.

- ✔ **Imposing undue restrictions on your actions:** A parent with AS may not allow you to do certain things because they conflict with what he or she wants to do or may cause him or her anxiety.

- ✔ **Unusual responses to sensory stimuli:** A parent's sensory difficulties may also affect his or her children. For example, children may constantly be asked to be quiet, play quietly and turn music down.

Be explicit with your parents and tell them how you're feeling and what that means.

Your parents do love you; they may just find it hard to express that love. Ask them to tell you more often, if their lack of open affection makes you feel sad.

Particularly as you get older, you may also feel that you have to sometimes be the parent. For example, you may have to explain a social situation or take control when a parent becomes anxious about something. If a sudden change in routine occurs that your parent finds difficult to cope with, you may be the one who understands how he or she feels and so can take control of the situation.

If you feel you need help, approach other family members, family friends or your teachers. You can also phone the National Autistic Society (NAS) Helpline on 0845 070 4004.

Focusing on the positives

Like any parent, those with AS will have their good days and bad days. But some things about AS make parents with these characteristics particularly great, for example:

- ✔ They're likely to be very honest with you, and you'll always know where you stand.

- ✔ They're likely to run a very organised household based on clear routines, which is excellent for children because they like to know what's expected of them and what will happen next.

- ✔ They may have fascinating interests or know lots of amazing facts about a subject.

Being a carer

As people who have AS get older, they may find themselves having to care for their elderly parents. However, for many people on the spectrum, family relationships have broken down. Parenting a child with AS is no easy task, and these frustrations may carry over into the relationship parents have with their adult autistic children. The parents themselves may be on the spectrum and have grown up in an era of less awareness and so not received any help. As a parent ages and suffers dementia, for example, he or she may begin to present challenges for an autistic carer. The parent may not be talking sense, and caring for someone who's confused requires an ability to guess what the person probably meant rather than what he or she actually said. Caring for a person with memory loss is like a never-ending game of charades. Social services departments are only just realising that adults with an ASC who aren't learning disabled require help, and helping them perform a carer's role is not yet on their radar.

The parents of a woman with AS are often disappointed that she hasn't produced grandchildren. This daughter may be coping with the caring role alone, earning nothing and unable to make savings for her own old age. We hope that things will improve as a result of more widespread understanding of this problem.

Relating at Work

You may assume that this section refers to people who've been open about their diagnosis, but many of the tips we offer for working with people on the autism spectrum are basically good practice for working with anyone. Most large organisations will have undiagnosed autists working for them, as well as people who just have a few autistic traits. Chapter 7 has more on AS and employment.

Because people with AS don't follow the usual rules about eye contact and they may say things without realising how those words sound to another person, people who have AS are often distrusted by colleagues whom they've only recently met. This situation is incredibly ironic because people on the spectrum are almost all scrupulously honest, reliable and persevering. They're often very good at following a process or system accurately and can often maintain their concentration for very long periods. Many are perfectionists, which can be a great asset to a company when their perfectionism is focused on important tasks (otherwise it can lead to a lot of wasted time). Practice makes perfect, and some people who have AS have practised their skills until they're almost unbelievably good.

Employing a person who has AS

Once you've taken the decision to employ someone who is on the autism spectrum, your next tasks are to make the person feel welcome, help the person fit in, and make sure that the team accommodates the person and his or her different styles of working and thinking. Just like anybody, the person who has AS will be less flexible and less productive if stressed or made to feel insecure, unhappy or unwelcome.

Other members of staff may not know that a person with an ASC finds social interaction and communication difficult, and may think their colleague is rude or unfriendly. Because you can't physically see ASCs, other members of staff may find understanding the person's differences more difficult.

Under the Disability Discrimination Act 2005, employers are required to make reasonable adjustments for individuals with an ASC diagnosis.

As the employer of a person with an ASC such as Asperger's, your biggest responsibility is to make sure that the expectations of the job are completely clear. You also need to pay attention to the work environment and ensure that all the unwritten rules of the workplace are made explicit. Consider drawing up a daily timetable for your employee with AS, so that he or she knows what's likely to happen each day and can mentally prepare for it.

When employing someone with AS, consider these tips:

- ✔ Before the person starts work, and whenever you ask the person to do something new as part of the job, make sure you provide sufficient training and mentoring.

- ✔ Meet your employee regularly. Bear in mind that shorter, more frequent meetings may be more acceptable.

- ✔ Be aware that the person may get stressed easily, particularly in group situations.

- ✔ Ask a colleague to act as mentor for the person, so that the person has someone to turn to if he or she encounters any problems.

- ✔ Provide a list of practical alternatives to deal with commonplace office hiccups. People on the spectrum are often perfectionists when it comes to work, and things like the photocopier breaking down can cause a huge amount of stress. If your employee finds these situations difficult, having a back-up plan — such as using the photocopier in the office next door — can help.

- ✔ Give direct feedback about your employee's work, rather than expecting him or her to pick up on social cues. If you need to criticise the person's work, do so in a clear, sensitive and consistent manner. Explain what you didn't like and how to do it differently in future.

- ✔ Give clear and direct instructions that are precise and leave no room for misinterpretation.

- ✔ Provide as much notice as possible of any changes to the workplace or the person's job.

- ✔ Allow the person with AS to share information about his or her diagnosis with whom he or she wants to, and to keep it private if he or she prefers.

You can get advice and information about employing people who have AS at www.autism.org.uk and from the NAS's training and employment service, Prospects (prospects.london@nas.org.uk).

Being a colleague of a person who has AS

Rule number one: be yourself and then adjust your behaviour to the person who has AS. Remember that people with AS often don't see the big picture.

People on the autism spectrum can't intuitively read other people and may not be able to tell if someone's too busy to talk, stressed or tired. Often people on the autism spectrum can't take hints, so you may need to make some adjustments to the way you communicate, and say what you mean rather than trying to be polite. People on the spectrum tend to be very open and honest themselves and appreciate these qualities in others.

Your colleague with AS may sometimes say something strange or appear rude. He or she may have misunderstood a situation, request or instruction at work. Check with your colleague what he or she means, and you'll be able to save hurt or hostile feelings developing as the result of a misunderstanding.

Not being able to "see" AS in a person's physical appearance doesn't make the person's differences and difficulties any less real.

Often people on the autism spectrum don't want to disclose their diagnosis to everyone in the workplace. Respect someone's privacy if he or she has told only you, as a trusted colleague. You may have to ask people to make allowances for your colleague with AS without really explaining why.

Being a Support Worker for Someone Who Has AS

Many people who have AS need support with various aspects of their daily lives, be it household management or getting out in the community, or may just need someone to pop in and see how they are every now and again. People employed to support those on the spectrum have a rewarding but challenging role. In this section, we offer you some basic tips and advice if you work with someone who has AS.

Your most important task is to get to know the person you're working with. As we repeatedly stress, everyone's an individual and, although some general tips apply when working with people on the autism spectrum, getting to know the person and developing a positive relationship with them is what counts.

The more questions you ask yourself about why the person you're supporting behaves as he or she does, and the more you find out about the autism spectrum, the better.

Although the rewards you gain from supporting someone on the autism spectrum may not be conventional, they are significant. For support workers who thrive on a challenge, working with people on the spectrum is endlessly rewarding because there's always more to learn.

Consider these tips for making your relationship with the person you support as rewarding as possible:

- ✔ Develop a detailed knowledge of how the person wants to be supported and when.

- ✔ Recognise that interactions will be much easier if your personality characteristics, interests, age and so on match the other person's. For example, an unfit middle-aged woman who likes knitting supporting a young man who enjoys hill walking and talking about football is unlikely to be the basis for a successful relationship!

- ✔ Get to know which situations may be difficult for the person to process, so you know when to allow extra time, avoid certain things or (verbally) back off.

- ✔ Understand the person's sensory differences, routines, rituals and anxiety triggers, so that you can be aware of them and pre-empt any problems.

- ✔ Encourage the person with certain things without being pushy; people who have AS often lack self-esteem and self-motivation.

- ✔ Don't interpret the person not saying thank you as ingratitude; he or she is very likely to forget social niceties, but it doesn't mean that he or she doesn't appreciate the hard work you do.

Support workers face the challenge of encouraging the person on the spectrum to try new things, broaden his or her experience and improve his or her independence, at the same time as taking account of, and respecting, the person's anxiety triggers, sensory differences, routines and rituals.

Communicating

Communication is often a difficulty for people on the autism spectrum, but if you constantly check the person's understanding of what's going on and explain things when the person hasn't understood, you overload the person with information, which can prevent him or her from learning, and may precipitate meltdowns. Sometimes leaving the person confused and less stressed is better. You may feel that you can't win! Again, getting to know the individual and adapting your behaviour and plans for the person you're working with is always the best bet. You're bound to make a few mistakes, but you'll soon work out how to make amends and continue building a positive relationship. Here are some tips about communicating successfully with the person you're supporting:

- ✓ **Work out how long it takes the person to process a verbal question:** Count (in your head, without moving your lips) the number of seconds it takes between you finishing a question and the person responding in various situations, so that you leave enough time for the person to process the information. By getting the timing right, you avoid repeating yourself too soon or asking in the middle of the person's thinking time whether the person has heard. Repeating questions, requests or instructions too soon can cause major problems because the person has to deal with even more information and may have to start processing the sentence he or she was working on from the beginning again, which is not only frustrating but can also contribute to a meltdown (see Chapter 6 for more on these).

- ✓ **Agree upon a sign that means the person is unable to cope with something:** The person may have days when he or she just needs to be left alone. Being able to signal this with a simple symbol or phrase allows the person to control the situation.

- ✓ **Be patient:** The person may take a long time to process each sentence that's spoken to him or her, particularly if the information is new or if it's provided in a crowded or noisy place in which the person must also cope with lots of other stimuli.

- ✓ **Phrase suggestions and requests in a different way for them:** The person may be generally anxious about trying new things, but have requested support doing so because he or she is bored with current activities. Asking "Do you want to try kayaking today?" will still be unlikely to get a positive response because the person doesn't really "want" to — he or she is anxious about it. Instead, try phrasing it like this: "We're going to try kayaking today. If you don't like it, we'll stop."

Dealing with anxiety and stress

If you're supporting someone with AS, you'll probably have to deal with the person's stress, confusion and fear. People on the autism spectrum often use routines and rituals as a way of managing their possibly constant sense of anxiety.

In new situations and in those that you know make the person worried, expect more routines and rituals.

Routines and rituals may be odd or time-consuming, making them frustrating or embarrassing to deal with. As a support worker, if you find someone's routines and rituals difficult to cope with, try asking the person how it feels if he or she is interrupted or stopped.

Understanding what a vital (and effective) role routines and rituals can play for someone managing his or her own anxiety can make such behaviour easier to tolerate.

Try to reduce the person's anxiety where possible. For example, if the person worries about getting lost, carry a map or sat nav. Doing so will also increase chances for interaction and learning. Work on skills such as managing the person's anxiety about getting lost only when the person is in a situation that he or she is very comfortable with. If the person is already in a challenging situation, he or she is unlikely to absorb new information and will probably become stressed or anxious as a result. If the person is trying something new, just focus on making it a positive experience rather than trying to maximise its learning potential.

In all situations, but particularly those that are already stressful, disagreement, confrontation, sarcasm, being emotional, raising your voice and using physical restraint all tend to make people on the spectrum more angry and agitated. Being upset means they're less able to mentalise and are more overloaded. Without the ability to think calmly, they can't control their emotions, however much they want to. Adding your emotions to the situation just makes matters worse.

When people who have an ASC are stressed, upset and overloaded, asking them what's the matter simply adds to their overload. They've already got a lot to think about without having to explain their feelings, and they're unable to think about their emotions (that is, unable to mentalise about themselves), because doing so takes a lot of brain power, which is currently in short supply because of the overload.

Regardless of the emotion — be it anger, frustration, panic or whatever — use a calm, quiet voice. Be firm, but not so firm that you come across as demanding or bullying. Knowing the cause of the upset is unimportant; you just need to relieve the situation. Understanding can come later.

Try to get the person to a more peaceful environment. Ask the person some questions about his or her interests to help the person think about those instead. Exercise may also have a calming effect.

Personalising support

Personalising support means that, rather than passively receiving a standard service, for example two days a week in a day centre, people actively make choices about what they do with their day and their life. At the moment, the Government provides people with a disability with their own individual budget, which they can spend on creating the life they want and getting the support they need. This situation is certainly preferable to the Government paying for everyone to receive the same generic support service, because it gives individuals much more control and choice over what they do each day. Person-centred planning tools can be used to help people explore what they would like their support to look like.

People who have an ASC such as AS, like everyone, have the right to make choices about their lives. Such choices include who supports them, what support they get and when. Your job will be much easier if the person you're supporting has had the opportunity to make his or her own decisions.

Hopefully, the person you're supporting feels able to talk to you about his or her likes, dislikes and ambitions. Maybe the person really wants to have a job or to go to the pub every Friday night. The person may want skiing lessons or to go on holiday. You can help the person in his or her choices.

Making choices about the unknown is often very difficult if you have AS, because you may find it hard to imagine what a place or activity is like. Visiting a place first, with no pressure, will help the person to understand the choice he or she is making.

Listen, and try to let go of any preconceptions you may have regarding what a person may or may not want to do with his or her life.

As a support worker, you need to spend time getting to know the person so that mutual trust and understanding can develop. You will usually get better results if you work with other professionals and the person's family to find out what support or opportunities the person on the spectrum wants or are possible. People who know the person you're supporting better than you do are likely to be around, so listen to what they have to say.

Keep an open mind about the person you support, because the person should have ultimate control over what he or she does during the day.

Some things the person you support wants to do may clash with your own beliefs or values. You may be uncertain whether you can support the person with the decision he or she has made. If you feel your beliefs contrast so much that you can't support the person, contact an advocacy organisation that may be able to provide someone who can give impartial advice about the benefits of a decision.

You may not be the perfect support worker for an individual, but this doesn't mean you can't be the perfect support worker for someone else. The value of personalised support in itself means that you can't be perfect for everyone. Try not to take things personally, and be brave and speak out. Tell the person and the person's support network if you think he or she may benefit more from a different support worker, and identify the skills and interests that the new support worker would need.

The organisations listed below provide tips and tools to help people personalise their support:

- ✔ Helen Sanderson Associates: www.helensandersonassociates.co.uk
- ✔ In control: www.in-control.org.uk
- ✔ Valuing People Now support team: www.valuingpeople.gov.uk

Many of the tools for personalisation need to be adapted for use with people who have AS, particularly in terms of the abstract terminology that's often used. For more information, go to the Social Care Institute for Excellence's website: www.scie.org.uk. Also see the *Person Centred Thinking for People who have Autism* mini-book (NAS and Helen Sanderson Associates), available at www.hsapress.co.uk/publications/mini-books.aspx.

Chapter 12

Sussing Out Sensory Difficulties

. . . .

In This Chapter
▶ Discovering the range of sensory problems
▶ Learning how to cope and adapt
▶ Applying what you know to the real world

. . . .

*S*ensory difficulties — essentially any problems related to sight, smell, touch, hearing or taste — probably affect everyone with Asperger's syndrome (AS) or any autism spectrum condition (ASC). (For more on the different diagnostic terms, see the Introduction and Chapters 1 and 3.) But because they don't stop and compare notes with other people, many on the autism spectrum assume that everyone experiences the world in the same way. On top of that, sensory difficulties are so little understood that many people can't talk clearly about them, just because the subject is so unfamiliar and they've never learnt the right words to use. This chapter makes everything much clearer and introduces you to all the technical terms that you may hear or read in connection with sensory problems. It's important you know what the terms are when you see them in a diagnostic report, and that you can understand a doctor who isn't very good at communicating in layman's terms (there are still plenty of them around!).

The whole area of sensory difficulties is still at the experimental stage as far as psychologists are concerned, so there's no one book that covers all of the sensory difficulties that someone on the spectrum may have. In order for you to be able to identify and research all of the problems relevant to your circumstances, we've tried to make this round-up of the symptoms as complete as possible.

Some of the ideas in this chapter about how to adapt your environment to make your life easier may seem obvious, but small changes can lead to big differences. Tackle one small problem, make a few small changes, and then move on to tackle another small problem. Dealing with one small change at a time doesn't sound very inspiring, but small changes are easy! Don't look at the size of the hill you're trying to climb — enjoy the walk instead.

Changing your environment to suit your sensory needs will make a significant difference: life will be less stressful and easier to deal with . Thinking about sensory problems will help explain why certain situations are particularly difficult, or more difficult than you expect, while providing ways to make such situations easier.

Recognising the Sensory Difficulties that Come with AS

Sensory difficulty has two obvious forms: too little sensation and too much sensation. Other common forms of sensory difficulty also exist, however, and a mixture of all or most of them is far more common than being just over- or under-sensitive. Because research into sensory effects is fairly new, researchers are still finding types of sensation that have never been reported before. So if you experience something that isn't in this chapter, that doesn't mean it doesn't exist or that it shouldn't be included in later editions of this book. Rather than going into detail about the very rarest sensations, however, we try to show the range of problems and where you fit into it.

This section starts with the various ways that senses can be affected and the terminology used to describe them. It then looks at each sense in turn.

Sensing too much or too little

Over-sensitivity is called *hypersensitivity* and can affect any of the senses we talk about in this chapter. You can do little about hypersensitivity other than avoiding the situations which are a problem most of the time, but pushing yourself to cope with slightly difficult situations on a regular basis will prevent hypersensitivity from getting worse. Reduce the intensity of the worst experiences with gloves, ear plugs, dark glasses or whatever, but don't use them all the time, because you're likely to make the problem worse in the long run. Try checking every hour or so to see whether you still need to be using them — although sometimes it'll be obvious, like needing ear plugs all the way through a film or train journey, or needing sunglasses all the time that you're out in the sun.

Try to cope with something that's a bit too much for you — noise slightly too loud, light slightly too bright, and so on — for a few minutes every day, because doing so will stop your over-sensitivity getting worse, and may result in it getting better. If it does improve, it means less stress for you, and that's got to be a good thing!

You may find that you're hypersensitive to certain foods. We don't cover the food you eat in this chapter — more on diet can be found in Chapter 15.

Unseeing things

You've almost certainly had the experience of walking into a shop, looking for something, not finding it and asking the assistant where it is. The assistant's then pointed and said something like, "There, next to the batteries." You've looked at the correct shelf but still not been able to see the familiar product you're looking for. What you experienced was a moment of poor visual discrimination when you looked at the display of products and just saw a mass of shape and colour — you were unable to focus on the important details you were looking for.

Under-sensitivity is called *hyposensitivity* (with the "o" pronounced long like "go"; this is especially important in this word, otherwise it sounds like *hypersensitivity*). Hyposensitivity involves being less aware of stimuli such as noise, temperature, light, and so on. Hyposensitivity can affect any of the senses described in this chapter.

Hard work and concentration can help you improve your sensitivity. For example, you could spend ten minutes each day deliberately paying attention to sounds of a pitch that you normally fail to respond to. You're never going to make your sense "normal", but the improvement you can achieve is often worthwhile.

Looking at poor discrimination

Poor discrimination can affect any of the five main senses, and can be quite a difficult idea to get your head around. *Poor discrimination* means not being very good at picking out relevant information. For an example of what this means, see the nearby sidebar "Unseeing things".

The easiest way to explain poor discrimination is to give you examples of what discrimination is in each of the five main senses — that's sight (technically called *vision*), hearing (*audition*), touch (*tactile sensation* or *tactility*), smell (*olfaction*) and taste (*gustation*).

- ✔ **Visual discrimination** allows you to pick out details of a scene. A child learns this, for example, from "spot-the-difference" puzzles. Camouflage is designed to make visual discrimination more difficult.

- ✔ **Auditory discrimination** is practised by anyone who can hold a conversation in a noisy place, picking out the other person's voice from the background hubbub.

- ✔ **Tactile discrimination** covers both the type of touch (soft, scratchy, wet, and so on) and what spot on your skin is experiencing that touch. Poor tactile discrimination can affect both type and sense of place.

Some forms of *tactile discrimination* are quite difficult for anybody, like being rubbed in two places by two different textures (say, velvet and sacking, one on the back of the right hand and one on the back of the left — keeping your eyes closed). Most people don't do very well at telling which texture is where, and the difficulty gets worse the closer your hands are together — just try this while they're crossed over! Most people get completely confused in this situation, being convinced that the velvet on their right hand is actually on their left hand.

- ✔ **Olfactory discrimination** is the ability to tell which smells make up the aroma you're sniffing, such as being able to tell that a perfume is a mixture of roses and violets. Being able to do this with tastes also counts as olfactory discrimination, like those TV chefs who can pick out thyme and dill from the taste of the gravy.

- ✔ **Gustative discrimination** completes the set, but taste is so closely bound up with smell that we cover both issues together later in this chapter.

Clear examples of poor discrimination are given in the various sections below which deal with touch, hearing, and so on. For another example, see the nearby sidebar "That's discrimination!".

Poor discrimination can itself be general or take any of several specific forms. Having more than one specific form of poor discrimination, but for the severity to vary with each one, is common.

As with hyposensitivity, poor discrimination can be improved with effort, so try spending ten minutes each day trying to pick out details that you have trouble with. Pick the sensory problem that will make the most difference to your life and work on that one alone. Trying to work on two at the same time doubles both the work and the frustration if you don't progress as fast as you'd like.

That's discrimination!

The Goth has *hyperacuity* (hypersensitivity to sound — amplified buskers often make him put his fingers in his ears) and very poor auditory discrimination, so is unable to hold a conversation whilst another one is going on next to him (well, unless the other person shouts). Poor auditory discrimination limits the ability to pick out a particular sound from all the sounds around it.

Poor discrimination can also be useful, however. Someone with poor visual discrimination will be sensitive to improvements in street signs, so makes a good consultant for the local council. In the Goth's case, he finds different makes and models of hi-fi equipment easy to distinguish, and is thus tempted to buy ruinously expensive systems with very low levels of background noise and distortion. His inability to discriminate between all the individual musical notes means that a hi-fi system which makes these differences even a tiny bit clearer sounds obviously better.

Catcher in the eye

The Goth is easily distracted by the way a glass (or any other reflective or transparent object) catches the light, and can end up staring at the glass until someone prevents him. He's deeply frustrated by the experience, because he's losing time out of his day and has no way to control the distraction or to break the spell. Distraction is particularly unpopular with employers, who are inclined to think you're wilfully wasting time or, if they know about your diagnosis, think that it's time that you need to think about stuff, and that they shouldn't disturb you. To make matters worse, no onlooker seems to be able to reliably tell the difference between when someone is usefully thinking about something important and when he or she is just absorbed in a distraction.

Take small steps and try to make the training fun — if you're improving your visual discrimination, use spot-the-difference and jigsaw puzzles, for example. With sound, try picking out a single instrument or note from different pieces of music.

As well as finding it difficult to focus on what is interesting or important, people with AS can also have difficulty telling which sense is sensing what. Technically, this is called _sensory confusion_. Unless you experience it yourself, confusion about which sense is providing information is probably the hardest sensory problem to understand. People hear something and think they've been touched, or cannot tell which sense the sound came from — whether it's a sight or a smell or whatever. It's almost impossible (maybe it _is_ impossible) for most people to imagine what that is like. If you don't experience this confusion yourself, your mind should now be boggling!

Getting distracted

We've all been in a situation where we're talking to someone and our attention is caught by a sound or movement. Most people may be distracted for a moment but are able to return to the conversation. For people with sensory problems, a particular stimulus such as a certain colour or sound can lead to them being caught up in the distraction to the point of devoting all their attention to it. It can be a great struggle, or even impossible, for such people to turn their attention back to the conversation without being prompted to do so. For an example of this, see the nearby sidebar "Catcher in the eye".

Distortion

Distortion could be seeing halos around objects or hearing distant sounds as nearby — it's any sort of change in normal perception. If a sensory problem you're experiencing isn't covered by one of the other sections here, then it's probably a form of distortion.

Seeing music and tasting words

Synaesthesia is a neurological condition where one sense is perceived not only by that sense but also by another one. The sensation of one sense can also trigger particular thought pathways. Common examples include seeing particular colours when you hear words or music (a particular note or word may be red, while another one may be blue). Different numbers may have particular personalities, for example the number 12 may be kind, or the number 399 angry. Synaesthesia can also be spatial, so months of the year are perceived as being in a particular location, for example at points around a circle. Some people hear sounds when they see movement.

Seeing the words you're reading as coloured is possibly the commonest form of synaesthesia. This form is a specific version of seeing shapes and patterns as colours, which most frequently affects letters and words — imagine what reading this page in a profusion of multi-coloured inks is like. Other common forms are:

- ✔ Hearing music and seeing colours
- ✔ Smells triggering colours
- ✔ Touch triggering colours
- ✔ Sounds giving the feeling of touch
- ✔ Sight giving feelings of touch
- ✔ Smell or taste giving the feeling of touch
- ✔ Sounds causing you to move (called *audiomotor synaesthesia*)

Various rarer forms also exist — this list is just the ones you're most likely to encounter. Some *synaesthetes* (people with synaesthesia) actually experience the extra perception; for others it's more like remembering, or just associating the two experiences. Some researchers restrict the definition of synaesthesia to those people who actually experience the extra sense. If you haven't experienced it yourself, saying that these black words are simultaneously brightly coloured doesn't make sense, but if you have that form of synaesthesia (actually experiencing words as colours), then that is exactly what you see.

You won't be able to spot synaesthesia in someone else very easily, but listen out for tell-tale expressions such as, "I don't like that book because the words are too green," or "I wish this song was a bit more purplish."

Synaesthetes have no control over how they perceive the world — it's not a choice and neither is it a hallucination or delusion. Rather, bits of the brain that don't have any direct connection in most people are wired together in people with synaesthesia.

While you can't do anything about synaesthesia, you can take advantage of it. For example, someone who sees words and symbols as coloured and can pay close attention to detail makes a good proofreader: even the tiniest errors stand out because they're the wrong colour.

Overloading your senses

Overload is one of the key problems in AS, and although it isn't strictly a sensory problem, we've never heard of people suffering from overload (for instance, being overwhelmed by their own thoughts) who weren't also suffering sensory overload (being overwhelmed by the information being fed to them by their senses). Sensory overload is unlikely to be associated with hyposensitivity but can be caused by any of the other sensory problems.

Trying to carry on while overloaded is always going to make you stressed, and will make it increasingly harder to act and react in situations. If you do nothing about the overload, then you get more irritable, upset and anxious. Eventually, you'll have no choice but to shout, scream, cry or have a full-on meltdown (see Chapter 6 for more on these). So learn to spot the build-up (although doing so isn't easy) and leave the situation as soon as possible. Don't worry about offending your friends; if they are friends, they'll understand. And don't worry about offending other people, because having someone abruptly walk away is less offensive and embarrassing than coping with a stranger who's having a meltdown.

Taking Problems One Sense at a Time

With so many alternatives to consider, building up an idea of all of your, or someone else's, sensory difficulties can be a lengthy process, especially as testing facilities are extremely rare and often not available on the NHS. Learning which senses can be affected, and in what way, is explained, one sense at a time, in the following sections, including tips on how to deal with the difficulties.

You may come across many therapies when you're researching what to do about your problems, but here we don't mention those which have no sound evidence of success — remember, anecdotal evidence shouldn't be relied on (see Chapter 13).

You're likely to find that your experience of sensory problems will vary. Sensitivity can be permanent — such as always hearing sounds of a certain pitch as more quiet than other sounds — or changeable if, say, the sounds that are quiet vary from day to day and minute to minute.

Teasing out difficulties with touch

You may think that starting with touch rather than sight or hearing is odd, but touch, including physical sensation, is probably the area that people on the autism spectrum have most problems with. The range of problems is vast: some find that they can only wear certain clothes, eat certain foods (because of the texture) or only sleep on the floor (because the enveloping sensation of a mattress is too intense). Others find skin-to-skin contact with another person almost unbearable. If you think clothes are uncomfortable and like to wander around the house naked, you probably have problems with touch. Conversely, you may like to wear the roughest clothes you can find, because only they make you feel like you're wearing anything. If you're at your wits' end because you can't seem to get your 8-year-old to keep his clothes on in the supermarket, spare a thought for how uncomfortable he must be. Even children with AS usually seek and enjoy parental approval, so to give that up, those clothes must be pretty unbearable.

Some people like a weighted blanket, which provides deep pressure without the need for a hug. You can buy these from specialist online retailers for about £100 (just do an internet search for "weighted blankets").

Some standardised tests for touch do exist. These tests usually measure how well you can discriminate between two different points of touch, or how soft a touch you can detect. However, touch is a complicated sense, and the response to touch after it's detected may be different in ASCs. Some people on the autism spectrum can tolerate an enormous bear hug while being unable to stand a very light touch. Others may be able to cope with the feel of cotton but not polyester, or the reverse. For some, a "prickly" touch is tolerable but a "woolly" one is unbearable. Try to imagine what it's like to travel on a rush-hour train when every time someone brushes past you it feels like a thump!

Unexpected touch often seems to be more problematic. If you want to give someone on the spectrum a cuddle, then give a warning first rather than going straight up and putting your arms around him or her. You could say "I'd like to give you a hug now, is that OK?" If the person would rather you didn't, he or she can always say "No".

Hypersensitivity to touch is seldom straightforward, but simple hyposensitivity to touch (that is, never really noticing light touch and always needing quite a knock to realise you've banged something) is more common. Tactile hyposensitivity can be dangerous, because you may seek out sensations that are so extreme they can cause injury, so someone with hyposensitivity will have to use their judgement and experience.

Some people with an ASC may be so hyposensitive that they don't notice if they are in pain. If this is the case for you, be extra careful when cooking (don't touch hot things, even if it doesn't hurt, because the burn will still be damaging) or when using sharp objects.

Poor tactile discrimination can mean that you can't tell the difference between wool and sandpaper, but they both feel scratchy unless you're hyposensitive. An example of distortion is feeling the roughness of something changing as you handle it. Distortion can also include normal clothing sometimes feeling loose and flappy or of a normal mattress feeling like it's swallowing you up like a scene from a cheap horror film.

If you're concerned that your child has tactile difficulties, look for these signs:

- ✔ Stripping off at every opportunity — we reckon that if this happens, you've noticed already!

- ✔ Persistent scratching or attempting to keep certain items of clothing away from the skin, like trying to keep a woolly jumper away from the neck and wrists.

- ✔ Frequently pulling or readjusting clothing.

- ✔ Favourite clothing always having the same texture (usually soft and smooth, but not always); putting up significant resistance to wearing clothes of a different texture.

- ✔ Liking tight clothing, big hugs, being lain on, and rough and tumble more than other children of a similar age.

- ✔ Avoiding shaking hands or kissing on greeting — most children go through a shy phase, but this may carry on indefinitely or they may be happy to engage in conversation on their own terms while maintaining this avoidance. Letting people tease them about it isn't helpful! Support them in their choice. More severe cases of this avoidance are diagnosed as *tactile defensiveness*.

- ✔ Being fussy about the textures of food. Everyone thinks there's something funny about the textures of kidney and mushroom; what differs is whether the person is put off eating these foods. Changing the texture of food (not cooking the mushrooms, or not cooking them for very long) can help get your child to eat a more varied diet if texture is a problem.

Careful choice of clothing and food plus a willingness to challenge yourself (or your child) a little — these are the main ways to cope with touch and to not end up retreating from life as you retreat from unpleasant sensations.

Sensing the problems with sound

Being unable to bear loud sounds (*hyperacuity*) is the obvious problem. However, poor auditory discrimination may be even more common, and no simple solution such as sticking your fingers in your ears exists. The sensitivity, or lack of it, may be very specific, affecting only sounds of a certain pitch — so people on the spectrum really do have an excuse for why the person they seem to be deaf to is their mother. Because of your sensory problems, you may not be able to recognise people's voices unless they're very distinctive.

Hypoacuity is selective insensitivity, for example affecting only certain pitches or types of sound (like hisses or short, sharp sounds). The term hypoacuity isn't usually used in its simple sense, as that's simply called being hard of hearing.

Poor auditory discrimination doesn't mean you're hard of hearing either. Separate to any insensitivity you have, if you find picking individual sounds out of background noise difficult, then you have poor auditory discrimination. So, if you're in a noisy shop and someone speaks to you, you won't be able to hear his or her words. You may, nevertheless, be exceptionally good at picking out details in the sound that you hear, just not necessarily those details that the person speaking to you thinks are important (his or her words!). Poor auditory discrimination, in other words, makes it difficult to pick out one sound among many.

If you have poor auditory discrimination, tell people about it. If you are meeting up with someone for a chat, or need to have an important meeting with your boss, make sure you organise it in a quiet place with minimal background noise. If you're asking your child to do something, switch the telly and any music off and make sure that siblings are quiet before you start talking.

Distortions include distant sounds seeming to come from nearby, someone you know sounding like someone else whom you know (or a character in a book or film), and a sound issuing from a specific place sounding like it's coming from all around you.

Ear plugs aren't recommended for constant use in preventing pain and discomfort, and shouldn't be used for more than four hours at a time, even in bed. Otherwise, the ear tries to hear through the obstruction and becomes even more sensitive to noise, making the problem worse rather than better. Prolonged use can also lead to earache and tinnitus (ringing in the ear).

Sophisticated headphones are available that cancel out background noise (prices range from about £50 to £300; the more expensive models offering more noise reduction and better build quality). These are certainly effective, but make sure you try the headphones you're thinking of buying, because the various models sit on the ear very differently, and some people find certain models unwearable. Ear defenders, as worn by road diggers, are also effective and cost just £8 or so for the best quality ones. These are significantly better at blocking out noise than cheaper pairs of ear defenders (costing about £3) or ear plugs. Some people who are sensitive to touch find them unbearable, though, because they press quite firmly against the head.

Looking at light

Over-sensitivity to light is called *photosensitivity*. But, as with other sensory issues, it is the subtler forms of sensitivity which tend to be more problematic. Some

people can see the flickering of fluorescent lights and computer screens —
even the newest flat screens — others become distracted by a certain shade of
red. Some can see clearly only in daylight, no matter how bright the artificial
light is. Others see objects surrounded by bright halos, a problem often made
worse by flickering lights or sunshine.

As with ear plugs, wearing sunglasses for prolonged periods isn't recommended, although because some light gets in around the edges, they are safer
than ear plugs, and can be used all day if the light really is far too bright. But
it's easy to forget about them and carry on wearing them when the light level
drops, which can lead to a weakening of the eyes as they strain to see.

The best-known form of poor visual discrimination is face-blindness (technically called *prosopagnosia*; pronounced pro-sop-ag-nose-ia), which makes it
difficult for people to remember and recognise faces, even of familiar people.
The inability to pick out details may also contribute to people with prosopagnosia easily getting lost: failing to recognise landmarks makes getting around
without someone's help almost impossible.

Visual distortions and some forms of photosensitivity can be alleviated by
using tinted glasses or contact lenses — you can try the Irlen method to determine which colour lenses may help you. Information on what the Irlen method
is and how to find an assessor — or "screener", as they're known — can be
found at www.irlenuk.com. Strictly speaking, only those tinted lenses the
colour of which was determined by the Irlen method should be called Irlen
lenses (or, if you're being very technical, Irlen filters), but you will come
across people who call any tinted lens an Irlen lens. Unfortunately, the Irlen
method isn't available on the NHS, so you'll pay at least £100 more than the
cost of a pair of glasses. The benefits to your stress level may well be worth
it though, and the screening process should weed out the majority of people
who won't gain, so only the screening fee has to be paid if you don't need to
buy the lenses.

Smelling and tasting trouble

What we think of as taste is actually two senses. One is technically called *gustation*: our tongues are able to distinguish five tastes (salty, bitter, sour, sweet
and umami, the last one being the taste of monosodium glutamate, which
is found in seaweed and other green leaves). In the last few years, researchers have identified other possible tastes, including "fatty acid" and metallic,
but the important point here is that a very small number of tastes exist. The
second sense involved in taste is smell: we smell the food in our mouths, and
we can distinguish thousands of different smells, giving us the full experience
of what we call taste. Because gustation is so simple, the sensory problems
associated with it are fairly straightforward and are also intimately bound up
with smell (olfaction) and the smelling aspect of taste. So we refer just to smell
here — but remember that we're including gustation.

Someone quite often has a particularly strong reaction to a certain smell. Cast your mind about and you can probably think of someone who makes a real effort to avoid a certain smell — coffee for instance — and gags and grimaces when he or she makes a mistake with a coffee-cream chocolate. Autism can make things much worse, adding the pitfalls of distraction and overload. Hyposensitivity to smell (*hypo-olfaction*) can lead to problems with nutrition, because without the impetus of interesting aromas, you won't be tempted away from what you're doing, and meals will be skipped. And you won't vary your diet if you don't find variation interesting.

Because smell is such an emotive sense and has such strong links to memory, smells cause overload and distraction very easily. Distortion of smells, also, can be influenced by memory. For example, if you associate the smell of grass with being bullied, then you may smell grass whenever you're in a situation that you think may be bullying, or the smell of grass itself can make you think that you're being bullied.

Poor olfactory discrimination can make combinations of smells into a confusing mess and cause you to eat each thing on your plate separately. This desire to eat things separately can also be caused by hypersensitivity, if it affects a wide range of flavours. If you put two flavours to which you're hypersensitive into your mouth together, the effect can be overwhelming. As a result, you may go to great lengths to prevent foods from touching each other on the plate.

As your senses mature, you may be able to start combining smells and tastes, however, so don't think that you'll be stuck eating one thing at a time for ever. Smell and taste seem to be the senses which are the easiest to change, possibly because they're the most primitive — even bacteria have a basic sense of smell, known as "chemical sensitivity". Don't feel you have to change, though — why shouldn't you eat everything separately if that's what you prefer?

Knowing where you are — proprioception, balance and motor control

Although often not thought of as senses, knowing where your body is without looking (*proprioception*), balance, and sensing the right amount of movement or force that's needed, are three very important senses. If you're hyposensitive in all three, you'll be the clumsiest of clumsies.

Balance itself is actually made up of a sense and a skill. The vestibular sense, which is provided by organs in your inner ears, allows you to know which way is up and how your head is moving. But to stand on one leg, for example, you also need dozens of muscles to be both coordinated and sufficiently strong; if your motor control is poor, you may never have learnt the necessary motor coordination nor built up sufficient strength in the muscles, so therapy to improve your motor control won't magically allow you to stand on one leg.

Hypersensitivity in proprioception, balance and motor control isn't necessarily a good thing, because small, unexpected movements, such as someone brushing past you on the street, can lead to overload and a sense that you're spinning or falling, which can then result in you trying to compensate for what you feel was a large movement and pushing yourself over in the opposite direction.

Problems with these three senses may result in a diagnosis of being *gravitationally insecure*, which means that you feel disorientated, especially when your feet aren't on the ground. You may also feel disorientated while you move, causing you to do so in short, sharp steps and with gestures, and always ending a movement with your hands touching fixed things like walls and tables.

Feeling the heat (and the cold, and the pain)

Strange as it may sound, it's possible for people to be insensitive to heat, insensitive to cold (wearing just a shirt all year round), come out in goose bumps and get the shivers when they feel a faint breeze on their skin, be unaware how bruises happened to them, and wince in pain when they walk. The degree of sensitivity to pain, for example, can vary around the body, one part being hypersensitive and another hyposensitive.

Almost everyone has had the experience, when they're in the bath, of the tap dripping onto their toe and not being able to tell whether the water is icy cold or scalding hot. Poor discrimination, distortions and confusion can be much more varied in autism, however.

If you're insensitive to pain, be very careful around hot objects like the cooker, for example, as you may not notice that you're burning yourself.

Exploring Sensory Difficulties in Everyday Environments

While the suggestions already given may help you to cope with your difficulties, certain situations involving other people may set up challenges where it's not clear what the best strategy is. We hope we offer some useful suggestions here.

Not all the suggestions will prove useful — you need to experiment to find what works for you. Also, be wary of blanket advice you may read on this subject. For example, some books say that children who have hypersensitivities become tense and very aware in over-stimulating places, but some will actually become absorbed and others distant. The coping strategies they themselves have developed will be individual, and no substitute exists for getting to know you or your child's sensory needs and finding the strategies that work for you.

Sensory "toys" may help people in all of the contexts described below. These toys may be highly textured or have lights or sounds which are interesting. They may be especially useful for individuals who seek out sensations and reassurance in stressful situations through familiar or calming sensations (the stressball is an example of a sensory toy that's used by many a stressed business person). A sensory toy doesn't necessarily have to be labelled as such — a piece of plasticine may do. If you're after something more sophisticated, then try specialist retailers online (search for "sensory toys").

Coping with sensory issues at home

More than other children, those on the spectrum are likely to need time to themselves, and you can trust them to choose environments that they can cope with (well, most of the time). Creating a safe, semi-private space for your child is one of your first steps towards making the home more of a haven. If you're not a child any more, then the advice doesn't change; altering the amount of sensory stimulation around you in order to reduce stress and increase the opportunity to be happy is still what's important, and you probably have more opportunity to make changes that suit you.

If a landlord tries to block your attempts to improve your home environment, point out gently and politely that the Disability Discrimination Act applies to landlords as well as employers — not only does the law say that reasonable adaptations must be allowed, but also that the landlord should pay. Be careful with small private landlords, though, as asking them to pay may make them stop renting out their properties, which means you're out of a home. (A small landlord isn't necessarily short, but it means a landlord who owns only a small number of properties.)

People with a tendency to suffer from visual overload are likely to benefit from a lot of magnolia or another paler plain wall colour. Try to minimise clutter and ornaments, at least in the areas where most time is spent, so that there's little visual distraction, especially at meals — at breakfast, the cereal packet will be distraction enough, even if you don't need to rush to school.

If background noise is a problem, completely reorganising the house may be in order: moving the sitting room to the back of the house, away from the road, say, or moving the bedroom downstairs so that your sleep isn't so disturbed by people you share with. Such changes can make for a house with a bit of an odd layout, but that isn't really important and needs to be weighed against the advantages. If you live in a flat or a bedsit, this isn't such helpful advice, but you can use these ideas to rearrange your room or when looking for a more suitable place to live.

Pay attention to how you feel, not what you like. Liking red isn't a good reason to paint all the walls that colour — such a place may actually make you stressed and make life harder for you. Look for signs of stress, and try to work out what's causing it. Then base your changes on getting rid of stress. Letting go of a favoured colour or other preference can be difficult, and you may be tempted to deny that it's a problem, so a bit of experimentation may help to sort things out.

You can work with your child's sensory problems — don't feel that you have to bring your child up to look "normal". If being squished and getting bear hugs are what your child likes, they can be used as rewards every bit as much as sweets or television. If other people think it's odd for you to be piggy-backing your child and squishing him or her against a wall, that's not your problem. Just try to make it clear that your child is enjoying it!

Occupational therapists may be able to help with sensory issues, in terms of altering the environment to minimise sensory stimulation, and suggesting ideas for how to cope with sensory difficulties.

Coping with sensory issues at school

Coping at school depends fundamentally on the attitude and willingness of the staff; you need them to accept an AS diagnosis, whether or not it's official. Many schools are reluctant to provide special provision for a child unless the child has a formal diagnosis, but you can still discuss the individual needs of your child and small adaptations which may help.

While many aspects of the provision will need to be tailored to the individual, two general ideas which are helpful in many cases are:

✔ Ask for your child to sit in a part of the classroom where there's less opportunity both for distraction and for bullying to happen — say, at the front of the class.

✔ If your child has visual problems, he or she needs a view with little visual distraction; similar considerations apply for other senses. Try to avoid seats near windows or colourful displays if the problem is visual, seats near the noisiest class members if the problem is auditory, and so on.

For more on coping within the school environment, see Chapter 10.

Coping with sensory issues in the community

The best, most effective coping technique in the community is teaching everyone that people have sensory issues and how hard those issues make life for them. Sadly, no way exists to magically make that happen in the next few years, and enlightenment is only going to occur slowly as we (the "autism community") continue to educate people about this common condition. In the meantime, try rehearsing conversations with shop assistants, ticket salespeople and all the rest, with the help of a family member or friend. Once a clear idea of how the interaction is likely to go has been learnt, the trip out should be less stressful and more attention can be paid to novel aspects of the experience, which will make these unexpected moments less challenging and reduce the need to retreat into routine.

Coping with sensory issues at work

Understanding of autism among employers is very limited, but as at school, the attitude and willingness to help of managers and colleagues is crucial to making any job a success. You need to help people at work who know about your autism to understand your particular case, because, unlike a school, where teachers will need to understand autism in all its forms, your employer simply needs to know how to work with you. If you're overwhelmed by forced eye contact, and your employer has read in a book that forcing eye contact helps make people pay attention, then you're going to find dealing with your employer very stressful and your employer is not going to get the best out of you.

The workplace also presents challenges. Fluorescent lighting in offices and factories is a significant hurdle for some people on the spectrum, as are the pervasive smells of carpets, paint, printers and photocopiers. Automated air fresheners, especially in the toilets, may present a problem. And many jobs require you to wear the company uniform, which is usually cheaply made from hard fabrics like polyester, with rough, scratchy stitching. Unfortunately, employers are very reluctant to change any of these things, even for the benefit of several employees.

The more you're able to explore your sensory issues and needs and identify ways to improve your experience, the better able you'll be to explain these to employers and colleagues.

Part IV
Discovering Therapies, Medication and Diet for Asperger's Syndrome

"Of course I'm capable, bright, trustworthy and successful – I have Aspergers Syndrome."

In this part . . .

With the (seeemingly) hundreds of different therapies, medicines, vitamin pills and unusual approaches for helping people on the autism spectrum, it can be really baffling to figure out what might help you or your child. We're here to help you to understand the different options.

In this Part we guide you through the different approaches that might help with communication, social skills and behaviour, and steer you away from unproven methods. You can also learn about the common medications that people on the spectrum might get prescribed and what to look out for and avoid in terms of medical procedures. If you are interested in how diet can help, we run through eating problems, allergies and intolerances in AS and point you in the right direction for understanding gluten- and casein-free diets.

Chapter 13

Navigating Behavioural Therapies

In This Chapter

▶ Finding out about non-medical therapies

▶ Deciding what approach is best for you

▶ Avoiding dodgy interventions

*F*inding your way around the world of therapies for ASCs is pretty over-whelming. You can find lots of different approaches and so far not much research to tell you which are good or which may work for you. When you look for information, you may hear words like *treatment*, *intervention*, *therapy*, *behavioural therapy* and *cure* in relation to *treating* autism and Asperger's syndrome (AS). In this chapter we introduce you to some common approaches to help you get to grips with what's out there.

Knowing What Therapy Can (And Can't) Do

You can't cure AS or any autism spectrum condition (ASC). In fact, whether we should be looking for a cure at all is debatable. However, you can find many educational and behavioural approaches that may help people with AS to improve their communication and social skills and quality of life. Covering the literally hundreds of different approaches in a single chapter is impossible (we'd need a whole book!), but by reading this chapter you can find out what questions to ask and what factors to look for when deciding which non-medical approach could be right for you. We discuss medical interventions in Chapter 14 and dietary issues in Chapter 15.

Sadly, individuals and companies still exist out there charging a great deal of money for unproven interventions. What's more frightening is that some therapies and interventions are dangerous. While we don't want to scare you, it is important that anyone looking for information about treatments, interventions or therapies for AS is aware of the dangers. This chapter helps you look out for the pitfalls and steers you towards places where you can find accurate information about helpful approaches.

Looking at Specific AS Programmes

Hundreds of programmes and ideas exist out there for helping people with Asperger's. However, for this chapter we've just chosen the most common or well-known approaches in the UK. Plenty more can be found on the Research Autism website (www.researchautism.net) and the National Autistic Society (NAS) website (www.autism.org.uk).

Early Intensive Behavioural Intervention

Early Intensive Behavioural Intervention (EIBI) is a behavioural teaching approach for individuals with autism that probably has the widest body of research behind it of any intervention for autism. It uses the principles of *Applied Behaviour Analysis* (ABA). You may hear the terms ABA and EIBI interchangeably, but in fact ABA is a technique used in the EIBI teaching approach.

Understanding how EIBI works

EIBI programmes are usually carried out at home by trained individuals. As the name suggests, EIBI is intensive: it happens on a one-to-one basis for up to 40 hours per week. It can therefore be very expensive (up to £20,000 per year). EIBI is usually used with children rather than adults, and is best started at a young age (ideally before 5 years, although it can be effective for older children and adults too). Some schools use the principles of ABA in their teaching methods, so look out for these if you don't want to set up a home programme.

When setting up a home-based programme of EIBI, parents often employ a consultant to design an individually tailored programme for their child. A team of therapists is employed to work in the home with the child on a one-to-one basis. You'll develop a strong relationship with your therapists, because they may come five to seven days a week, for up to six hours a day!

Therapists in the EIBI programme use ABA principles to teach a wide number of skills, including communication, social and daily life skills. New skills are taught by breaking them down into small achievable chunks. Once broken down, each skill is taught in a structured way, building more difficult aspects of the skill on top of easier ones. In technical language, this process is called *Discrete Trial Training*. Children are rewarded when they do something right (by praise or by giving them a favourite toy, for example), and prompted when they're not sure. When a child behaves in an inappropriate or undesirable way, the EIBI therapist analyses the causes and consequences of the behaviour. Once these are understood, alternative behaviours can be taught, and undesirable behaviour is discouraged through redirection or by ignoring it.

Researching the effectiveness of EIBI

ABA, the behavioural approach used in EIBI, was originally developed in the 1960s by Ivar Lovaas, a psychologist from Norway. His research claimed that, after intensive ABA, children with autism became "indistinguishable" from "normal" peers. Based on this finding, EIBI has become one of the most popular and widely known interventions for autism. Subsequent research has found that some people who go through an intensive programme of EIBI make really good progress in terms of IQ, communication, social and daily living skills. But it is only some individuals that improve, not everyone. Over 20 research studies evaluating EIBI have shown a lot of variability in outcome, and we still don't know why EIBI works for some people but not others.

We need much more research that compares EIBI to other interventions and that looks at the long-term outcomes of EIBI before we can truly know when it works and for whom. This means that EIBI may work for you, but it may not. However, claims that it can make people on the autism spectrum "normal" are unfounded and misleading.

Be very wary of anybody claiming they can "cure" autism or make people with AS "normal": so far no evidence shows that any intervention, therapy or teaching method can do this.

Finding out more about EIBI

Useful organisations that you can go to for more information about EIBI and ABA include the following:

- ✔ Research Autism (www.researchautism.net) has information about research and effectiveness.

- ✔ The NAS offers a wide range of useful information and links (www.autism.org.uk).

- ✔ Parents for the Early intervention of Autism in Children (PEACH) provides information and support to families interested in using EIBI (www.peach.org.uk).

- ✔ The Lovaas website (www.lovaas.com) gives further information about its ABA approach.

Getting a properly qualified therapist

The skill and experience of a therapist may have an impact on how well the intervention works (see the nearby sidebar "Factors that may influence intervention outcomes"). You're entrusting your child to a professional for up to 40 hours per week for a good few years, so choosing therapists that fit with your family ideals and who are qualified, or supervised by someone qualified, is important. Lots of families find recruiting therapists difficult, but here are a few tips:

✔ Look for a case manager or consultant on one of the following websites:

- www.autismpartnership.co.uk

- www.big4autism.com

- www.peach.org.uk

- www.abascotland.co.uk

- www.ukyap.org

✔ Look for therapists with qualifications. Therapists can get a degree in ABA, or look for the letters BCBA (Board Certified Behaviour Analyst) or BCABA (Board Certified Associate Behaviour Analyst) on their CVs. See www.bacb.com for more information.

✔ Know the right place to advertise or search for therapists. Publications and websites where therapists and families can place adverts are:

- PEACH (www.peach.org.uk)

- British Psychological Society (www.bps.org.uk)

- ABC Therapists (www.abctherapists.com)

- Autism Jobs (www.autismjobs.org)

Some people also advertise through local universities and colleges for students whom they can train to become EIBI/ABA therapists.

Make sure that anyone you take on has a Criminal Records Bureau (CRB) check before you employ him or her.

Factors that may influence intervention outcomes

In every research study evaluating every approach for autism, outcomes vary enormously. Some individuals do really well, some moderately well, and some don't respond to intervention at all. We still don't have enough information to know what factors are important in predicting who will do well in a given intervention. Some factors that may be important are:

✔ The age of the individual

✔ The intellectual ability of the individual

✔ The communication skills of the individual

✔ How much involvement the family has

✔ The intensity of the intervention (that is, how many hours per week)

✔ How long the intervention lasts for (for example, six weeks or one year)

✔ The skill and experience of therapists

Getting funding for EIBI

The postcode lottery of services for people with ASCs means that where you live determines whether your local authority will pay for EIBI programmes for your child. In some areas, the local authority will pay for part or all of the programme, but in others it won't contribute at all. The PEACH organisation provides good advice about getting funding for EIBI. You're often asked for evidence that EIBI works, so keep track of your child's progress so that you can use it as proof if necessary.

The Son-Rise Programme

The Son-Rise programme, also known as the *Option Approach,* was developed in the USA in the 1980s by two parents whose son had autism. Son-Rise, like EIBI, is an intensive one-to-one home-based programme that's usually used with young children. Most families who use this approach have children with more severe forms of ASC, but it can also be used with children with higher functioning forms, including AS. Anecdotal evidence also suggests that older children benefit from the Son-Rise programme.

Understanding how Son-Rise works

The Son-Rise programme is led by the child rather than by a parent or therapist. This means the child dictates the pace of learning. Parents usually act as "therapists" for their child, although they may also employ others to help run the programme.

The Son-Rise Institute believes that the best way to help a child is to follow the child's lead. The emphasis is on having a loving and accepting attitude towards your child. The first step in a Son-Rise programme is to accept your child as he or she is, including his or her difficult or socially inappropriate behaviour. Parents or therapists are asked to mimic the child's behaviours (including repetitive behaviours) and join in with the activities the child does, rather than attempting to teach a preset list of skills. The idea is that, by copying your child, you enter your child's world, and your child begins to trust you. Once you've built up a trusting relationship, you can use the child's own interests to motivate him or her to learn new skills.

Mimicking the child's repetitive behaviour may sound silly, but the Son-Rise Institute believes it gives social meaning to whatever the child is doing, so that retreating into repetitive behaviour no longer becomes a way to block out the rest of the world. Once the child welcomes you into his or her world and begins to attend and interact with you, the parent or therapist can then expand on the shared activity and try to develop new social interaction and communication skills.

You need to set up a dedicated playroom to carry out the Son-Rise programme. This room must offer no distractions, be calm (so no sensory overload) and safe. The playroom needs to be the place where the child finds it easiest to relax and relate to people around him or her, and so should help maximise learning.

Researching the effectiveness of Son-Rise

Although anecdotal reports on the effectiveness of the Son-Rise programme abound, so far no research evidence shows whether it works. Some have criticised the Son-Rise Institute for providing false hope of curing autism, without having carried out any formal research on the effectiveness of the approach.

Look for evidence that an approach works: don't believe the hype, because it's not always true. Check out www.researchautism.net for accurate information on the effectiveness of interventions.

Based on anecdotal evidence, Son-Rise may work better for young children with at least a moderate level of intellectual ability. Again, it's up to the parents and the individuals with AS themselves to work out what's right for them; useful information pointing people in the right direction given their individual circumstances just isn't available yet.

Setting up a Son-Rise programme

Setting up a Son-Rise programme is a big decision because doing so can be very expensive and you may have to travel to the USA to go on a training course. These training courses can cost up to $11,000, not including travel expenses. A few courses are available in the UK, but these are expensive too. Also factor in the potential expense of re-arranging your home to create a playroom.

Bear in mind that you'll have to dedicate many hours each week to running and organising the programme. Even if you recruit volunteers to help you, you still need to coordinate and oversee everything. You can understand why some parents give up their jobs in order to run Son-Rise.

The fact that no strong research evidence demonstrates whether Son-Rise works makes the decision to set up a programme feel like a risky one. The only advice we can give is to talk to other families who've done it, and to read as much information about it as you can, from as many different sources as possible — for example, from your child's school teachers, psychologists, books and reliable websites such as www.researchautism.net. If it seems right for you, and you can afford the time and the money, by all means give Son-Rise a try. Keep track of your child's progress, and also of the impact the programme's having on the rest of your family, because the programme can be stressful. Be brave enough to stop if you think it's not working for you (easier said than done if you've invested a lot of time, emotion and hope). This goes for all approaches, not just Son Rise.

Finding out more about Son-Rise

The Son-Rise Institute provides lots of information on its programme and recommends books and courses: www.autismtreatmentcenter.org. The NAS website has a list of articles and books on Son-Rise that may be useful, as well as great descriptions of many different interventions: www.autism.org.uk. Also remember to look at www.researchautism.net for information about research into the Son-Rise programme.

Learning to TEACCH

The Treatment and Education of Autistic and Communication Related Handicapped Children (TEACCH) programme is an educational approach widely used in special education classrooms that focuses on the role of structure in the learning environment of children on the autism spectrum. Psychologists at the University of North Carolina, USA, developed it in the 1970s. TEACCH isn't a specific method but more of a philosophy of learning. It works on the strengths of individuals on the spectrum and makes use of lots of different teaching techniques that can be tailored to individual needs. TEACCH's primary goal is to help children learn the skills necessary to have meaningful lives at school, home and in the community. The programme is usually used with school-age children on the spectrum, although many of the principles are useful for people throughout their lives.

Understanding how TEACCH works

Structure and routine are crucial elements of TEACCH and they contribute to its success as a teaching method for students with AS. Structure, routine and predictability are really important for people with AS, so any approach that incorporates them will be more successful than ones that don't. Through TEACCH you can learn skills involving academic subjects, develop social and leisure skills, and undertake communication training and vocational preparation.

TEACCH uses several key principles that it may be useful to learn about, whether or not you go on to use the programme:

- ✔ **Physical organisation of the learning environment.** A structured classroom layout makes it easier for people with AS to know where they should be sitting or standing for a particular task. Assigning different areas to different activities works really well.

- ✔ **Visual timetables and work schedules.** You can use pictures, symbols, tick lists, words, objects, or whatever is useful for the individual to make a schedule of activities for the day or week. This means children can see what is happening, and when, in pictures as well as words. Visual schedules help with transitions between activities and make it easier for people with AS to remember what to do next (verbal instruction alone may be harder to remember). They also make the day more predictable.

✔ **Predictable routines.** Knowing what comes next, how long it will take and who you're doing it with is really important in AS. Routines create a sense of order and reduce anxiety. However, allowing for some flexibility within the routine is also important, so that people don't get too attached to a particular way of doing things. TEACCH professionals often vary the schedule slightly each day to stop strict adherence to rigid routines.

✔ **Structured activities for learning.** Having visual examples of the task in hand and clear steps to take is helpful. Organisation of the activity is also important; for example, having everything ready for a task before you start but keeping some necessary objects out of sight so that they don't cause a distraction.

Researching the effectiveness of TEACCH

Anecdotal evidence suggests that TEACCH is effective. Research studies have also shown positive results from the programme. But the research studies are small and may not always be objective (for example, some are carried out by the people running the TEACCH programme, who may be biased). Also, because TEACCH is so individualised, generalising findings from one person to another is difficult. Staff skill may also be a big factor in intervention outcome (see the sidebar "Factors that may influence intervention outcomes" earlier in this chapter). As always, more high quality independent research is needed.

Finding a TEACCH programme

You can find out more information on TEACCH from the following websites: www.teacch.com and www.autismuk.com. Many schools use methods from TEACCH in their curriculum, so ask around and see if a school near you uses the approach.

Training programmes for parents and professionals are run by the NAS (www.autism.org.uk/training), Autism Independent UK (www.autismuk.com) and Autism NI (www.autismni.org). Initial training usually lasts three days and can cost up to £600.

Early Bird training

The NAS's Early Bird programme is an early training approach for parents whose children have recently received a diagnosis of an ASC, which includes Asperger's. The programme runs for three months and is a combination of group sessions with about six families and individual family support with a professional. This means that you meet others in a similar situation, while getting a high level of individual attention.

Understanding how Early Bird works

Early Bird is a way of supporting parents in the period between a child receiving a diagnosis and starting school or nursery. The three main aims of the programme are:

✔ To help you understand about autism

✔ To learn ways to communicate with your child and to help improve your child's social communication and interaction

✔ To learn about your child's behaviour and to use structure to help your child cope with everyday life

If you're a parent of a child with an ASC, Early Bird can help you to communicate more effectively with your child and give you lots of strategies for coping with difficult behaviour. It also provides tips on how to help your child communicate with you. The programme builds your confidence for dealing with difficulties associated with autism, such as social and behavioural problems. Helping you to understand autism and providing strategies to improve communication, social interaction and behaviour from really early on is great, because it may pre-empt difficulties developing at a later date.

The Early Bird programme is used for children under 5 years old (though an Early Bird Plus also exists for children aged 4–8 years).

Joining a parent support group and finding ways of meeting other parents who have children with an ASC is really important. You can get to know people and share stories and helpful tips.

If you sign up for an Early Bird programme, a professional conducts a home visit and may video you playing with your child. Don't panic, because this person is not trying to judge you on your parenting skills. The videos are used to help show you ways of changing your communication and interaction to be more autism specific. The feedback you receive is really useful as a way of helping you see how you're getting on (though there's no getting around the fact that seeing yourself on film is a bit embarrassing). You have to commit to a group session or home visit every week for the duration of the three-month programme, and to practise the strategies.

Researching the effectiveness of Early Bird

Research into Early Bird is thin on the ground. As this chapter stresses, not much high quality research evidence exists for any intervention or therapy for ASCs! That said, anecdotal evidence from parents suggests the programme's been really helpful, and it's quite widely available across the UK free of charge or at minimal cost.

Finding out more about Early Bird

If you're interested in going on an Early Bird or Early Bird Plus programme, contact the NAS Early Bird team via www.autism.org.uk or earlybird@ nas.org.uk, or phone 01226 779 218.

Finding an Early Bird Course

Early Bird courses are often run by NHS child and adolescent mental health services or by local authorities through educational psychologists or specialist autism teaching services. Contact these people to find out more. If no course takes place in your area, then contact the NAS Early Bird team using the details in the previous section.

The Picture Exchange Communication System (PECS)

In the section on TEACCH earlier in this chapter, we talk about creating visual schedules with symbols to help people with AS to know what's happening in their day. Visual symbols have another really important use — in communication. Sometimes, people with AS don't see the need to communicate. If you don't understand that other people have thoughts or beliefs that are different to yours, then you may not see the point in communicating ('cos they know what you know, right? So why bother talking?). Helping with communication and explaining the desire to communicate are really difficult, but visual symbols can certainly help.

The Picture Exchange Communication System (PECS) was developed as a way to help people with autism to communicate what they need and to request objects. Rather than using words, you can exchange a symbol of what you want for the actual thing you want. Basically, PECS is a method for helping people with autism to communicate by using symbols. Figure 13-1 shows some examples of these symbols.

Understanding how PECS works

To start with, children are shown how to exchange a small card showing a symbol (usually a line drawing) for a toy or piece of food they really like and really want. Adults physically prompt children by guiding their arms to model how to exchange symbols for things they want, rather than just grabbing what they want. Adults also say the word of the object (for example, "biscuit") while exchanging the picture, so that the child learns to associate the word "biscuit" with both its symbol and the actual biscuit. Soon children begin to learn that, by exchanging the symbol, they get the toy or piece of food that they want. Gradually, they're introduced to more symbols for more objects.

Individuals with AS find generalising what they learn in one situation to a different situation difficult. For this reason, use generic symbols such as line drawings. For example, if you use a photograph of a particular brand of biscuit instead of a generic line drawing of a biscuit, the person with an ASC may think the picture represents only that brand and not biscuits in general. This misunderstanding may make things tricky.

I want		I see		thank you	
drink	biscuit	apple	cake	crisps	banana
book	sand	bricks	pens	farm	puzzle
shoe	jumper	trousers	coat	sock	hat

Figure 13-1: Examples of PECS symbols (taken from www. widgit. com).

Widgit Symbols and Pictures © Widgit Software 2004-2010 www.widgit.com Produced using Communicate: In Print, published by Widgit Software

Once children can exchange pictures for objects, you can then show them how to select a picture in order to request something they want. For example, if they want a drink, they go and get the symbol for drink, and bring it to show you. You then know that they're thirsty and want a drink (rather than having to guess).

You can build up a communication book containing lots of different pictures to keep with you and use wherever you go. Eventually you can use PECS symbols to create sentences. You can also use PECS symbols as a way to make choices. If you show two or three symbols for available meals or activities, the person on the autism spectrum can make a choice by picking the symbol he or she wants.

Although it may seem that PECS is most useful for children who don't speak, the symbols can also be really helpful in AS, even though that person may have fluent language. Sometimes it helps to have a symbol as well as a word to listen to in order to understand things properly. Sometimes a person with an ASC may not want to talk, for example if he or she is in a new situation or feeling overwhelmed, but may be happy to communicate through symbols. Symbols and pictures can also be extremely helpful in Asperger's for creating timetables, schedules and instructions for how to do things (for example, instructions for using the bathroom can be displayed using symbols).

Researching the effectiveness of PECS

Research and anecdotal evidence shows that PECS is effective at helping children with an ASC to communicate using symbols. It doesn't necessarily follow that non-verbal children who use PECS will start to speak, though. PECS is inexpensive to use (you can even make your own symbols), and fairly straightforward, but you need training to use the system properly.

Finding out more about PECS

You can get more information on PECS from Pyramid Educational Consultants UK Ltd (www.pecs.org.uk; pyramid@pecs.org.uk; 01273 609 555). Symbols can be found at www.dotolearn.com, and software for making symbols at www.widgit.com.

Checking Out Other Techniques

As well as formal programmes, various other options are also available to you. Although the overall therapies may seem less tailored towards AS, you can usually find experts within each category who know how to mould their therapies accordingly.

Speech and language therapy

Speech and language therapy doesn't just deal with problems with speaking. This approach is used to help people with communication difficulties in every sense (from speech production difficulties such as stuttering, to speech comprehension and high level social communication). Speech and language therapy is widely available for people with AS and can be helpful for people of all ages.

Understanding how speech and language therapy works

Qualified professionals (unsurprisingly called "speech and language therapists") carry out assessments to see what your speech and language needs are. From their assessments, they develop a programme of work to help you to improve in areas of difficulty. With AS, common areas include understanding body language, how to hold a conversation and social skills, although the areas of work will depend on your individual needs.

Speech and language therapy isn't one single technique or approach. In fact, therapists use lots of different approaches depending on what you want help with. They may use PECS, described in the previous section, or run social skills classes, or utilise something else entirely. Each therapist has a "toolbox" of strategies and skills that he or she can use to help with social and communication difficulties of many varieties. The therapies offered can therefore be individualised to your particular needs.

Speech and language therapists generally work as part of a team including teachers, psychologists and other health care and education professionals. If your child is receiving the therapy, you'll also be included in the team of people deciding what skills to work on, and if you're the recipient, the same applies. Sessions may be held in a school, hospital, health centre, day centre or at home.

Researching the effectiveness of speech and language therapy is difficult because of the wide range of techniques it uses. However, it does use techniques (for example, PECS) that have been researched and shown to be helpful.

Finding out more about speech and language therapy

As a first port of call, contact your local NHS speech and language therapy services. Your GP can also make a referral for you. Information is also available from the Royal College of Speech and Language Therapists: www. rcslt.org.

Make sure you go to a properly qualified therapist who's registered with the Royal College of Speech and Language Therapists and the Health Professions Council.

Social skills groups

Social skills groups are usually facilitated by a professional in the field of autism and aim to help people with AS to develop their social understanding and social skills.

Social skills groups take many varied forms and happen in many different settings (for example, in school or run by speech and language therapy services). Groups may include only individuals with ASCs, or also others with different social communication difficulties. Individuals with no social difficulties may attend the group as "role models" (this often happens in school settings). Social skills groups are suitable for individuals of all ages with AS.

Understanding how social skills groups work

Usually a social skills group follows a set structure whereby you're taught about different social skills one at a time. You may be shown models of good social interaction, watch DVDs demonstrating social skills or practise role-plays of social interactions and social scenarios. Lots of time is usually provided for discussing social interactions (for example, why do people ask you "how are you?" if they don't really want to know the answer, and you're supposed to say "I'm fine" even if you're not?). You'll also meet people with similar difficulties, which can be really helpful.

Topics covered in social skills groups may include the following:

- How to start and end a conversation
- Taking turns
- Understanding body language and facial expressions
- How near or far away you should stand in a conversation
- What to talk about and what not to talk about
- Making friends and having romantic relationships
- How loudly or quietly you should speak

Many different types of social skills programme exist, but few have been researched to evaluate how well they work. Most research studies have shown the programmes to be helpful, but often the skills learnt in the group setting aren't transferred to daily life.

Learning skills in lots of different settings (wherever the skill may be used) is very helpful. Doing so helps you generalise what you've learnt to lots of different situations.

Finding out more about social skills groups

If you want to join a social skills group, contact local autism charities (the NAS, for example), because they may run some. Ask school teachers to set one a group, or you may be able to join a group run by a speech and language therapist. Sometimes the NHS provides a service for people with AS, which may run social skills groups. If you're feeling proactive, Jessica Kingsley (www.jkp.com) publishes a range of books on different techniques for running social skills groups, which may be helpful.

Social skills groups differ from social groups, which may not teach specific skill sets. Instead, social groups are usually gatherings of people on the autism spectrum who do social activities together, such as go to the cinema, the park or the pub, or otherwise have some social interaction time together. Social groups are a great way of spending time with like-minded people.

Cognitive behavioural therapy

People with AS often develop anxiety, obsessive–compulsive disorder, depression or other psychological problems. Cognitive behavioural therapy (CBT) is one method used for anyone with these difficulties, and it can be adapted for people with AS. CBT isn't used to address the core difficulties in AS, such as social understanding, communication and stereotyped behaviour (although some academics are working on this), but it can be helpful for associated anxiety, obsessive–compulsive disorder and depression. This therapy can be used at any age, and is usually provided on the NHS, although private practitioners also exist.

Understanding how CBT works

CBT is a way to help people change the way they think, so that anxiety, depressive thoughts and anger don't become overwhelming. The idea is to help people recognise their thoughts and to realise that some thoughts are wrong (for example, "If I don't touch the stair banister 15 times, I'm going to die"). In CBT, a trained therapist (often a psychologist) individually works with you to help you recognise your thoughts and feelings and understand when your thoughts are unhelpful, and to give you ways of changing these thoughts to reduce your anxiety, depression and anger.

CBT involves several stages. First, you're assessed using standardised questionnaires and interviews with the therapist to work out what problems you may be having. You then have a certain number of individual sessions with the therapist in which you talk and do different activities to help you to recognise your thoughts and their connection to how you feel and how you behave. The third stage in CBT is helping you to change the thoughts that are untrue or unhelpful so that your anxiety and/or depression are reduced. This all sounds very easy when written down, but the process is hard and you shouldn't expect changes to happen overnight.

Using CBT for people with AS used to be criticised because such people typically have difficulty reflecting on their thoughts and feelings — a fundamental part of this therapy. However, if the psychologist carrying out the therapy has a sound understanding of AS as well as the CBT techniques, then the therapy can be really helpful. Actually, doing CBT can help the person on the autism spectrum to reflect on his or her inner thoughts and feelings, which in itself can be beneficial.

Finding out more about CBT

Several studies have shown that CBT helps reduce anxiety, depression and anger in children and adults with AS. Your GP can refer you for CBT, or you can search for a therapist privately. You may find there's a waiting list for treatment. Make sure the therapist has had experience of working with people with AS and is accredited by the British Association for Behavioural and Cognitive Psychotherapies. In the meantime, try reading *Cognitive Behavioural Therapy For Dummies*, by Rob Willson and Rhena Branch (Wiley), to gain an understanding of this approach.

Computers and other technology

Computer programs and other technology are becoming increasingly popular as ways to help individuals with AS cope with daily life, get organised and learn. Some people with AS prefer working on a computer rather than in traditional classroom situations, because it reduces the need for social interaction and they can focus better on the task in hand.

Several computer programs aim to help individuals with AS learn emotions. A few are listed in the nearby sidebar "Computer programs to teach emotion recognition". Many other resources are out there, so look around and ask teachers and friends what's been useful for them.

In addition to computer programs, many people find handheld computers and mobile phones really useful tools for staying organised, for example by sending reminders to themselves. Smart phones have a number of applications that can be extremely helpful for people with Asperger's, for example with organisation, independent living and social interaction. Getting the bus into town may seem less worrying if you have got the bus timetables to hand, reminders about what to do if the bus is late loaded onto your phone, and GPS to know how to get to the shops. And if you're stressed, you can play your favourite music on it or browse the Internet (but beware of spending lots of money on the Internet if the phone has Internet access!).

Complementary therapies

Music, art, drama and pet therapy, homeopathy and lots of other therapies are also used by people with AS. They may be really helpful in increasing self-esteem and confidence, learning to express emotions, controlling anger and reducing stress. Some research is investigating the benefits of these complementary approaches, but so far not much evidence exists either way. Many people anecdotally say different complementary therapies have been helpful for them. If a therapy appeals to you and works for you, go ahead, but make sure your therapist is a professional with suitable qualifications and understands AS.

Computer programs to teach emotion recognition

Below are some computer programs designed to teach emotion recognition. Lots more are available, but these are probably the most well known:

✔ *Mind Reading: The Interactive Guide to Emotions* DVD-ROM (www.jkp.com) catalogues over 400 emotions and situations in which you may feel them. This resource is useful for teenagers and adults with AS who want to learn more about facial expressions, tone of voice and the context of emotions.

✔ *The Transporters* DVD (www.transporters.tv) is a cartoon series based on vehicles with facial expressions. It's designed to teach young children with autism to understand emotions.

✔ *Fun with Feelings* CD (www.ultimatelearning.net/products/funwithfeelings.html) is designed to teach school-aged children about emotions.

Music therapy

Music therapy may help people with Asperger's to express and explore emotions. Communicating feelings through music may be easier than communicating through words, and some studies have shown that music therapy can improve communication skills in people with ASCs. Music therapy may also help with social skills and self-other awareness.

In music therapy, a trained therapist works on skills such as turn taking, play, imitation, expressing feelings and listening, all through the use of music. Many different musical instruments can be used, ranging from simple percussion to the piano or the voice. The individual receiving therapy can usually choose a favourite instrument to start with, although new instruments will be explored. You don't need any particular musical skill or to know how to play an instrument in order to benefit from music therapy. Usually, therapy happens in a one-to-one setting, although it can be done in groups.

Music therapy may be offered at school for a child, or you can look up qualified therapists through the Association of Professional Music Therapists (www.apmt.org) or find out more at the British Society for Music Therapy (www.bsmt.org).

Drama therapy

Drama can be beneficial for people with Asperger's, because through role-play and rehearsing different scenarios you can practise different social skills. Drama can also be of great benefit to self-confidence. Many people on the autism spectrum enjoy performing, and having the opportunity to perform in front of an audience can be extremely rewarding.

Even if a final performance isn't the ultimate goal, theatre activities are great ways of learning about emotions, particularly facial expressions and body language. You can also practise conversation skills and strategies to cope with various different social scenarios, tell stories and practise the use of your voice.

Some drama therapy is specifically run for people with ASCs, but these groups are few and far between. Drama groups of any kind may be beneficial, as long as the group leader is sympathetic to the needs of group members with Asperger's. Drama at school is also widely available.

For more information about drama therapy, see the British Association of Dramatherapists (www.badth.org.uk) and Roundabout (www.roundabout.nildram.co.uk). The book *Acting Antics: A Theatrical Approach to Teaching Social Understanding to Kids and Teens with Asperger Syndrome* by Cindy Schneider (published by Jessica Kingsley) also has some useful information.

Assessing Your Options

Before going ahead and choosing a therapy, make sure you're fully aware of all the pros and cons. In this section we try to help you decide which therapies to avoid and which ones may work for you.

Entering "Asperger's syndrome and therapy" in Google brings up over 900,000 results. No wonder people who've just received a diagnosis of AS for themselves or for a member of their family feel overwhelmed and confused. Very few of the many interventions out there have good research evidence supporting how effective they are. No single "treatment" or one magic approach works for everyone. At the moment, there isn't even enough research to show which approach may work for which types of people and circumstances. Finding what's useful for your individual circumstances is therefore very much up to you.

Knowing what doesn't work and what's potentially harmful

You've probably gathered that lots of different interventions, therapies and approaches exist for helping people with AS and other ASCs. Before you do more research to decide what's right for you, read this section to find out which approaches have been shown to be ineffective, dangerous or harmful.

The Research Autism website (www.researchautism.net) lists the following interventions and medications as having *very strong negative evidence* (meaning they probably don't work) or as being *hazardous* (harmful) or *extremely hazardous* (dangerous). You need to think very hard before trying the approaches listed in Table 13-1.

Table 13-1	Interventions to Think Twice About		
Intervention	*Description*	*Is it Harmful? Does it Work?*	*Possible Hazards*
Auditory integration training	Listening to music with high and low frequencies removed and volume controlled. Claims that you gradually get less sensitive to sounds that are distressing, so behaviour improves.	Evidence it doesn't work Possibly harmful	May help those with sensory difficulties, but not effective for social and communication difficulties. May damage hearing.

Intervention	Description	Is it Harmful? Does it Work?	Possible Hazards
Dolphin therapy	Swimming with dolphins or using swimming with dolphins as a reward for doing a task.	Insufficient evidence that it works Potentially hazardous	Risk of aggression from dolphin and of spreading disease.
Facilitated communication	For non-verbal individuals. Someone physically supports person to point to pictures or symbols so the person can communicate his or her needs.	Strong evidence it does not work Hazardous	All communication comes from the facilitator rather than the child. Unsubstantiated reports of child abuse from people using this approach.
Holding therapy	Therapist or parent holds child by force until child stops resisting, makes eye contact, or a certain amount of time has gone by. Different from a cuddle or hug because involves force.	Insufficient evidence that it works Harmful	May cause pain and discomfort for individuals with tactile oversensitivity. Forced holding from someone you love can cause psychological damage.
Patterning therapy	Based on the simplistic view that autism is caused by mild to severe brain injury. Person does physical exercises and activities intended to "rewire" the brain.	Evidence that it doesn't work	None.

Don't be taken in by sweeping statements and wild claims that something works — especially if it's expensive and the person making the sweeping statements also developed the intervention! Do your homework and read up about interventions before you try them.

Working out what's right for you

Finding out what's helpful and what isn't may seem like an impossible task. But as long as you do your homework and go to trustworthy sources of information before trying an intervention, you're likely to be fine. If your chosen therapy works for you, great. If it doesn't, stop and try something else. If your friend said it worked for him or her, just remember that it may not work for you, because everyone's different.

AS and ASCs affect everyone differently. Just because something worked for one person, doesn't mean it will work for you, and the reverse is also true.

If you're looking for information on interventions, try the following places and people:

- ✔ Your GP
- ✔ Your local authority
- ✔ The doctor, psychologist or psychiatrist who made the diagnosis
- ✔ The NAS (Helpline, 0845 070 4004; website, www.autism.org.uk)
- ✔ Research Autism (www.researchautism.net)
- ✔ Local autism charities

Before starting any intervention, make sure you get information about it first. If you read research articles about an approach, have a look at the nearby sidebar "Interpreting evidence" to know what to look out for.

Treatments to beware of include:

- ✔ Treatments that cause pain, distress, fear or anxiety
- ✔ Evaluations of therapies that are carried out by the people who developed the therapy (especially if they're making lots of money out of it)
- ✔ Studies showing great improvements that have included only individuals with very mild difficulties to start with (the same improvements may not be seen in people with greater difficulties)
- ✔ People who say or imply that no improvement will happen unless you "take my drug", "use my intervention" or "believe in my therapy" People can improve over time, and many different approaches may help.

Always remember that short-term improvements may not translate into long-term improvements, so don't be fooled by quick-fix solutions.

Interpreting evidence

When you're looking for information about a particular intervention, you may be shown articles or literature making claims about what it can do for you. Here are some tips on what to look out for when interpreting research evidence and evaluations:

✔ How many people were in the study? (The more the better.)

✔ Was there a control group who didn't receive the intervention or experienced an alternative intervention? (A comparable control group is necessary because otherwise you can't know whether people got better because of the intervention or just because they got older or because something else happened.)

✔ Was the research carried out independently or by the person who's selling the intervention? (It should be independent, because the person selling the intervention will be biased and will want to show how good his or her approach is.)

✔ Is there a long-term follow up of people who had the intervention? (You want to know how people do in the long term, not just after six weeks of therapy; it could be that after the therapy stops, so do the improvements.)

✔ Can you be sure that the results were due to the intervention rather than anything else?

Chapter 14

Understanding Medication and Medical Procedures

In This Chapter

▶ Investigating medication and Asperger's syndrome

▶ Finding out about harmful medical procedures

▶ Understanding what medication can and cannot do

*I*f you have Asperger's syndrome (AS) you may need medication, but medicines certainly aren't a "cure" for AS. Like anybody, people on the spectrum may need to take medication from time to time for particular medical conditions. Most medication that is prescribed is for conditions that are in addition to AS, and may not be related to AS at all.

In this chapter, we describe some of the medications you or your child may be prescribed to help with conditions associated with AS, such as anxiety and depression. We're not recommending particular medication, but want to make you aware of what a doctor may prescribe for a person with AS and why.

We're not going to keep saying "you or your child or the person you're caring for" every time. Mostly, we just say "you", and if you're reading this book because you're a parent or carer, you know what we mean.

This chapter also covers some of the medical procedures that are sometimes proposed for people on the autism spectrum but which aren't supported by evidence that they work. We also warn you about harmful medical procedures you should avoid.

Understanding Medication and Asperger's Syndrome

Doctors don't prescribe particular medication when diagnosing a person as being on the autism spectrum. No medication will "cure" an ASC or "treat" the social and communication difficulties a person on the spectrum may have. See Chapter 13 for more on therapies which may help people with AS, but which certainly aren't cures.

Like everyone, people on the autism spectrum will have individual health needs, many of which won't have anything to do with ASCs. So people with AS may take medications for the same reason everyone does. You go to your GP if you're unwell, and you may be prescribed medications that may improve your well-being. If you're healthy and have never needed to go to the doctor's, then you probably aren't taking any medication. Some people may take medication for a short period in their lives, and then not need to take any again.

Some people may find certain medications helpful for easing anxiety, depression or other health-related conditions. We don't go into a lot of detail about medication in this chapter because we're not medical doctors and the best thing you can do if you're feeling unwell, stressed, anxious or depressed is to go and see your GP. Only they will be able to determine if any medication will help you given your individual circumstances.

In this section we provide an overview of what medications people on the spectrum may come across.

We aren't suggesting you take any particular medication. Medication is highly individual and only a qualified medical doctor has the knowledge and ability to prescribe to people. Doctors take into account all your individual needs and health concerns.

Finding out about medications your doctor may prescribe

In this section we introduce some of the medications that may help people with a diagnosis of AS with the difficulties they face. In particular, epilepsy, anxiety, depression and hyperactivity are associated with autism spectrum conditions (ASCs), although many other conditions are too (see Chapter 4). Many of these conditions improve if you take the right medication. Some of the more common medications for these conditions are described in this section.

These medications must be prescribed by a medical professional and can be dangerous if taken without the appropriate medical guidance and supervision.

Anticonvulsants

Some people on the spectrum have epilepsy and may need to take medication that suppresses epileptic seizures and also reduces their severity, called *anticonvulsants*. Some have claimed anticonvulsants can ease the social and communication difficulties of people on the spectrum, but no evidence exists to support this, and anticonvulsants shouldn't be used for this purpose. If you're on the spectrum and have epilepsy, talk to your neurologist and follow his or her advice about taking the correct anticonvulsants.

Anticonvulsants can also be useful to treat *bipolar disorder*, which used to be called manic depression. So if a person on the spectrum also has bipolar disorder, he or she may be given a type of anticonvulsant to help with extreme mood swings. Anticonvulsants used for this purpose are usually prescribed by psychiatrists, whereas anticonvulsants used to control seizures are usually prescribed by neurologists.

Anti-depressants

Many people with AS suffer from depression and may need to take medication to help them cope with the symptoms. *Selective serotonin reuptake inhibitors* (SSRIs) are the main anti-depressants prescribed. SSRIs are used to treat the symptoms of both depression and anxiety (see the nearby sidebar "Sorting out SSRIs") and produce good results. Cognitive behavioural therapy (CBT) can also be used to treat the symptoms of depression and anxiety (see Chapter 13 for more on this) and may be used as well as or instead of medication. As with most things, treatment of depression is based on individual needs and preferences.

Anti-depressants may have serious unwanted side effects in children, and should only be used under very close medical supervision.

SSRIs aren't recommended for treating the symptoms of ASCs and aren't effective for this purpose. They should only be used if a person on the spectrum is suffering from depression or anxiety.

Don't believe the media hype about "drugs to cure autism'. Any such claims are inaccurate and not based on sound evidence.

Sorting out SSRIs

Serotonin is a chemical that plays a part in brain development, social behaviour, aggressive behaviour and sleep. Some research has found that children on the spectrum have higher levels of serotonin in their blood than is normal. This research has led some people to believe that medications called *selective serotonin reuptake inhibitors* (SSRIs) may help improve the symptoms of autism.

SSRIs can suppress the action of serotonin in the brain and were frequently used to treat autism in the 1980s. However, studies show that their effectiveness varies , and SSRIs are no longer recommended to treat the core features of ASCs. You just don't know how someone may respond to SSRIs or how effective they will be. More importantly, some people who take SSRIs for autism have side effects such as chills, agitation, confusion and nausea. Not things you want to experience.

Neuroleptics

Neuroleptics (which are also called major tranquillisers) are used to reduce signs of psychosis. *Psychosis* is a loss of contact with reality, often resulting in hallucinations (experiences of things that aren't there), delusions (beliefs that aren't true) and confusion, particularly about whether your thoughts are inside your head or coming from outside. Some neuroleptics are also useful for reducing signs of severe anxiety and dementia. They may be used to treat the most challenging problems faced by those on the spectrum, such as extreme aggression, intense hyperactivity, serious self-injury and the most repetitive behaviour.

People on the spectrum who suffer with severe irritability, hyperactivity and repetitive behaviour are sometimes prescribed a neuroleptic called risperidone, which can have unpleasant side effects.

Anxiolytics

Many people on the spectrum suffer from additional anxiety disorders, and anti-anxiety medications, called *anxiolytics*, may be prescribed to help. The group of medications called the benzodiazepines (also still sometimes called the minor tranquillisers) are often used as anxiolytics. Diazepam is the most well known of these – originally patented and sold as Valium.

Stimulant medications

Some stimulant medications can be used to treat *attention deficit hyperactivity disorder* (ADHD). Some people on the spectrum have problems with attention and hyperactivity, so they may be prescribed medications such as methylphenidate (originally marketed as Ritalin) or dextroamphetamine.

Sorting out side effects

People on the autism spectrum are often more sensitive than other individuals to medication. Mention this fact to your doctor or psychiatrist, because these people may not be aware of it if they're not experienced in prescribing medication for people on the spectrum. They may recommend starting on smaller doses and increasing the doses more slowly than usual.

Don't be afraid to talk about the possibility that you may be more sensitive than other people to medication. Raise the issue with your doctor, because he or she may not know about it, and you're the one who is at risk of suffering increased side effects.

Many medicines have nasty side effects, but these can be minimised by taking medicines in the way your doctor suggests. Suddenly stopping any medicine can also cause problems, so in most cases your doctor will advise you to decrease doses slowly if you plan to come off a particular drug.

Don't stop taking your medication without the advice of a doctor, because doing so will increase the chance of your developing nasty side effects or withdrawal symptoms. And if you do stop, don't start again without seeing your doctor first and discussing it.

Introducing the Hormones

Hormones act as chemical signals in your body. The hormone *testosterone* has been linked with the development of autistic traits. This doesn't mean that testosterone causes autism, though! Taking testosterone-reducing pills won't get you anywhere if "curing autism" is your aim (see Chapter 2 on causes of AS, and Chapter 13 on therapies). *Secretin* is another hormone that some people claim is involved in autism but, again, taking secretin is no miracle cure. *Melatonin*, a hormone involved in sleep, might be useful for some people on the spectrum who have sleeping difficulties. You can find out more about each of these hormones in the following sections.

Melatonin

Melatonin is a hormone that regulates sleeping patterns. You feel sleepy when the amount of melatonin in your body goes up, and your body usually produces melatonin when it gets dark, making you want to go to bed. Melatonin's also produced early in the afternoon, making you fancy curling up for a nap instead of getting on with work! Eating certain foods such as turkey can also boost your production of melatonin (they're high in the substance your body uses to make melatonin), which is why people often feel sleepy after a meal, especially a big Christmas dinner.

Some studies have suggested that the release of melatonin is unusual in people on the autism spectrum, which could make their sleep patterns irregular. Many parents of children on the spectrum report sleep problems in their children, and many adults with ASCs bring up difficulty sleeping as a major issue in their lives. Many possible reasons for sleep difficulties exist, but one potential source of the problem is this irregular melatonin production.

If you're having problems dozing off or staying asleep through the night, get in touch with your GP. He or she can give you some tips about how to improve the chances of good sleep without the need for medication, and can prescribe melatonin if changing your sleeping habits doesn't work. Chapter 6 has more on getting a good night's sleep.

Melatonin is only available on prescription in the UK.

If you're having trouble sleeping and want to talk about it with your GP, consider keeping a sleep diary for a week or two before your appointment. Write down when you sleep throughout the day (including naps), how long for, and any problems you experience to do with sleep, such as not feeling rested afterwards, feeling groggy or having bad dreams. You can find some autism-specific tips for better sleeping in Chapter 6.

While melatonin itself can only be prescribed by a doctor, some foods can help increase your levels of the hormone. Not much evidence supports the idea that eating these foods helps with sleep, but you can try if you like. Keep a note in your sleep diary to work out if any melatonin-rich foods could possibly be helping. These foods include:

- ✔ Turkey
- ✔ Oats, sweetcorn and brown rice
- ✔ Ripe tomatoes, pumpkin, parsley
- ✔ Bananas, dates, brazil nuts
- ✔ Cottage cheese, soya

Chapter 15 on diet has more on melatonin.

Oxytocin

Recently, some media attention has focused on the hormone oxytocin as a potential medical therapy for ASCs. *Oxytocin* is involved in social behaviour and social understanding. Mothers produce oxytocin when they give birth and when they breastfeed their children. The emotional bond between the mother and her child may be strengthened by the release of oxytocin, because it's also produced when you're cuddled.

Scientists are now examining whether a nasal spray of oxytocin can help people on the autism spectrum to recognise emotions, and reduce social difficulties. So far, only preliminary studies have been carried out and, as usual, they're inconclusive. Small-scale studies can never tell us whether something could be used as a therapy for ASCs, yet the media hype suggests oxytocin could be the next big thing. More research is needed before we know for sure whether oxytocin can be helpful, and currently doctors in the UK are unable to prescribe it for ASCs.

If you read something in the newspaper about a medication or therapy you think might be good for you, always do more background research. The Research Autism website (www.researchautism.net) provides a reliable list of medicines and therapies for autism, rated by the evidence for their effectiveness. It also offers signposts to more detailed information.

Testosterone

Testosterone is a male sex hormone. Higher levels of testosterone in the foetus may be one of the causes of autistic traits. High levels of testosterone don't cause autism, though. So far, the research linking testosterone levels in the womb and autistic traits has only been carried out in people who don't have an ASC (remember, we all have some degree of autistic behaviour).

Some people have jumped on this testosterone bandwagon and suggested that taking drugs to reduce testosterone levels will reduce the signs of autism, but this is not true. Research thus far has only examined testosterone levels in the amniotic fluid in the womb in pregnancy, and hasn't even looked at people on the spectrum yet. Also, testosterone levels in amniotic fluid aren't the same as levels of testosterone in the blood of fully grown adults. So, taking drugs to reduce blood levels of testosterone doesn't make logical sense and is unlikely to have any effect on the signs of autism.

Secretin

Secretin is a hormone involved in digestion. Some people believe that people on the autism spectrum have too little secretin, which isn't good for their digestive systems. Others believe that poor digestion means that harmful chemicals from food can reach the brain. Secretin hit the headlines in the late 1990s as a potential therapy for autism. Anecdotal reports of improved or even "cured" autism followed. Nobody knows for sure whether secretin is involved in bowel problems in people on the spectrum. However, taking secretin doesn't improve the symptoms of autism. Many rigorous research studies have shown that people on the spectrum who take secretin show no improvement (one study even found that taking salty water produced better results!). Secretin can also have harmful side effects.

Considering Medical Procedures

No medical procedure can cure autism, so if anyone claims it can and tries to sell a particular medical procedure to you, that person doesn't have your best interests in mind and may just be after your money.

Electro-convulsive therapy

Electro-convulsive therapy (ECT) applies carefully controlled electric shocks to the brain and is used to treat a variety of psychological conditions. In autism, ECT has most recently been used for people who also have catatonia. *Catatonia* is a serious condition whereby people repeat words and behaviour and have a grimace-like facial expression. People with catatonia may find moving and talking very difficult or impossible and they may freeze in one position for very long periods of time (even weeks). Electrically shocking the brain while the person is sedated can cause a reduction in catatonia in people on the autism spectrum, although nobody knows why or how this works.

Electro-convulsive therapy isn't recommended for people on the spectrum unless they have catatonia that can't be treated in any other way.

Hyperbaric oxygen therapy

The bends is what happens when divers come up too quickly from a deep or long dive. During these dives, nitrogen from the air they're breathing dissolves in the blood (because the water pressure forces more nitrogen into the blood). By coming up slowly, divers allow the nitrogen to leave their blood gently. If they come up too quickly, the nitrogen forms bubbles in their blood, which cause damage to the heart and other organs. The treatment for the bends is repressurising the diver in a large canister called a hyperbaric chamber. (*Hyperbaric* means high pressure.)

Some claim that hyperbaric oxygen therapy can be used to alleviate stress, social difficulty and communication problems in autism, but no rigorous research has been carried out, and only anecdotal reports suggest it works. At the moment, no one really understands whether hyperbaric oxygen therapy really works for autism, and if it does, why.

Chelation

Chelation (pronounced "key-LAY-shun") is a medical procedure used to treat people who've been poisoned by toxic metals such as lead. Soldiers poisoned by gas in the First World War, for example, were treated by chelation.

Some people believe that ASCs are caused by toxic metals in vaccines, even though no research evidence supports this idea. As a result, they've tried chelation as a way to treat autism because they think that if you remove the toxic metals in the blood, then you can "cure" the autism. But ASCs aren't caused by toxic poisoning from heavy metals (see Chapter 2 for more information about the causes of autism), so chelation won't work.

Chelation is a tricky medical procedure that should only be used in true cases of toxic metal poisoning. You're more likely to come across chelation therapy for autism in the USA rather than the UK, but if you do come across it, bear in mind that it can be extremely harmful and can even be fatal if it's not done properly.

Increasing immunoglobulin

Some think autism is caused by problems of the immune system. *Immunoglobulin* is an antibody found in blood or other bodily fluids, which is used by the immune system to identify and neutralise foreign objects such as bacteria and viruses. Some people claim that injecting or swallowing immunoglobulin will improve the immune system and, as a result, the symptoms of autism.

No evidence supports the use of immunoglobulin, and it can have potentially harmful side effects such as rashes, dizziness, fever and upset stomach. It may also cause kidney failure.

Assessing the Risks

Medication is only a good idea if prescribed by a medical doctor who's taken your medical history and made an assessment of your individual needs and circumstances. Medication is highly individual, so what works for one person may not work for another.

Certain medications and medical procedures are definitely not recommended for people on the spectrum, because no research evidence exists to support their effectiveness and they might actually cause harm.

Do your homework and read about medications and medical procedures to discover as much information as possible. Talk to your GP; he or she will know what's safe and what isn't.

Go to the "Interventions" section of the Research Autism website (www. researchautism.net), which lists medications, medical procedures and therapies and their effectiveness, supporting research evidence, proven validity, side effects and so on.

If in doubt, do lots of research to find out as much as you can about any medication or medical procedure you're considering. Talk to other people and seek advice from qualified medical professionals. Don't take unnecessary risks, and don't let people take advantage of your vulnerability or desperation to get better.

Research into the causes of ASCs is advancing all the time. As we learn more, new medications and therapies are likely to develop, which may help improve the lives of people on the autism spectrum. Further research into existing approaches will tell us which ones really are useful and which ones do nothing.

Chapter 15

Digesting Diet

Many people who have Asperger's syndrome (AS) notice that certain dietary changes improve digestion and make them feel better. In fact, most people would feel better for avoiding certain foods for a few months (or just when they're ill) — you don't have to be on the autism spectrum to benefit from improving and varying your diet. Plenty of evidence links both moody and impulsive behaviour with poor diet, and autism seems to make some people particularly sensitive to dietary changes. Gluten- and casein-free diets have sparked particular interest, and you can find out about these approaches in this chapter.

Very few dietary supplements — which are mostly vitamins and minerals — have been shown to have any measurable benefits. No sound evidence supports taking even vitamin C, which almost everyone believes helps you fight off a cold. Research actually shows that any extra vitamin C you eat or take over the equivalent of an orange a day doesn't make you feel any better, nor does it get rid of the cold more quickly. Those supplements that have been shown to have a positive effect are described in their own section in this chapter.

Just because you think you are fine doesn't mean that you won't gain from experimenting with your diet. Many people, especially if they're on the spectrum, don't realise that they could feel better than they do. Only by trying some different diets can you find out how to feel at your best.

Knowing When Things Aren't Right with Your Guts

Lots of people who have an autism spectrum condition (ASC) such as Asperger's put up with digestive problems because they always have done and don't realise that they can do something about them. Pain, constipation and diarrhoea are the three main problems, and if they don't have a specific cause such as an allergy, they're likely to fall under the diagnosis of irritable bowel syndrome (IBS), covered in the following section.

Eczema is another problem which can be influenced by diet. If this is a problem for you, try eliminating certain foods from your diet (an approach we describe later in this chapter). If no obvious improvement occurs, try discontinuing your eczema cream (check with your doctor first). Steroidal creams such as hydrocortisone creams treat the symptoms of eczema and usually make the skin look better without actually stopping the eczema from forming. Because the skin looks better, any improvement related to changes in your diet can be difficult to spot, so you may only see clear improvement when you stop using the cream.

Investigating irritable bowel syndrome

Irritable bowel syndrome (IBS) is a problem of the intestines that can cause constipation, diarrhoea and severe pain — or any combination of these symptoms. Experts refer to it as a negative diagnosis because only by eliminating other possible conditions do you arrive at IBS — it's all that's left! No clear diagnostic line can be drawn between IBS and having one or two food sensitivities or intolerances. But typically someone with IBS will have several such sensitivities and intolerances. So you might have constipation, diarrhoea and stomach cramps, generally feel off colour, or none of these. IBS is very hard to define.

Because the situation is so complicated, we recommend reading *IBS For Dummies* by Patricia Macnair, Carolyn Dean and Christine Wheeler (Wiley), but also note that leading UK experts reckon that insoluble-fibre sensitivity is the root cause of IBS. Insoluble-fibre sensitivity is so important that we provide a whole section on it below.

Understanding the role of dietary fibre

Two types of fibre exist in your diet:

- **Insoluble fibre:** The main role of insoluble fibre is to absorb water, which — how shall we put this? — makes the contents of your guts softer and thus able to move through the system better. Too much insoluble fibre can therefore be a bad thing. In extreme cases, runniness is the problem, because diarrhoea means that some of the nutrition from your food just flows straight through you, and your guts don't have time to absorb it. But even in mild cases, the swelling fibre causes painful bloating. Too little insoluble fibre can also be a bad thing if you're prone to constipation.

- **Soluble fibre:** Soluble fibre dissolves in water and becomes invisible, just like salt and sugar. This type of fibre is crucial for digestion because it's eaten by your gut bacteria, and the friendly ones produce substances for your benefit — that's why we call them friendly.

You need to have the right amount of both soluble and insoluble fibre in your diet in order to be healthy, but some people suffer from sensitivity to insoluble fibre. Doctors estimate that this sensitivity affects 15 per cent of people. Fortunately for most people, the solution is very simple and relatively quick. Go on a wheat-free diet for three months and then very gradually reintroduce wheat. Take at least another three months to build up the "dose" (the amount of wheat you eat), starting from just a crumb of bread a day. No one knows exactly how slowly you need to reintroduce things after elimination, but this is definitely slowly enough.

This diet works for insoluble-fibre sensitivity because the principal source of insoluble fibre in the western diet is wheat. However, the diet also causes some confusion, because wheat is also the principal source of gluten. So if you eliminate wheat from your diet and you feel better, this could be because you have a gluten problem or an insoluble-fibre problem. Studies have found that people who suffer from gluten sensitivity make up between 10 and 30 per cent of the population, but the problem with this figure is that it may include many people with insoluble-fibre sensitivity. For all anyone really knows, gluten sensitivity could be very rare.

Surviving restricted diets

You may choose to experiment with avoiding various foods to see whether you feel better. But you might also avoid some foods because you find their texture too unpleasant to cope with or you have a strong dislike of certain colours (for example, you hate yellow and so don't eat bananas or lemons).

Some people on the autism spectrum will eat only apples and oat biscuits, for example. Many won't tolerate different types of food being on the same plate, or may eat only a certain brand of food. While being picky is a problem if malnutrition affects a person's health, if the person is healthy, there's not much to worry about — unusual eating habits simply make life a bit more complicated.

You may be distressed by your child's lack of a balanced diet, but the human body is very resourceful, and eating only fried chicken and chips for an entire lifetime is perfectly possible. Your child's health won't be perfect; he or she may be shorter, be ill more often and have problems with his or her skin — but your child will be alive. So there's nothing that people *must* eat. If someone you love is very particular, don't worry and have patience. You could try vitamin supplements, but no hard evidence exists that they work (except in people who are severely malnourished) — and there's no substitute for a healthy diet! Be tolerant of your child's relationship with food and sooner or later he or she will try something new.

To encourage someone to try something new, lead by example! Eat a dish you're totally unfamiliar with, and do it in front of the other person.

Cajoling someone into trying something that he or she won't eat doesn't work. Sneaking foodstuffs into other food doesn't work for very long either, and destroys trust. Being seen eating these things yourself and occasionally commenting on how nice they are is the best approach. Every so often ask the person who has AS if he or she would like to sample what you're eating. If you get a straight no, that's no, but if the person hesitates, he or she is probably thinking about trying it. Gently allow the person who has AS to take some of the food (again, don't push it towards the person or do anything to make him or her feel cajoled), and if the person tastes some, say "it's nice, isn't it?" Never make comments about the person being unadventurous, stubborn, difficult, boring, or having any other negative characteristic.

If you're very particular about what you eat, the last paragraph probably sounds very familiar. But eating a wide variety of things is to your advantage. A balanced diet is healthier, and not adhering to a rigid set of foodstuffs makes life easier when you're in a shop, café or restaurant.

Learning to enjoy a varied diet is important, because by eating a variety of foods, you're more likely to get all the nutrition your body needs.

Avoiding accidents (of the lavatorial kind!)

"Avoid eating anything that gives you diarrhoea" is the number-one tip. The runs are generally a bad sign, because they prevent you from gaining nutrition from everything you eat, not just the problem food.

While you're working out what the problem foods are, and assuming that you don't want to resort to wearing nappies, we suggest a two-strategy approach.

First, you need to strengthen your pelvic floor. Any pelvic floor exercises are good, but the simplest is to lie on your back, bend your knees, put your feet flat on the floor, and clench the muscles that you use to stop yourself having a lavatorial accident. Hold the clench for five seconds then relax. If you're new to this exercise, do it just five times, one after the other, each day. As your muscles get stronger you can build up the number of times to 30 or more. You can do pelvic floor exercises anywhere, in any position, without anyone noticing. Getting through a whole morning (or afternoon or evening) with galloping diarrhoea and without accident is possible if your muscles are strong enough.

Don't make a habit of holding in diarrhoea for long periods: this technique really is just for emergencies! Once you need to go, you should try to get to a toilet as quickly as possible.

The second strategy is to plan your day so that you always know where the nearest toilet is. This strategy is often quite impractical, but little choice exists until you get your guts under control.

Working Out What's Wrong with Your Diet

Many people on the autism spectrum have digestive problems. Fundamental to understanding why these problems might occur is understanding diet, full stop. Your digestive system is basically robust and adaptable. And this is true even if you think that yours is constantly playing up. If you experience digestive problems and the disruption seems to be caused by what you're eating, there are three possible ways in which this can happen: allergy, intolerance or sensitivity. In this section you can learn what sensitivities, intolerances and allergies are, and think about whether these signs of digestive distress affect you.

Many people use these terms interchangeably, as though they all mean the same thing — they don't:

✔ **Allergy:** You may have an *allergy*. In an allergic reaction, your body mounts an immune response to a specific substance (called an allergen) — the sort of response that should happen when you're invaded by disease-causing microbes. The symptoms of allergies are the same as for disease: fever, mucus, phlegm, sore throat, rashes, aching, vomiting, diarrhoea, and so on. (This isn't a complete list of the possible symptoms.) Which symptoms appear varies, just as the symptoms vary with different diseases. Some signs may be mild, and others may be serious such as in anaphylactic shock, when immediate medical attention is required (you may have heard of peanut or shellfish allergy sufferers going into anaphylactic shock). Serious allergies such as this are usually discovered at a young age and diagnosed by a doctor.

If you know you have allergies and you come down with an illness, for example a cold, you should avoid even mild allergens, because the allergic reaction will affect your ability to fight it off. If you believe you may be allergic to a particular allergen, ask your GP to refer you for testing.

✔ **Intolerance:** In an *intolerance*, your body is unable to digest a particular foodstuff, and so doesn't gain nutritional benefit from it. The most common sign of intolerance is found in the loo, but we don't suggest you investigate — leave the search for undigested food to professional pathologists, especially as microscopes and chemical testing kits are involved. Intolerances to casein and gluten are the two we examine in this chapter.

> ✔ **Sensitivity:** If you have a food sensitivity, your body over-reacts to a certain substance, especially when you're stressed. Feeling sick, having stomach cramps or running to the toilet are the usual signs. Food sensitivity has a wide range of causes: if you eat, say, a banana, and then feel ill, it's possible that for years afterwards you'll feel unwell when you smell that fruit, even if it was not actually the banana that made you ill. In this example, the sensitivity to bananas has a psychological origin, but this isn't the only common type of food sensitivity: sensitivity to insoluble dietary fibre can occur as a result of having too much insoluble fibre in your diet, for example, or as a result of a bout of flu. Because fibre doesn't have a smell and is present in almost all foods, it's almost impossible to develop a sensitivity to it that's psychological in origin. We look at sensitivity to casein and gluten later in this chapter.

The crucial distinction that identifies an allergy is that blood tests show it. Blood tests don't show any sign of an immune response if the problem is a sensitivity or an intolerance, and symptoms are also less sensitive to stress in an allergy. Intolerance differs from sensitivity and allergy in that you fail to gain nutritional benefit from the food: it just goes through you and provides unusual amounts of food for your gut bacteria, the excessive growth of which can lead to further symptoms. Sensitivity to food doesn't prevent you gaining nutritional benefit from it and doesn't produce an immune reaction.

People who have an ASC may be more susceptible to food allergies, intolerances and sensitivities. Some people (parents and people on the spectrum) have found that changing diet improves not only digestive difficulties, but also some of the supposedly unwanted characteristics of ASCs. However, the jury is still out in the research community about whether special diets can change fundamental aspects of ASC. But just like anyone, if you are on the autism spectrum and have a digestive problem, then altering your diet may well help improve your digestive problem.

For information on digestive problems that are much more common in classic autism than AS, such as leaky-gut syndrome, see *Understanding Autism For Dummies* by Stephen Shore and Linda G. Rastelli (Wiley). Here, when considering AS, we focus on foodstuffs that have hard evidence against them.

The elimination diet

Just as for weight loss, various people have suggested many different diets for AS, often just on a hunch or because they work for the family of the inventor of the diet. Very little evidence exists proving that any of these diets work. So in this chapter, we mention only diets and dietary interventions which have evidence to support them.

If you're experiencing problems with your guts, there's no better way to obtain evidence about how your body reacts to a particular foodstuff than to avoid eating it for a month and then gently reintroduce it to your diet (that is, don't binge on it straight away). This approach is often called the elimination diet. The results are even more conclusive if your family can arrange it so that you don't know when the particular food was reintroduced. Keep a diet diary of what you eat and drink, when, how full you feel, your mood, your trips to the toilet, how much energy you have, and any symptoms of illness. After a food is reintroduced, look back over your diary and see whether the reintroduction can be identified from a change in how you felt. You can then draw your own conclusions.

Common problem foodstuffs (for anybody) are:

- Nuts
- Fish
- Shellfish
- Soya
- Sesame
- Wheat
- Cheese
- Dairy products
- Caffeine (found in tea, coffee, chocolate and cola)
- Very acidic foods such as fizzy drinks, tomatoes and pineapple (not to mention vinegar and alcohol)
- Citrus fruits
- Beef
- Chocolate
- Sugar
- Chilli, mustard, pepper and other strong spices

Speed things up by eliminating several things at once, but only reintroduce them one at a time.

If you've eliminated lots of foods and are still ill, seek professional advice. Professionals usually recommend the "few-foods diet' or a variation of it while they investigate your problems. This diet involves eating only things like plain rice cakes which don't cause any sort of reaction. You may actually find that your problems aren't caused by your diet; see the nearby sidebar "Placebos aren't always sugar pills".

Placebos aren't always sugar pills

Experimenting on yourself can be tricky, because the expectation that you'll see a difference can cause a difference — the placebo effect. There's no way around this. If someone else puts something in your food as a test, the person is likely to behave differently around you, which can influence your reaction even if you remain unaware of the person's change in behaviour. This all makes working out your dietary problems complicated. Problems with food boil down to whether you can convince yourself you have a problem. The human mind is a powerful thing, and food sensitivities can be conquered just by the belief that you can overcome them. Equally, if you believe that you can't defeat your problems with food, they can spiral out of control and you progress to ever-more-restricted diets; the health problems that you blame on foods may then actually be caused by the poor nutrition of a restricted diet. If you find yourself being boxed in by your own thoughts like this, check out Chapter 6 for more about developing a healthy attitude to life and the ability to relax.

Gluten- and casein-free diets

Gluten is a mixture of two proteins and provides the main source of protein in wheat. Casein, another protein, is the main source of protein in milk. Gluten and casein can cause a variety of digestive and nasal problems, and seem to do so more often in people who have AS.

Many parents whose child is on the autism spectrum and individuals on the spectrum themselves have tried gluten-free and/or casein-free diets, based on the belief that digestive problems may be causal in ASCs. While there is no evidence that diet or any other environmental factor causes ASCs (see Chapter 2), gluten-free and casein-free diets have become popular, and some people think that they help. If you have AS and experience dietary problems, then it's worth trying a gluten- or casein-free (or GF and CF) diet to see whether it improves your digestive symptoms. For more detailed information see *A User Guide to the GF/CF Diet for Autism, Asperger Syndrome and AD/HD* by Luke Jackson (Jessica Kingsley), which is still one of the best sources of information for people who want practical and detailed help with trying to go gluten- and casein-free. As an interesting aside, Luke Jackson may be one of the most famous people who has AS, because he wrote the well known book *Freaks, Geeks and Asperger Syndrome* (Jessica Kingsley), which is definitely worth reading. Another useful book, covering just a gluten-free diet, is *Living Gluten-Free For Dummies* by Sue Baic, Nigel Denby and Danna Korn (Wiley).

Getting to grips with gluten

Gluten is found in only one family of grasses, which has three members: barley, rye and wheat. One closely related species, oats, contains a closely related protein called *avenin*, which appears to be a cause of sensitivity in some people. Think of the word "brow" to remember these four, because it's made up of their initial letters. Wheat has the most gluten, barley has about a quarter the gluten of wheat, rye has less than a tenth as much gluten as wheat, and oats have none but have as much protein (in this case, avenin) as rye, which makes oats less of a problem than rye in its ability to cause symptoms.

Gluten is a protein complex (in chemistry, a *complex* is a state in between a *molecule*, where atoms are strongly chemically bound, and a *mixture*, where the constituents aren't chemically bound) made of two proteins: glutenin and gliadin. These aren't found separately in any food and are extremely difficult to separate even in a chemistry laboratory. That's what *we* call complex!

So going gluten-free means not eating:

- ✔ Bread (except rice bread, of course, because it's made with rice flour)
- ✔ Pasta
- ✔ Rusk (used to bind the mince together in sausages so that they don't fall apart when you cut them)
- ✔ Cake (fruitcake, sponge cake, pastries, and so on)
- ✔ Noodles (except rice noodles, which are rare)
- ✔ Most breakfast cereals
- ✔ Batter
- ✔ Flour (except cornflour, which is made from maize)
- ✔ Wheat starch, modified or otherwise (often used to thicken sauces and to stick flavourings onto crisps and other snacks)

Gluten intolerance causes coeliac disease, which is relatively uncommon (affecting 0.2–1.2 per cent of people) but can be quite serious. Gluten sensitivity is estimated to affect between 10 and 30 per cent of people (but considerable doubt is expressed about the validity of this figure; see the "Understanding the role of dietary fibre" section earlier in this chapter). People on the autism spectrum are three times as likely as people in general to have a problem with gluten.

Given what we usually eat — things like breakfast cereals (even some brands of crispy rice cereal contain gluten), sandwiches, fish and chips, and processed foods — going gluten-free can make eating very tricky. The number one tip is: learn to love rice cakes! Making traditional "meat-and-three-veg" meals gluten-free is actually quite easy, though. And buffet-style eating (that is, just a collection of things you can eat, all put on a plate) is great. Gluten-free food doesn't have to imitate your old diet — all sorts of gluten-free breads are available, for example, but they're expensive and most have an odd texture that some people don't like; most also fail to taste like bread and all are much more crumbly than real bread. So why bother? Because people don't want too much upheaval in their diet. Well, tough: going gluten-free is an upheaval, and you just have to make the most of it.

Most gluten-free food is aimed at people who are very health-conscious, and so contains very little salt. Make sure you get at least 1 gram of salt every day (a bit less is okay for children); more if you're sweating a lot because of illness or exercise. You also need more if you use low-sodium salt. Falling seriously ill while your body's low on salt (catching flu, say) can be life-threatening. This obviously contrasts with the usual advice to keep your salt intake down. The average person in the UK eats nearly 10 grams of salt a day. Government advice is to keep your salt intake below 6 grams a day, so there's no contradiction with the 1-gram minimum.

Casing out casein

Casein is a protein found in dairy products. Milk from goats and sheep has about a quarter of the casein of cow's milk. Going casein-free means no:

- Milk
- Yoghurt
- Cheese
- Cream
- Cake (unless dairy- and egg-free, of course)
- Pastry (the same)
- Meringue
- Meat that's been marinated in yoghurt (tricky to spot, this one)
- Lactose (you have to read the ingredients carefully; it can be found in foods as diverse as olives and sliced ham)

Like gluten, casein intolerance makes a normal diet tricky: no milk on your cereal or in your tea, no butter on your toast or on your sandwiches. Rice, soya and almond milk are among the alternatives available to replace milk. Be aware that each of these has its own distinct flavour, so, for example, you can't expect tea to taste the same. You can use olive oil or hummus as alternative ways of moistening your food.

Discovering Dietary Supplements

Hype surrounds dietary supplements: bear in mind that it's generated by marketers, and that many claims are made for which no sound supporting evidence is ever given. In this section we cover the three supplements which are relevant to Asperger's and which have good evidence to support them.

Zoning in on zinc

Of all the vitamins and minerals on sale, zinc is the only one with clear, sound, scientific evidence supporting its health benefits. Zinc is needed by your immune system to fight off infections, and also to help you absorb iron from your diet. Evidence also suggests that people on the autism spectrum have weakened immune systems more often than most people.

Because zinc helps you absorb iron, it can use up all your spare iron and make you anaemic. So you shouldn't take zinc supplements all the time. You can't get around this by taking an iron supplement as well; iron is even more difficult to absorb from supplements than zinc. Exactly why taking the two together doesn't work isn't clear, but what is evident is that taking iron with zinc supplements doesn't solve the problem.

Zinc is most effective if you (an adult) take about 120 milligrams per day for four days before you become ill, and carry on taking it while you're ill. Try to take about a third of this dose with each meal to make up the total daily dose. (That's the same as 530 milligrams of zinc sulphate, the best form of zinc supplement for adults. Some companies produce zinc sulphate in 200-milligram tablets, so you could take one tablet with each meal.) Obviously, you need to guess when you're going to get ill for this tip to be most effective! If you fall ill and you haven't been taking any zinc, just start taking it until you're better.

The eagle-eyed among you will have noticed that 120 milligrams is 800 per cent of the recommended daily allowance of zinc (15 milligrams). Don't worry: taking this amount is perfectly safe because zinc is both difficult to absorb and water-soluble, so any of it that your body can't use will just pass out of you in your urine. Overdosing on zinc is possible, but you'd have to take a significantly larger dose than this. Nevertheless, *do not* try this tip with children, because their systems are less developed and more vulnerable to nutritional imbalances.

Meditating on melatonin

Melatonin is a hormone vital to healthy sleep and other daily biological rhythms. A surge in melatonin is what sets off the chain of events that makes you feel sleepy (see Chapter 6 for more on this). Plenty of evidence exists for sleep disturbance in people on the spectrum, and also some evidence that extra melatonin can help. However, melatonin is available only on prescription in the UK, because of the risk of serious damage being caused by an overdose. If you or your child is suffering significant sleep problems, consult your GP. Buying melatonin without a prescription, including on the Internet, is illegal in the UK.

Befriending friendly bacteria

Everyone needs a healthy balance of gut bacteria. The two things most damaging to your gut bacteria are antibiotics and yeast infections. So, especially after a course of antibiotics or a yeast infection but also if you've recently been ill or are feeling rundown, a month's course of one-a-day bacteria capsules can re-establish your gut bacteria. The capsules should contain *Lactobacillus acidophilus*, and may contain bifidobacteria (sometimes incorrectly called *Lactobacillus bifidus*) and other friendly bacteria.

Without healthy gut bacteria, if you eat any of the foodstuffs we mention in this chapter you will have worse symptoms than if your gut bacteria are healthy.

Yoghurt drinks containing friendly bacteria have no sound evidence supporting them. Your stomach acid will kill all the bacteria before they get into your gut. This doesn't mean that yoghurt drinks are no good: they're still nutritious and tasty, and can make you feel good about yourself and so you'll be healthier — this anecdotal evidence (people saying they feel healthier) is usually what's quoted in support of yoghurt drinks. Bacteria capsules contain bacterial spores, which are the equivalent of bacteria in hibernation. Bacterial spores are much more robust and able to survive in your stomach for long enough to get into your gut, where they can begin to feed and grow.

Part V
The Part of Tens

"And do you think having Asperger's Syndrome
has held you back in your business career,
Sir Gerald?"

In this part . . .

As this part is called the *Part of Tens*, we've come up with three lists of 10 things (or thereabouts!) that you might want to find out about.

Even if you read right through this book, learning more is always important, so we've made a list of organisations who can give you more information, advice and help when you need it.

We know that living with AS is certainly not all bad. We've made a list of the ten best things about being on the spectrum — you may have your own to add!

Finally, for those of you who've ever wondered whether Isaac Newton had an ASC, in this Part you can find out about our top 10 famous characters from fact and fiction who may have been on the spectrum.

Chapter 16

Ten (Or So) Sources of Support and Information on Asperger's Syndrome

This book provides a comprehensive overview of what Asperger's syndrome (AS) is, what life with AS is like and what things might help. You may also have looked at other books, read articles, accessed websites and watched documentaries. A vast amount of information on autism spectrum conditions (ASCs) including AS exists out there and is very hard to navigate!

Don't think you have to read everything or be an expert in everything all at once. Find out things as and when they apply to you. Ask people for help. Throughout this book we refer to various sources of help so you'll be ahead of the game in knowing where to go when you need more detailed information.

In this chapter, we run through useful organisations to approach for more on AS and all ASCs. Not all will be useful for you, and we certainly haven't listed all the possible websites to look at — because hundreds exist. But have a browse, explore the websites of the organisations we suggest, and enjoy finding out more.

National Autistic Society

We mention the National Autistic Society (NAS) a lot in this book, probably because this organisation is (in its own words) the "UK's foremost charity" for people affected by ASCs. Here's a quotation from the NAS website:

We champion the rights and interests of all people with autism and aim to provide individuals with autism and their families with help, support and services that they can access, trust and rely upon and which can make a positive difference to their lives.

The NAS started out in 1962 as a group of parents with children on the spectrum who met up to discuss their difficulties. It set up the first school for children with autism in the UK. Nowadays the NAS has over 18,000 members and 90 branches across the UK. Here's a list of services provided by the NAS for people with ASCs and those who work with and support them:

- ✔ Autism Helpline
- ✔ Information about ASCs
- ✔ Advice for individuals on the spectrum and their families
- ✔ Information and training for professionals
- ✔ The Lorna Wing Centre for diagnostic services and professional training
- ✔ Training and support for parents
- ✔ Specialist resource centres
- ✔ Advocacy for people on the spectrum and their families
- ✔ Specialist residential and supported living services
- ✔ Specialist outreach and day services for adults
- ✔ Specialist schools and education outreach services for children
- ✔ Out-of-school services for children and young people
- ✔ Employment training and support for students and adults
- ✔ Social programmes such as befriending and social groups
- ✔ Magazines

Not all NAS services are provided in all parts of the UK. Check on the website (www.autism.org.uk) to find out what's available in your area.

Autism Helpline and Signpost

The NAS runs the confidential Autism Helpline (Tel: 0845 070 4004). People on the spectrum and their families (including brothers and sisters) who live in the UK can call Monday to Friday from 10 a.m. to 4 p.m. to talk about ASCs, find out more information, and discuss any difficulties or worries they may have. You'll initially be put through to a helpline assistant who'll then pass you on to a helpline adviser. Helpline advisers know a lot about AS and have a database of resources to share. They'll do their best to answer any questions you have.

The NAS's Signpost service is a web-based service (www.autism.org. uk/signpost) that provides individually tailored information about how Asperger's may be affecting you, what services and support (provided by the NAS or other organisations) are available where you live, and what rights and benefits you may be entitled to. All you have to do is fill in a short online form giving some information about yourself (such as your age, diagnosis, gender and where you live).

Autism Helpline: 0845 070 4004.

Asperger United

This may seem a gratuitous plug, but we'll mention it anyway! The Goth edits a quarterly magazine called *Asperger United*. Surprisingly, given its title, *Asperger United* is a magazine written by and for adults who have an ASC. All articles and letters are written by people who have ASCs. Occasionally articles are written by professionals with those on the spectrum in mind. Highlights of the magazine (aside from the fact that it's free!) include personal accounts of being on the spectrum, a pen pal page, letters to the editor, poems, short stories and artwork. *Asperger United* is suitable for people 16 years old and above (although some parents are happy to subscribe on behalf of a younger child). Currently, *Asperger United* is only available by post, although you can download the latest issue from the NAS website (www.autism.org.uk/aspergerunited). Gratuitous plug over!

NAS campaigns

An amazing amount of work goes on behind the scenes at the NAS. A very dedicated group of people work hard to campaign for the rights of people on the spectrum at local and governmental level, with tremendous success. Thanks to the hard work of the NAS Policy and Campaigns team, the UK Government passed a law in 2009 called the Autism Act to begin to address the needs of adults who have an ASC. The Autism Act supports the adult autism strategy, which will require local authorities to explicitly state how they're meeting the needs of adults with ASC in terms of health, social care, employment and training. This is a really good start to helping improve the lives of people on the spectrum.

If you're interested in getting involved in the latest NAS campaigns, visit www.autism.org.uk.

Lorna Wing Centre

The Lorna Wing Centre is a diagnostic, assessment and advice service for children, adolescents and adults affected by AS and all ASCs. The centre specialises in people who show a complex presentation of difficulties. The DISCO (the Diagnostic Interview for Social and Communication Disorders) was developed by staff at the centre, and is a comprehensive assessment to assess individual needs in many areas associated with ASCs. The centre provides training for professionals in the use of the DISCO and an approach to diagnosis of ASCs which covers all aspects of development and each individual's pattern of skills and difficulties.

Research Autism

Research Autism is a charity providing information and advice about interventions, treatments and therapies (whatever you want to call them) for ASCs. You can find out really useful information about many different approaches to ASCs, from medicines through to diets and behavioural teaching approaches. Its website (www.researchautism.net) provides an A–Z list of these approaches. Many of these have also been rated by a team of experts in the field of autism, based on the evidence supporting (or not) their use. So, if you're considering using a particular teaching approach, taking a dietary supplement, or have been prescribed some medication, check out the pros and cons here.

Research Autism also commissions and carries out independent research into the effectiveness of some approaches designed to help people who have an ASC. Articles describing the outcomes of this research can be found on the website. The views of people on the spectrum and their families, as well as the opinions of professionals and academics, are important in establishing the charity's research priorities.

Some interesting conferences have been hosted by Research Autism, such as discussions about autism and girls, mental health and ASCs, and sleep and autism. The conferences are open to anyone, although most require that you book in advance if you want to attend.

If you're looking for the latest information about the safety, success and appropriateness of any behavioural approach, teaching strategy, medication or diet for ASCs, go to www.researchautism.net.

Autism Education Trust

The Autism Education Trust (www.autismeducationtrust.org.uk) is an organisation working to improve education for children on the spectrum in England. It raises awareness of educational provision for those on the spectrum, brings organisations involved in such education together, provides information about education, and shares good practice.

The website contains some great resources and ideas for children, parents and professionals. The Kids Zone on the website has some fun games, videos, tips, puzzles and facts for children on the spectrum.

If you're a teacher or parent who wants more information, tips and ideas about education for children and young people on the spectrum, go to www. autismeducationtrust.org.uk.

OAASIS

OAASIS (www.oaasis.co.uk) provides information for parents and professionals about all ASCs. OAASIS is part of Cambian Group, a specialist education group for children and young people on the spectrum (www. cambianeducation.com). It offers a helpline and free publications with information on the following topics:

- ✔ Autism and AS
- ✔ Other learning disabilities
- ✔ Educational issues
- ✔ Adult AS (with specific information for partners)

The OAASIS helpline (Tel: 0800 197 3907) is for parents and professionals who have questions they need answering or want someone to talk to.

Jessica Kingsley Publishers

Jessica Kingsley publishes hundreds of books about all aspects of ASCs. The company also publishes books on other topics, but we assume the ones about ASCs will be most useful to you, seeing as you're reading this book!

Titles range from those aimed at professionals such as speech and language therapists, psychologists and teachers through to those aimed at parents, siblings or partners of people on the autism spectrum. Many people who have Asperger's and their parents have published personal accounts of life with AS that are often moving and highly informative.

You can order books directly from Jessica Kingsley through the company's website at www.jkp.com.

Autism Research Centre

The Autism Research Centre (ARC; www.autismresearchcentre.com) is part of the University of Cambridge. It carries out research into ASCs in order to understand their biomedical causes as well as develop methods for assessment and intervention. Professor Simon Baron-Cohen, the director of the centre, is a leader in the field of research in this area and has written many papers and books on the subject. The ARC's work includes that on perception and cognition, screening and diagnosis, intervention, hormones, genetics and neuroscience. If you want to take part in the ARC's research, you can sign up to the volunteers' database at www.autismresearchcentre.com/volunteers.

Autscape

Autscape is an annual conference specifically for people with ASCs. Unlike the majority of conferences you'll come across on ASCs, people on the spectrum run the conference. The majority of presenters and participants are also on the spectrum. The needs, interests and sensitivities of autists are the first consideration, so the environment, schedule and communication styles are appropriate for their needs, as far as possible. Autscape aims to provide an opportunity to present and discuss ideas related to ASCs, meet other people on the spectrum, and have a social gathering.

People who aren't on the spectrum are also encouraged to attend, so long as they respect the needs of the participants and have an open mind. Autscape usually lasts three days and includes lectures, workshops, structured discussions, leisure activities and social events. If you're interested in finding out more, go to www.autscape.org.

The Many Organisations Named "ASPIRE"

Probably because "aspire" means to have strong ambition or strongly desire something, and the acronym for Asperger's syndrome is AS, many organisations supporting people with AS (and other ASCs) have called themselves ASPIRE. This situation can be quite confusing, so below is a summary of the different ASPIRE organisations and what each of them does.

Impetus ASpire

Impetus is a charity in the Brighton and Hove area. Its ASpire project provides mentoring and social activities for people on the spectrum, and training about AS for parents and professionals. For more information, go to www.bh-impetus.org and follow the link to "ASpire".

Autism West Midlands ASpire

The ASpire programme in the West Midlands is an employment service for people with AS, and can be found at www.autismwestmidlands.org.uk.

Aspire: Asperger's Syndrome Association of Ireland

This organisation provides support, education and training services for people with AS and their families in Ireland. The website is at www.aspireireland.ie.

Romsey Mill Aspire Programme

This is a programme for young people with AS and high functioning ASCs in Cambridgeshire who are in mainstream education. Social clubs and activities are provided three times a week with a variety of activities. Go to www.romseymill.org/pages/aspireprogramme.asp.

Fife Aspire

This is an employment support service for people with AS living in the Fife area. For more information, go to www.fifedirect.org.uk and search for Aspire in the A–Z directory.

Asperger Syndrome Partners & Individuals Resources, Encouragement & Support (ASPIRES)

This is an online resource for partners, spouses and family members of adults on the spectrum. You can join the ASPIRES email list to share information and support about relationship experiences, resources and survival tips. For more information, go to www.aspires-relationships.com.

Asperger and ASD UK Online Forum

Asperger and ASD UK Online Forum (www.asd-forum.org.uk) is a website for people affected by ASCs. You can chat online about ASC-related issues or just general topics of interest. The forum aims to bring people together who may be feeling lonely or isolated, and who may be in similar situations to each other. Hopefully, they can support each other and share practical advice on ASCs. Discussion topics on the forum are

- ✔ Meet and greet
- ✔ General discussion
- ✔ Education
- ✔ Help and advice
- ✔ Medication, diet, vitamins, supplements, remedies
- ✔ Resources
- ✔ Beyond adolescence (for further education, diagnosis, benefits, employment and so on)
- ✔ Off topic (for non-ASC related chat)
- ✔ Techie corner (on how to use the online forum)

Aspie Village

Aspie Village (www.aspievillage.org.uk) is a social networking website for people on the spectrum. As of April 2010, as a result of overwhelming demand, you can now only join if a friend recommends you. Once you're in, though, you can discuss issues related to ASCs such as:

- ✔ Everyday difficulties
- ✔ Friendships
- ✔ Romantic relationships
- ✔ Work and education

You can also discuss non-ASC-related topics, chat about your interests or participate in the greetings, personal news and meet-ups section of the website. Gaining access to this website will offer the opportunity to make new friends and link up with others who share similar interests.

Asperger's Syndrome Foundation

The Asperger's Syndrome Foundation (www.aspergerfoundation.org.uk) is a charity which provides support to individuals and families affected by AS. You can find information about all aspects of AS for children, adults and parents. The charity also runs training seminars for parents and professionals, which include topics such as social and personal relationships, sensory issues, anger management and developing social competence. The foundation also has useful links to other organisations and websites related to autism and AS.

Aspies For Freedom

Aspies For Freedom (www.aspiesforfreedom.com) is a website that has forums, chat rooms and information for people who have Asperger's, or who are affected by ASCs. Anyone is welcome to join the site, including parents of children who have Asperger's or other ASCs.

Chapter 17

Ten Positives about Living with Asperger's Syndrome

In This Chapter

▶ Realising why it's good to be you

▶ Recognising why you're a good friend and colleague

▶ Looking at bad things that are actually good

At times you may dwell on the downsides of Asperger's syndrome (AS): the loneliness, the anxiety and the lack of understanding. But the majority of people who have an autism spectrum condition (ASC) want to be themselves *with* their ASC. If you have AS, you're very unlikely to be the sort of person who wishes that he or she were someone else. For example, you may want to be a musician, and if you do, you probably don't wish you were John Lennon or Mika. You just want to be you and a successful musician. So here are ten reasons why AS is a good thing, both for you and for society.

You See Details that Other People Miss

You may not be some sort of detail-spotting phenomenon, but everyone we've ever met who's on the spectrum has been good at noticing certain sorts of things. Exactly what thing varies from person to person, but it may be numbers, shoes, fabrics or anything else.

You may be able to develop a skill from your detail-spotting, such as working in drapery (fabric sales) and being able to identify and match materials quickly — and this job needn't involve working with the public. Or maybe you can hear subtle auditory differences that allow you to tell what make and model a musical instrument is just from its sound.

People Always Want You to Join their Quiz Team

Even if you're not any good at quizzes, people always seem to want you on their team (we assume this is because they have a stereotyped view of AS which tells them that you must have a good memory and have stored up lots of facts). Don't worry about whether you're any good: if you think you can enjoy the venue (such as coping with the noise if it's in a pub), just go along and socialise. If you're worried that you'll let the other team members down, warn them that you don't think you'll be any good. You never know, you might surprise yourself!

You May Have an Exceptionally Good Memory

In fact, the Goth reckons everyone has an exceptionally good memory *for something*. The memories may not be very useful (even in a pub quiz), but you'll have some subject about which you can remember an exceptional amount. One person has a vivid and detailed memory of everything they saw and did while living for a few years in a certain market town. Questions about the three blue bricks in the red-brick wall of what was once the butcher's are unlikely to come up in even the most bizarre quiz, but that doesn't take anything away from the remarkableness of the memory.

Quite a few people on the spectrum can remember the names of all their infant-school classmates, and maybe their heights and shoe sizes too. Again, this sort of information is unlikely to come in handy, but it demonstrates an exceptional memory, and you can learn how to apply your memory to whatever you want. You just have to practise.

You might, perhaps, have an interest in learning all there is to know about house prices in your area. Both the Land Registry and your local council have offices where this information is needed, and having someone who just knows the details saves a lot of looking up and improves the quality of the services they can offer. Any information that has commercial value can help you get a job — just remember to let them know that you know it on the application form.

You Are Trustworthy

Whether you just find that being manipulative is too difficult to get right or you abhor the idea of not being honest, people can trust you. You do a lot to keep your life simpler and less stressful, and that includes following rules. So when you're told to keep a secret, you keep it; when lent something, you give it back. You're not perfect, but in terms of trustworthiness, you're a lot more reliable than most people.

You Are Loyal

A consequence of being straightforward with people is that you're loyal towards people you like, even people you've never met whom you've come to know through the media.

You present some difficulties to people who want to be your friend: you can be rude, unfeeling, self-centred and pedantic. But you can also be trusted to give an honest answer to a straight question. You appear to deal with news calmly, no matter how un-calm you may feel inside, which can be a great help to people who are struggling to cope with unwelcome news. And part of being unmoved by day-to-day events is that you maintain your loyalty to people even when events challenge your friendship: you're not quick to throw away something of value just because of a temporary blot.

You Are an Individual and Don't Succumb to Peer Pressure

Most people feel peer pressure — the psychological need to fit in with friends by copying them. Group norms can influence — or dictate — your hairstyle, clothes, shoes, watch, jewellery, the way you walk, how you talk, whether you have a tattoo, or even just how you wear your clothes, for example boys wearing their jeans halfway down their backsides.

Dressing so that you fit in with everyone else is called *urban camouflage*, and is a social norm found all over the world. Not that many people realise that fitting in also includes walking the way other people walk. You might be aware that certain American gangs walk in a distinctive way, but this is actually true of almost everyone. Very few cultures around the world walk in an entirely natural, entirely unlearned way. Changing the way you walk is in response to a very subtle form of peer pressure, which people aren't usually conscious of, and all sorts of behaviour can be affected like this.

Peer pressure can also mean doing things that other people do, even if you don't particularly enjoy doing them. For example, many teenagers start smoking because their friends do or because doing so's fashionable and cool. People who have AS are less likely to be pressured into doing something they don't like just because other people are doing it.

However, you make your own decisions, which may or may not include the decision to try to fit in with some of the people you spend time with or whom you see in the street.

You Can Live Outside Social Norms

Many people fret about drawing attention to themselves or being gossiped about. As well as not being afraid to do your own thing, you often don't care about what other people think of you. And you shouldn't care. If you want to dress like a Victorian gentleman and write with a quill, your colleagues may think it's a little odd, and you'll certainly get talked about, but you're doing no harm and you're satisfying yourself, which is important. You are free to question any and all of the rules people lay down about how normal lives are lived. And within the law, you can change any you don't like. Be aware, though, that you may draw attention to yourself, which you may find stressful. Think about what you can cope with before embarking on a lifetime of eccentricity, and be aware that causing yourself stress isn't always worth it. So here's to owning a pet otter, painting your house magenta and wearing flip-flops in winter.

You Are Creative

Creativity isn't the result of some fantastic ability; it mostly just involves not thinking in the same way as everyone else. According to Einstein, "The secret to creativity is knowing how to hide your sources," which sounds like cheating, but bear two things in mind: Einstein had a mischievous sense of humour, which is expressed in this quote, and he was getting at a deeper truth. Deep truths are difficult to express in simple language and, in the same way that an explained joke is no longer funny, expressing deep truths in basic words reduces them in some way. But here goes anyway. Creativity, according to Einstein, involves taking other people's ideas and developing them in ways that their authors or inventors never thought of, so that the sources are changed beyond recognition (they're "hidden"). And this applies to any sort of creativity: coming up with new ideas, drawing in a distinct style, improvising and interpreting music — anything. All creativity relies on not just slavishly copying someone else, but taking the ideas further or in a different direction.

Some creative people admit to feeling like frauds. They don't feel comfortable accepting praise when all they've done is take other people's ideas (their sources) and changed them a bit. Even when they try to point out that they owe their work to their sources, other people just call them modest and self-effacing.

So, to get back to the point, you are creative. And you're creative because you don't think in the same way as most people. You probably have an unusual set of interests which act as a unique and very different set of sources for your ideas.

You May Have a Steely Determination

Maybe it's the result of your perfectionism or your very keen interest in a certain subject, or simply because you enjoy the repetitive process of, say, piecing together a broken vase and gluing it together again. Whatever the cause, lots of people on the spectrum will persevere with tasks that most people would give up on or not even start.

Always let people know if you enjoy, or at least get satisfaction from, tasks that others find tedious, especially at work. Otherwise, boring jobs tend to get shared out and everyone has to do some. If you tell people that you prefer to take on the whole task, you can then ask to be let off doing something that you don't like — answering the phone, for example.

You May Feel Stupid

Many of the world's most successful people admit to feeling that their work isn't good enough and they don't really know what they're doing or why people think their work is so good. Fear of not being good enough can push people to try harder, and the people who are both talented and try very hard are the most successful in their field or profession. So if you sometimes feel stupid, you share that experience with lots of very successful people — it's not a feeling associated with failure or mediocrity.

As Mark Twain said, "Keep away from people who try to belittle your ambitions. Small people always do that, but the really great make you feel that you, too, can become great."

Chapter 18

Ten Famous People (Some Fictional) Who May Have Had Asperger's Syndrome

*I*dentifying famous people as having Asperger's syndrome (AS) or some other "fashionable" condition has become something of a game in the media and on the Internet. Often, however, no explanations are provided of why certain people are identified as such, beyond picking out a few Asperger-type traits.

We aren't trying to trivialise the diagnosis of AS in this chapter — we just want to show that people who have AS can be and have been very successful. They've also been represented as heroic in various works of fiction, which shows that plenty of people view Asperger's in a positive light.

Here we give you a few more reasons for our choices, but we don't want to bore you, so we don't list all the traits that make each person a candidate, just some of the more important.

No traits are purely representative of AS: only when a person demonstrates dozens of such traits can you describe them as being on the autism spectrum. Trying to identify someone you don't know, and whose childhood history you also don't know, as having AS is extremely difficult, because the information you need is seldom available. And you can't formally diagnose someone who's dead — no such procedure has been developed and isn't likely to be in the foreseeable future either. The more successful someone on the spectrum is, the more likely it is that the person will be successfully compensating for (that is, disguising) his or her autistic traits.

The *broader autism phenotype* (BAP) is the technical term that refers to people who don't quite qualify for a diagnosis, usually because either they don't show symptoms across the full range of autistic traits or they are "functioning" well in all areas of their lives, including socially, romantically and in employment. By definition, someone with a diagnosis is sufficiently disordered to need a diagnosis, and that means that the person's condition is having a significant effect on at least one part of his or her life. If you're single and content, that is still considered to be functioning well. But if you're romantically or socially lonely or unable to earn enough money to live on, and such problems persist in your life, then you're not functioning well from a diagnostic point of view.

Albert Einstein is probably the most famous person suggested as having AS, but because he had many friends, a wife, numerous infidelities and a spectacularly successful career, he can't really be diagnosed as having anything more severe than autistic traits. He hated teaching, which may imply that he had problems coping with the social skills involved, but, again, this isn't enough for a diagnosis. Even in his late teens, had he been referred for diagnosis he'd have been seen as functioning well. The only blot on his life at the time was failing the entrance exam for Zurich Polytechnic, which is not an autistic trait — a significant number of intelligent people either fail or drop out at some point.

Trying to identify people who are long-dead or fictional as having AS is very difficult. Standards of behaviour have changed, which adds its own difficulties. For example, displaying a certain stiffness at a social gathering was considered appropriate behaviour (but not the only appropriate behaviour) among the upper classes at the turn of the nineteenth century. So there's no way of knowing whether the underlying cause of a person's behaviour was just upbringing or social convention — Mr Darcy in *Pride and Prejudice*, for example, thus cannot be diagnosed by behavioural criteria.

With fictional characters in general, the fundamental diagnostic point is whether the author set out to depict a character who has AS. This doesn't mean the author has to know about AS, just that the author is trying to describe a certain personality. It's been suggested, for example, that Lisa, the elder daughter in *The Simpsons*, has AS — but did the writer, Matt Groening, intend her to have it? We very much doubt it, because Lisa plays the role not of the autist but of the parent, while Homer, the father, is the irresponsible teenager. What can be perceived as her being a bossy little professor, a classic Asperger's trait, is actually her in the role of nagging parent. Role reversals like this are widely used in comedy, so speculating whether comic characters have AS is particularly difficult.

Another convention of literature is also often mistaken as a sign of AS: the *explanatory ingénue*, that is, a character ignorant of normal conventions, a naive person, who gives the author the opportunity to explain the conventions without seeming to patronise the reader or viewer. Famous examples of explanatory ingenues are Mr Spock and Data from *Star Trek*, who allowed the writers to talk about basic human traits and emotions without appearing to talk down to the viewer, and Luke Skywalker in the first *Star Wars* film, *Episode IV: A New Hope*.

So, although all three characters have been ascribed AS, none of them can be considered to be on the spectrum.

Bearing all these barriers to diagnosis in mind, here we whittle the list down to ten people and characters whom we think are the most likely to have had AS. But we only allow ourselves one person from any particular background or career, so this isn't just a list of ten famous physicists. We look at a mathematician, a detective, a time lord, a painter, a singer–songwriter, a composer, a film director, a philosopher, an author and a lawyer.

These historical (and fictional!) figures show that, despite the difficulties created by the combination of AS and society's ignorance of the condition, success and achievement are possible. And achievement will be so much easier when the government and health and social services realise that a bit of help now can reduce their costs in the future. Even though AS itself isn't a disability, it has disabling symptoms (and different symptoms in different people) which shouldn't be ignored, no matter how tight the budget.

As a way to pass a rainy hour or two, or a long journey, pick a historical figure or famous person and identify all his or her AS traits, then decide whether you think the person is on the autism spectrum or not.

Isaac Newton

In the case of Isaac Newton (1642–1727), so much biographical detail exists that is indicative of AS that for once we can be fairly confident that he did have it.

Newton came from a yeoman family, meaning they were small landowners; in wealth and social standing they sat between merchants and the gentry. Within the yeomanry, the family seems to have struggled financially to maintain the outward appearance of its station, and Newton would probably have been under pressure to marry the right girl. However, he never appeared to show any interest in anyone, never married and is believed to have died a virgin. An inability to cope with personal relationships and a subsequent retreat from the stress and confusion of such interactions (often despite severe loneliness) is a common AS trait.

Newton is most famous as the genius physicist who made great progress in the disciplines of optics and gravitation, but fewer people realise that physics and mathematics represent only about one-sixth of his writing. The rest of his output concerns witchcraft, biblical prophecy and alchemy, and he seems to have developed an obsession with these topics. Charms to ward off witches and their curses were cut into the plaster of his house. In dwelling on these subjects, Newton was a man of his time — he lived in an age of puritanism and witch trials. You can still visit his house, at Woolsthorpe-by-Belvoir in Lincolnshire, and see these charms along with the famous orchard that was visible from his study. Sitting at his desk, he watched and pondered why apples always fell to the ground.

At the age of 24, Newton became a fellow of Trinity College, Cambridge, where he displayed some of his most autistic behaviour. He hated being wrong, and would argue bitterly for years over both trivial and important matters, showing no perspective of the situation. His pettiness was famous among academics all over Europe. As a fellow, one of his duties was to lecture undergraduates, and he apparently delivered his lectures even when nobody arrived to hear them. The hall was empty, but he was being paid to lecture and he felt duty-bound to do so, regardless. This strict adherence to the rules is probably the single most persuasive piece of evidence that Newton had AS.

Sherlock Holmes

Sir Arthur Conan Doyle started his medical studies in Edinburgh in 1877. The detective Sherlock Holmes (circa. 1840–1920), his most famous creation, was based on Conan Doyle's professor at medical college, Dr Joseph Bell. Bell was incredibly quick at spotting details and he taught his students to make deductions from them.

Detecting illness

Dr Joseph Bell's skills at deduction when meeting a new patient were described in the *Lancet* (18 August 1956). Here we provide a translation of the patient's Scots dialect, because it may be difficult for some readers to understand:

A woman with a small child was shown in. Joe Bell said good morning to her and she said good morning in reply.

"What sort of crossing did you have from Burntisland?"

"It was good."

"And had you a good walk up Inverleith Row?"

"Yes."

"And what did you do with the other small child?"

"I left him with my sister in Leith."

"And would you still be working at the linoleum factory?"

"Yes I would."

"You see, gentlemen, when she said good morning to me, I noted her Fife accent, and, as you know, the nearest town in Fife is Burntisland. You noticed the red clay on the edges of the soles of her shoes, and the only such clay within 20 miles of Edinburgh is in the Botanical Gardens. Inverleith Row borders the gardens and is her nearest way here from Leith. You observed that the coat she carried over her arm is too big for the child who is with her, and therefore she set out from home with two children. Finally, she has dermatitis on the fingers of the right hand, which is peculiar to workers in the linoleum factory at Burntisland."

Some people have suggested that Bell himself was on the spectrum, but not enough evidence exists to be sure. His abilities seem almost superhuman; see the nearby sidebar "Detecting illness".

Such attention to detail and careful deduction, often based simply on the most likely rather than the definite, is characteristic of Sherlock Holmes, who wrote monographs (essays on specific subjects), one of which described 140 different types of tobacco ash (as mentioned in *The Sign of Four*). If that's not obsessive attention to detail, we don't know what is!

Bell's unegotistical and precise view of the world was characterised by his response to a letter from Conan Doyle, in which the author praised Bell's skills and paid him the compliment of confessing that Holmes was based on him. Bell replied, "You are yourself Sherlock Holmes and well you know it." Clear, concise, accurate, and piercing straight through the flattery — the very essence of Holmes!

Bell was also a very sociable man, but this doesn't preclude him from being on the autism spectrum, especially as he lived at a time when socialising was more formal, based on more clearly laid-out rules. However, Holmes's more asocial side seems to have been based on parts of Conan Doyle's own character rather than on Bell's. Conan Doyle was a scrupulously honest and conscientious man with a particular abhorrence of injustice. He was also intolerant of ignorance, despite being duped by fake spiritualists and trying to convince the conjurer and escapologist Houdini that his spiritualist-type tricks were actually caused by his (Houdini's) genuine psychic powers. It is only in Sherlock Holmes, however, that Bell and Conan Doyle's characteristics are merged and a large number of autistic traits are evident.

Doctor Who

Born on Gallifrey, in around 131,240 (new galactic calendar), the being known to us only as "the Doctor" completed his studies at the Prydonian Academy in the "year of 92" and became a Time Lord. The Doctor had an unusual, one could say reckless, youth, before falling in love with a remote little planet called Earth. He has since made it one of his obsessions to care for — some would say interfere with — this planet and her citizens. He knows a lot of things that he wishes he didn't (and the Goth wishes he could remember which incarnation of the Doctor said that — possibly the fifth).

Hero and explanatory ingénue are the main two literary conventions of the Doctor's role, and these make it difficult to view his traits in isolation as either autistic or not autistic. He is, after all, an alien with two hearts, so diagnosing him with a human condition isn't entirely appropriate, even though his mother was human.

However, one regeneration of the Doctor in particular displays a large number of autistic traits, and that's the sixth, played by Colin Baker (1984–1986). Sometimes referred to as the "busybody Doctor", Baker quite deliberately chose to play him as unlikeable, which is a bold move with such a loved character. He was pedantic, irritable, intolerant of other people's mistakes and of their ignorance. Like every regeneration, he was intense, obsessive, talented and didn't suffer fools gladly, a loner who nevertheless got lonely and sought company, grudgingly in Baker's portrayal. He was the most arrogant of the regenerations, a trait relieved by the good-natured side of David Tennant's (tenth) Doctor.

Paul Cézanne

Many artists, particularly Impressionists and Post-Impressionists, have been identified as possibly being on the autism spectrum, but Paul Cézanne (1839–1906), son of a wealthy banker, is the one about whom no real doubt exists. He abandoned his studies in law to pursue his painting in Paris. He went through long periods of obsessive painting during which he didn't wash and often forgot to eat. After such a marathon, he'd turn up at a friend's place or café, and it still wouldn't have occurred to him to wash. Despite this, he was sufficiently loved by his friends, including Emil Zola the author, that they supported the struggling artist when he was, as he often was, without money.

Cézanne's art is also revealing: he made studies of his subjects in extreme detail, and for a time tried to capture his subjects in three-dimensional detail, looking through one eye and then the other and painting aspects of both views to produce a sort of heightened reality. Some of his most famous paintings such as the series of *Mont Sainte Victoire*, consist of many pictures of the same scene all painted simultaneously: he would switch from one canvas to the next (and then maybe switch back again) as the light changed during the day. Cézanne was never satisfied with his painting and is one of a very select group of painters who've mastered several genres, in his case landscapes, portraits, still lifes and figures. Always, he used many small, repetitive brush strokes.

Cézanne was aware of the shortcomings of his vision, and it's been widely assumed that those shortcomings were the same as anyone else's, but we suspect his were rather worse. He was very aware of how different things could look when viewed from varying angles or in diverse lights, and seems to have had some difficulty in recognising that different views of someone were still the same person. Everyone has some difficulty recognising someone from behind, but Cézanne seems to have struggled recognising people at all: just approaching them from the side could leave him confused and unsure until they turned to look at him. He almost certainly had mild face-blindness (see Chapter 11) but had problems recognising objects from different angles as well as people. He was also peculiarly sensitive to light and the effect it had on the appearance of things, and he may have only been able to see clearly in sunlight.

Cézanne's combination of obsession and love of light contributed to his death: in his 60s he allowed himself to get soaked by a storm while painting in a field near his home in Aix-en-Provence. He stood in the rain for two hours and died a few days later.

Ian Curtis

Various singers and musicians have been put forward as having AS, but of those who are or were unaware of the diagnosis, Ian Curtis (1956–1980) is the most clear. His manner was quietly odd, he made odd eye contact, he moved in a peculiar manner at times and he had odd, jerky mannerisms. Picture after picture of the band shows him looking off-camera at something that no one else is focused on. Curtis became depressed, in part due to his inability to make his marriage work, the distress caused by his epilepsy, and his loneliness, which was accentuated by the fact that he was surrounded by people.

Being Curtis's friend was sometimes difficult, but not for the usual prima-donna behaviour that makes many lead singers hard work to be around. He was academically very able, but chose not to go into higher education. The tone of his singing voice is, well, to avoid using the word "odd" again, strange. It's not exactly without expression, but it lacks the intonation and rise and fall of most vocals. You can hear this most clearly on Joy Division's debut album, *Unknown Pleasures*.

Curtis was also a talented writer, and his writing features feelings of emotional isolation. He was a very troubled man who failed to cope with the demands of touring in a rock band and whose epileptic seizures often struck when he was at his most stressed and overloaded — including a number of times when he was on stage, performing.

Curtis's most famous and haunting song describes beautifully the anguish, hope and fearfulness of relationship: 'Love will tear us apart'.

Mozart

Whether all child prodigies show autistic tendencies has been a subject of debate — after all, as far as anyone knows, everyone on the planet fulfils at least two diagnostic criteria for AS. Because autism is a spectrum that merges smoothly with the characteristics of the rest of the population, diagnosticians have to decide where to draw the line. This line divides people who are very similar. Imagine lining up everyone in the world rated from the least to the most autistic. The line doesn't have to be single-file, which is handy because it would go all the way around the globe dozens of times. Somewhere near one end you're going to have to say "here" and everyone beyond that point gets a diagnosis (about 100 million people), and the 100 million or so just to the other side are said to have the broader autism phenotype. If a real connection exists between autism and giftedness, you can expect a lot of prodigies in these groups, and it seems that there are.

Studying prodigies who aren't clearly diagnosed is one way of shedding light on the grey area between those who get a diagnosis of autism and those who definitely won't get one. But the success, if it comes, gives prodigies the things they need to appear as though they're coping: a social life, romantic interest and work. That doesn't necessarily mean that they really are coping, and allowances have to be made for such circumstances.

Johann Chrysostom Wolfgang Amadeus Mozart (1756–1991) was a quiet, withdrawn child who didn't play with other children. He behaved selfishly all his life, and at times, had he not had a demanding father (or, as an adult, had he any money), you could have called him spoilt. His behaviour was exaggerated for the film *Amadeus*, so don't base your idea of him on that (easier said than done), but even so it's fair to characterise him as lacking in social skills.

Although Mozart was celebrated across Europe, and we think of him today as famous, his was just another here-today-and-gone-tomorrow career in the pop music of his time: the wealthy sponsors of composers were always keen to employ the latest sensation, but expected some respect and deference, someone who wouldn't argue with them in private and who wouldn't embarrass them in public. Mozart never got the post of master of the king's music, which he hoped for, and left several well-paid positions for a variety of selfish and disciplinary reasons, the most well-documented being his protracted argument with Archbishop Colloredo of Salzburg. From Mozart's point of view, he was under-utilised — many people thought that court music declined under Colloredo — and underpaid. Colloredo was annoyed that Mozart would leave without telling anyone where he was going, sometimes being unavailable when he was required to perform. Mozart was 21 when he left, an age by which people were expected to show they could behave like adults, but he never mastered this particular skill.

Alfred Hitchcock

Hitch, as he was affectionately known, was one of the most famous film directors in the world. His career in the film industry began in 1920, and his films from *The Thirty-Nine Steps* (1935) to *Frenzy* (1972) were all huge hits, despite varied critical reactions. Each one contains elements which have been copied many times by other film-makers. The film *Psycho* was the first to use strident, discordant violins going "eek! eek! eek!" to build up tension — a technique that has now become such a cliché that it can only be used tongue-in-cheek.

Alfred Joseph Hitchcock (1899–1980) was born in London and most clearly showed his autistic tendencies while still at school. He was reserved, often only speaking when spoken to and even then was difficult to engage in conversation. He developed an outsider's view of society. School friends, on being interviewed about the famous director he had become, paint a picture of a boy who didn't understand how to interact with people, but who enjoyed observing human interaction from the sidelines — sometimes quite literally, during school football matches! These observations were useful to him in his career, giving him his understanding of the human condition.

Hitchcock married Alma Reville, who was a quiet, slightly awkward, but very competent film editor and, by the time they married, his assistant director. She paid great attention to detail, and their understanding of each other cemented their relationship. Being married seems to show that Hitch had some social ability, but this doesn't mean he didn't struggle in other areas. In fact, Alma may have been instrumental in smoothing over ruffled feathers. So, on balance, Hitchcock was probably on the spectrum.

Ludwig Wittgenstein

Author of what's often called the most complex book ever written, the surprisingly short *Tractatus Logico-Philosophicus* (generally known just as "Wittgenstein's *Tractatus*"), Ludwig Josef Johann Wittgenstein (1889–1951) studied at Cambridge under the great philosopher and pacifist Bertrand Russell. The book is about language and truth. He wrote the *Tractatus* while serving as an artillery officer on the Austro–Italian front in the First World War, and it was eventually published in 1921.

After the war, feeling as though the *Tractatus* "solved" philosophy, and having been appalled by the warfare he'd been a part of, Wittgenstein gave away his money and became an elementary-school teacher. In school, however, he displayed his lack of understanding of other people and his inability to cope with the social pressures of the classroom.

After Wittgenstein failed as a teacher in Austria, to keep his mind occupied and his spirits up, his sister asked him to help design a new house. This took Wittgenstein two years of intensive and painstaking work from 1926 to 1928, during which he displayed his mind-numbing attention to detail: he didn't just tackle the architecture, he designed the doorknobs, the radiators and even the window catches — a unique and very effective design, although very expensive to manufacture.

On his return to Cambridge in 1929, Wittgenstein was persuaded to submit the *Tractatus* as his doctoral thesis. The examiners, one of whom was Bertrand Russell, did not, in Wittgenstein's opinion, understand the book, and after Wittgenstein was awarded his doctorate, he and Russell would spend whole afternoons with him explaining what he meant in it. Russell once commented that, after an entire afternoon's work, he would've gained a reasonable understanding of one or sometimes two pages.

After Wittgenstein had become professor of philosophy, in 1939, he said that he no longer understood a single thing that he had written in the *Tractatus*, and the Goth really, really wants this to be literally true. But what Wittgenstein meant was that his ideas had evolved and he no longer understood the man who'd written the *Tractatus*, his younger self, and without an understanding of the man, he no longer had a grasp of what the man meant in his writings. The language was now as foreign to him as it had been to Russell.

Wittgenstein continued as the shy, bookish professor who only really came alive when talking about his subject, until 1947, when he retired.

Jane Austen

It is a truth universally acknowledged that any writing on Jane Austen has to start with "It is a truth universally acknowledged" — the opening words of *Pride and Prejudice*. Whether or not Jane Austen (1775–1817) was on the autism spectrum is a tricky and contentious question. She certainly didn't conform to the social expectations placed upon her, and her humour was considered shockingly bold when her novels were first published, but these details aren't enough to diagnose her.

Pride and Prejudice tells the story of Elizabeth Bennett, an unconventional and outspoken young woman. As mentioned in the introduction to this chapter, it seems very unlikely that Mr Darcy — the love interest — was on the spectrum, but stronger cases can be made for other characters in the novel: a young clergyman, Mr Collins, one of Elizabeth Bennett's suitors, and Elizabeth's sister Mary can probably be diagnosed as having AS.

Mr Collins is an awkward and very precise man. So much fun is made of his manner, however, that considering it a portrait rather than a caricature is actually rather difficult. That said, we still reckon Mr Collins displays enough traits to make AS a strong possibility.

Mary is the Bennett sister who finds social situations most difficult. She enjoys playing and singing in public — a common entertainment in the 1700s, with anyone who was willing taking turns to do so — but her behaviour can be inappropriate at times, such as getting up to sing before giving the party a chance to invite her. She was unable to respond to "silent entreaties" on one occasion when her sister tried to stop her talking. She is also prone to making unhelpful and self-righteous comments without considering their effects, such as when her youngest sister has shocked the family by eloping. Overshadowed by her more sociable sisters, Mary reads sermons and educational books rather than the latest novels and romances, as her main pastime. These behaviours can all be related to AS.

Jane Austen, like any novelist, must have drawn on her real life in order to depict these characters, so she certainly knew people who displayed the full range of AS traits. Some would say she displayed many herself.

Austen wrote to her brother, Edward, in relation to a joint writing project: "What should I do with your strong, manly, spirited sketches, full of variety and glow? How could I possibly join them on to the little bit (two inches wide) of ivory on which I work with so fine a brush, as produces little effect after much labour?", which clearly attests her painstaking attention to detail.

She was the seventh child of eight and the younger of the two daughters, and, being a bit different, may have found securing a husband whom she herself respected enough to marry rather difficult. Her father retired when Jane was 25 — an age when most women would already have children and considered very old for a single woman — and he moved the family to Bath. Perhaps he hoped that Jane would find a wealthy husband, but she disliked society events and parties. She found it a strain to talk to people about nothing.

Many biographies state that Austen was one of seven children. Her brother George is often overlooked because he didn't live with them but in the care of a family who also looked after her uncle. Both these men had some sort of mental disability — George also had fits and may have had problems with his vision and hearing. This disability could easily have been autism with epilepsy, which increases the chance that AS was in the family.

Mr Grewgious

Who? Okay, we agree, Mr Grewgious isn't famous. Not even a tiny, tiny bit famous. He is to fame what cocoa is to copper mining. But there's a reason why he should be. More than 70 years before Hans Asperger first described boys severely affected by the syndrome which now bears his name, Charles Dickens drew the character of Mr Grewgious in his last book, *The Mystery of Edwin Drood* (published in 1870), which was left unfinished at his death. He is the legal guardian of the heroine, and the model of honesty, conscientiousness and reliability.

Mr Grewgious must surely have been based on one or more people whom Dickens met and observed, and it's a tribute to his skill in depicting characters that he can describe someone so unlike himself, and do it so clearly and affectionately — for Mr Grewgious is a character to be loved by the reader. He comes across as a little lonely and, although he has a career in the law, he's supported by a wealthy family.

Although Dickens doesn't make the point, Mr Grewgious was no doubt able to work because of his attention to detail and his prodigious memory. A widely held belief now exists that the combination of computerised records (which reduce the need for a good memory) and the growth of the "service economy" (jobs that involve serving customers, and thus need good social skills) has made life more difficult for people on the autism spectrum.

Mr Grewgious is, in his own words, "such a very Angular man" who is extremely conscientious and loyal, socially and conversationally uncomfortable, who keeps his rooms immaculately tidy, whose face lacks expression, who moves in an ungainly fashion and talks in a dull voice . . . indeed, so many AS traits are displayed clearly and simply by him that listing them all would be dull, pedantic and, well, very AS.

If anyone comes across an earlier depiction — real or fictional — of someone who very clearly has AS, we'd love to hear from them (modern biographies of people don't count as early; the date of the depiction is what counts). But for now we think that this is the earliest known clear description of AS.

Appendix A

A List of Books You Might Like to Read (And Some Discs)

· ·

In This Chapter

▶ Finding the details of that book you were interested in

▶ Coming across other books you might be interested in

▶ Listing more books (and discs)

▶ There really are a lot of books listed in this chapter!

· ·

We've mentioned a lot of books in the rest of this book, so to save you having to search the text for the book that you wanted get, we're listing them all here, along with a few other important books that will get you started in your quest for information.

General Books about Autism, Asperger's Syndrome and ASCs

Understanding Autism for Dummies **by Stephen Shore and Linda Rastelli (Wiley).** If you know someone at the more severe end of the autism spectrum, this is a good place to start, although some of the health and financial advice is very American.

The Complete Guide to Asperger's Syndrome **by Tony Attwood (Jessica Kingsley Publishers).** Not, as the title implies, a complete encyclopaedia about AS, but the most complete technical book on AS yet published. Everything gets a mention, but some things get very little explanation. It's written for any reader, including professionals, which is why it's technical in places.

Autism and Asperger Syndrome: the Facts **by Simon Baron-Cohen (Oxford University Press).** A neat summary of everything we know. Again, it's written from an academic viewpoint, so it's quite technical in places.

The Oaasis Guide to Asperger Syndrome by Patricia Romanowski Bashe and Barbara Kirby (Crown Publishers). A guide for parents, teachers and professionals working with someone who has AS, including tips on diagnosis, education, social skills and growing up.

Nobody Nowhere by Donna Williams (Jessica Kingsley Publishers). One of the first autobiographies by an autist. We're avoiding mentioning many autobiographies here, as people tend to find useful biographies that are about people who have personalities and mannerisms that the reader recognises and identifies with. *Nobody Nowhere* has a particularly wide appeal.

Freaks, Geeks and Asperger Syndrome by Luke Jackson (Jessica Kingsley Publishers). An amazing book written by Luke when he was 13, he writes about being a teenager and being in a family.

Dasha's Journal by TO Daria (Jessica Kingsley Publishers) This book is "written" by a disinterested observer of a family of pet humans. Dasha is a cat who's made a special study of how a family with an autistic member lives and interacts. It's full of insight into why all the members of the family behave the way they do.

Asperger's and Girls edited by Tony Attwood (Future Horizons). This book discusses the difficulties faced by girls and women who have AS, including education, growing up, friendships and relationships. It has lots of tips for women on the spectrum and professionals.

Pretending to be Normal: Living with Asperger's Syndrome by Liane Holliday-Willey (Jessica Kingsley Publishers) An autobiography of a woman who has AS, telling her story of how she accepted her AS through her life. It's particularly insightful if you are a woman on the spectrum or interested in understanding more about women on the spectrum.

A History of Autism: Conversations with the Pioneers by Adam Feinstein (Wiley-Blackwell). Full of conversations with the scientists, clinicians, lobbyists and parents who have shaped the development of autism in both research and policy.

Defeating Autism: A Damaging Delusion by Michael Fitzpatrick (Routledge). This book, written by a GP and father of a child with autism, highlights the fact and fiction of therapies for individuals with an ASC. The book highlights bad practice and pseudoscience in "treating" ASCs and is useful for anyone thinking of trying medical interventions.

Books about Health and Self-Improvement

***Cognitive Behavioural Therapy for Dummies* by Rob Wilson and Rhena Branch (Wiley).** CBT is one of the best ways to tackle depression and anxiety, and this book sets out all you need to know.

***Cognitive Behavioural Therapy Workbook for Dummies* by Rhena Branch and Rob Wilson (Wiley).** The authors provide a structured course for learning and improving your CBT techniques, so once you've learnt about CBT, this book is excellent for people who need a structure to focus their efforts.

***Asperger Syndrome and Anxiety* by Nick Dubin (Jessica Kingsley Publishers).** A fantastic book for understanding anxiety and learning how to deal with it.

***Neuro-Linguistic Programming for Dummies* by Romilla Ready and Kate Burton (Wiley).** For those who really like to get their head around something and not for those who want something easy, NLP is a fascinating way to understand and improve your social interactions.

***Neuro-Linguistic Programming (NLP) Workbook for Dummies* by Romilla Ready and Kate Burton (Wiley).** Again, if you need a structured approach to learning what you've been reading about in NLP for Dummies, this is the book for you.

***A User guide to the GF/CF diet for autism, Asperger syndrome and AD/HD* by Luke Jackson (Jessica Kingsley Publishers).** An invaluable guide to the gluten-free and casein-free diet, though written at a time before the effects of insoluble fibre were well-known.

***IBS (irritable bowel syndrome) for Dummies* (UK edition) by Patricia MacNair (Wiley).** A good guide to the symptoms, strategies and diets for IBS, which may affect people with AS.

***Living Gluten-Free for Dummies* (UK edition) by Sue Baic, Nigel Denby and Danna Korn (Wiley)**Aimed at people with coeliac disease, this book nevertheless provides a useful guide to a gluten-free diet for anyone.

***Positive Psychology for Dummies* by Averil Leimon and Gladeana McMahon (Wiley).** If you can't stop yourself fretting about how your life isn't good enough or people are always telling you not to be so defeatist or pessimistic, then this book is for you.

Mental Health Aspects of Autism and Asperger Syndrome by Mohammad Ghaziuddin (Jessica Kingsley Publishers). This book provides a wealth of information about psychiatric problems found in ASCs including schizophrenia, depression, anxiety, and tic disorders. It gives advice and guidance on early detection and treatment.

Books about Social Skills and Relationships

We've grouped these books into four separate categories, depending on your likely needs.

For adults

The Other Half of Asperger Syndrome by Maxine Aston (National Autistic Society). Maxine is a professional couples' counsellor who has AS, which makes this a very useful book for anyone struggling with a relationship.

An Asperger Marriage by Gisela and Christopher Slater-Walker (Jessica Kingsley Publishers). Gisela and Christopher have been married for 10 years and this book describes what they've learnt about marriage, relationships and his AS.

Asperger Syndrome and Long-Term Relationships by Ashley Stanford (Jessica Kingsley Publishers). Ashley is in a long-term relationship with a man who has AS. She provides plenty of information about the condition and coming to terms with the discovery that your partner has AS.

Love, Sex and Long-Term Relationships by Sarah Hendrickx (Jessica Kingsley Publishers). A markedly different relationship is described by Sarah in this book, which has contributions from her AS partner.

Flirting for Dummies by Elizabeth Clark (John Wiley and Sons). A handy guide, but not written with an autistic reader in mind, so you'll need to be quite good at body language before you can really benefit from this book.

For anyone

Body Language for Dummies by Elizabeth Kuhnke (John Wiley and Sons). All the basics about body language, clearly presented.

Making Sense of Sex **by Sarah Attwood (Jessica Kingsley Publishers).** A comprehensive guide to sex, sexuality, feelings and how sexual relationships relate to friendship.

Asperger's Syndrome and Sexuality **by Isabelle Hénault (Jessica Kingsley Publishers).** A large-format book that covers the basics with great clarity and lots of diagrams.

For children

How do you feel, Thomas? **(Egmont Books Ltd).** This interactive book is a fun way for young children to learn about emotions.

Different Like Me: My book of autism heroes **by Jennifer Elder (Jessica Kingsley Publishers).** This book is aimed at 8—12 year olds and writes about famous people in the fields of science, comedy, philosophy and more who may have had AS.

Tobin Learns to Make Friends **by Diane Murrell (Future Horizons Incorporated).** This book is about an engine called Tobin who has trouble making friends. The story talks about many friendship skills and social skills, such as sharing, being polite and taking turns.

Books for Parents and Siblings

Hitchhiking through Asperger Syndrome **by Lyse Piles (Jessica Kingsley Publishers).** This is written by a parent and gives a matter-of-fact and thoughtful account of one family's experiences of living with AS.

The red beast - controlling anger in children with Asperger syndrome **by K I Al-Ghani (Jessica Kingsley Publishers).** This book has some great tips on helping children with an ASC who have problems controlling their anger.

Asperger syndrome and difficult moments: practical solutions for tantrums, rage and meltdown **by Brenda Smith Myles and Jack Southwick (Autism Asperger Publishing Co.).** Provides practical solutions for everyday challenges facing individuals with AS and their families. This book is aimed at parents and professionals.

The incredible 5-point scale: assisting children with autism spectrum disorders **by Kari Dunn Baron and Mitzi Curtis (Autism Asperger Publishing Co.).** This book is aimed at children aged 7-13 and shows them how to help with behaviour such hitting, obsessions, inappropriate touch, anger and anxiety. It has suggestions for understanding feelings and how to deal with levels of emotion on a 5 point scale.

Sleep better! A guide to improving sleep for children with special needs **by V. Mark Durand (Paul H Brookes Publishing).** This has lots of information and suggestions about improving sleep.

My brother is different: a book for young children who have a brother with autism **by Louise Gorrod and Beccy Carver (National Autistic Society).** This booklet was written by a mother of a son with autism to help his siblings to understand what autism is, and why their brother did the things he did. More suitable for younger children.

Can I tell you about Asperger syndrome? A guide for family and friends **by Jude Welton and Jane Telford (Jessica Kingsley Publishers).** A useful book that might help you or your child tell others about their diagnosis.

Autism, Discrimination and the Law: A Quick Guide for Parents, Educators and Employers **by James Graham (Jessica Kingsley Publishers).** This easy to follow book outlines how the legal requirements of the Disability Discrimination Act 1995 can be met for students and employees with an ASC. Useful to make sure you're informed about what reasonable adjustments to education and work you can legally expect for your child.

More Than Words: Helping Parents Promote Communication and Social Skills in Children with Autism Spectrum Disorder **by Fern Sussman and Robin Baird Lewis (Hanen Centre).** This book provides strategies for helping parent—child communication and shows parents how to turn everyday activities into opportunities for interaction and communication.

TalkAbility: People Skills for Verbal Children on the Autism Spectrum: A Guide for Parents **by Fern Sussman (Hanen Centre).** This book gives practical strategies for parents to help their children develop an understanding of the social aspects of language that are important in conversations and friendships.

The New Social Story Book **by Carol Gray (Future Horizons Incorporated).** This book goes through how to write social stories to help children on the spectrum different social skills, behaviour skills and daily life skills.

Comic Strip Conversations **by Carol Gray (Future Horizons Incorporated).** This book teaches conversation skills and appropriate behaviour skills to children on the spectrum using comic strip illustrations.

DVDs and CDs

Being Me (**The National Autistic Society**). This is a DVD and CD-Rom set for individuals who have just received a diagnosis on the autism spectrum. It is suitable for teenagers and adults. People on the spectrum talk about their experiences and the user is encouraged to think about what having a diagnosis on the autism spectrum means for them personally. The CD-Rom has session plans for individuals or professionals to work through the issues raised.

The Transporters (**Changing Media Development Ltd., www.thetrans porters.com**) This is a DVD for young children with an ASC to help teach emotion recognition. The DVD is a set of stories about toy vehicles who experience different emotions in their daily adventures. Real faces show the emotions, and quizzes and games are included to help children learn.

Mind Reading (**Jessica Kingsley Publishers**). This is an interactive guide to emotions for children and adults on the autism spectrum. It includes a library of over 400 different emotions, and the different ways these emotions can be expressed (face, voice, context). A learning centre and games zone are also included to maximise learning.

Fun with Feelings (**Ultimate Learning**). A DVD designed to teach children to recognise emotions. Visual, verbal and contextual clues are taught to help children understand emotions in a fun way.

Appendix B

Glossary

● ●

*Y*ou will find brief explanations of many of the technical terms in this book listed in the glossary. If you want to know more, you should look the word or phrase up in the index. Some words and phrases used in the book have been deliberately left out because we couldn't find a useful way to describe them briefly, and we didn't see the point of entering them here only to say "see page . . .". . If we had included full explanations of everything, the glossary would be over 300 pages long!

We've tried to make the explanations useful, to minimise the number of times you'll need to refer to another part of the book. Doing this makes the glossary quite a bit longer, but you're not expected to read it through, so don't be put off.

We have also listed some terms which we don't mention in the book. We did this because we think you're likely to come across them when you learn about Asperger's and other forms of autism and we're trying to make this glossary genuinely helpful.

Each term is marked in **boldface** so that you can skim through the glossary easily. Within each definition, terms in *italics* have their own entry in the glossary.

ABA *Applied behavioural analysis* involves taking well-known psychology, applying it, then analysing the effects and changing what you're applying in order to achieve a better result. Then you repeat the process. A number of psychologists have developed this technique for autistic children, which is why you will find some people who think ABA is a technique developed specially for autism. The most well-known programme of teaching and training that uses ABA is *Early Intensive Behavioural Intervention*.

Acute depressive episodes are usually between nine and eighteen months long. The *depression* is very severe (acute) and it's normally during one of these episodes that someone with *clinical depression* is first diagnosed. After an acute episode you might recover, or you might continue to suffer from *chronic* clinical depression or chronic *sub-clinical* depression. Acute depressive episodes are the same as *major depressive episodes*.

ADHD Attention-deficit (hyperactivity) disorder. Sometimes still written AD(H)D, but people often leave the brackets out. People with ADHD show impulsive or very energetic behaviour or have difficulty concentrating on just one thing, or show any combination of these things. ADHD is only diagnosed if your schooling, work or social life are affected by your *signs* and *symptoms*.

Affective, strictly speaking, is a technical term referring to the *signs* of emotion, and excluding the *symptoms*. So it refers to things other people can see, like your smile, but doesn't refer to what you are feeling. Even *psychiatrists* often use it more loosely to mean both how you appear and how you're feeling, but this is old-fashioned and the younger generation use the correct term, *mood*, which includes signs and symptoms.

Anti-social personality disorder (ASPD) is characterised by failure to conform socially, deceitfulness, impulsivity, irritability, irresponsibility (especially towards others and the safety of others) and a lack of remorse. ASPD is officially the same as *psychopathy*, although some researchers disagree. ASPD was a frequent misdiagnosis for *ASCs*, especially Asperger's, though the number of misdiagnoses has been dropping as better awareness of ASC among professionals has developed.

Anxiety is, technically, a negative feeling whose cause is either unavoidable or unknown. The feeling is called fear if the cause is avoidable or known. If you've never experienced *clinical* anxiety it's hard to imagine how disabling it can be. Drugs (*anxiolytics*), *cognitive behavioural therapy* and meditation can be used to treat anxiety problems.

Anxiety attacks are the same as *panic attacks*, though some people use the term to mean less severe panic attacks. When you have a panic attack you might breathe hard, have a thumping heart, sweat, have a dry mouth, shake, feel detached from reality, feel sick, feel dizzy, have chest pain and in severe attacks you might wet yourself, soil yourself or collapse. People often fear that they are having a heart attack or are going to die, but these aren't ever a result of a panic attack.

Anxiety disorders are all disorders which induce fear, *anxiety* or *panic attacks* (*anxiety attacks*). Another diagnosis is usually present as well, such as *depression* or *ASC*, technically called a *comorbid* diagnosis. Anxiety disorders are treatable both with and without *anxiolytics*.

APD is a confusing abbreviation which is usually used for *antisocial personality disorder* but not always. Sometimes it stands for anxious personality disorder, which is listed in this glossary under the modern name of *anxious (avoidant) personality disorder*. We do not use the abbreviation "APD" in this book, but you're likely to come across it if you read a lot of books about Asperger's and conditions related to it or confused with it.

AS — Asperger's syndrome (or Asperger syndrome). See the whole book!

ASC — autism-spectrum condition (or autistic-spectrum condition) means the same thing as *pervasive developmental disorder*. "*Autism*" is often used to mean the same thing as well.

ASD (Autism-spectrum disorder or autistic-spectrum disorder) is the same as *ASC*, see the entry immediately above, and autism-spectrum disorder is also the new diagnosis proposed for *DSM*-V which does not distinguish between various different types of ASC because the distinctions are unreliable (doctors disagree on which diagnostic type a certain person comes under).

ASPD — (Anti-social personality disorder) is characterised by failure to conform socially, deceitfulness, impulsivity, irritability, irresponsibility (especially towards others and the safety of others) and a lack of remorse. ASPD is officially the same as *psychopathy*, although some researchers disagree. ASPD was a frequent misdiagnosis for *ASC*s, especially Asperger's, though the number of misdiagnoses has been dropping as better awareness of ASC among professionals has developed.

Asperger's disorder (or Asperger disorder) is the official *DSM* name for Asperger's.

Atypical autism is used to mean the same as *pervasive developmental disorder — not otherwise specified* by most experts, but some define it as a separate form of autism. To make things more confusing, these experts use different definitions of what atypical autism is. So we can't tell you much more unless we write another book!

Autism can be used to mean either the whole autism spectrum or just classic autism (see the section *Terminating confusion over terminology* on page X of the introduction to the book).

Autism-spectrum condition (or autistic-spectrum condition, ASC) means the same thing as *pervasive developmental disorder*. "*Autism*" is often used to mean the same thing as well (see the section *Terminating confusion over terminology* on page X of the introduction to the book).

Autism-spectrum disorder (or autistic-spectrum disorder or ASD) is the same as *autism-spectrum condition*, see the entry immediately above, and autism-spectrum disorder is also the new diagnosis proposed for *DSM*-V which does not distinguish between various different types of ASC because the distinctions are unreliable (doctors disagree on which diagnostic type a certain person comes under).

Autistic traits are the behaviours, preferences, mannerisms, sensitivities, talents, disabilities and thinking styles which are associated with *autism* (but which can be found throughout the general population). There are at least 400 autistic traits. Traits are not at all the same as *diagnostic criteria*.

Black-and-white thinking describes thinking in terms of either/or. For example, everyone's either your friend or your enemy. Every book on autism is either brilliant or rubbish. Every topic is either absolutely fascinating or terminally boring. This way of thinking is over-simplified, and also causes extra stress when facts or experience contradict the expectations of black-and-white thinking..

Broader autism phenotype (BAP) is the technical phrase that describes everyone who has a lot of *traits* but who doesn't actually qualify for a diagnosis. Everything about you is your phenotype, so if you have brown hair, the phenotype of your hair colour is brown. If you and your partner have brown hair, and one of your children has red hair, then one of you must carry the red-hair gene, and so must have a hair genotype of red+brown. Phenotypes always match the genes you carry, so you can't be red+brown and have blond hair (bleaching excepted!).

Bulimia nervosa is the desire to binge on food, and then make yourself sick or take laxatives so that you don't put on weight. Sometimes, if you have bulimia, your weight will stay fairly steady, or you might be one of those who balloon up and then go on a long stretch of purges until your weight is down again. Some people with bulimia are very thin; many are various sizes of normal.

Catatonia is a state of extreme isolation from the world. People showing this *sign* are always unresponsive, often not even looking at something held out to them. They can be lethargic, rigidly immobile or extremely fidgety.

CBT (cognitive behavioural therapy) is the name for any therapy that aims to change your behaviour by getting you to think about your behaviour (thinking is technically called cognition). Some experts use "cognitive behaviour therapy" to mean something slightly more specific, but the difference is very technical and not used by all experts.

Childhood disintegrative disorder (CDD) is the scary name for a severe form of regressive autism where the first two or more years of childhood are normal, language develops, social skills develop, motor skills develop, potty training is successful, and so on, then there is a relatively sudden and significant regression in two or more of these areas of development. After regression the child often meets the *criteria* for classic autism and has the same expected course of development from then on.

Classic autism is used to refer to the specific diagnosis of autism, because the word "autism" on its own is often used to refer to the whole autism spectrum (see the section _Terminating confusion over terminology_ on page X of the introduction to the book).

Comorbid in its broadest sense describes any medical conditions that occur in the same person. So if you have a cold and a broken leg, these conditions are comorbid in you. More narrowly, it's used to mean conditions which occur together more often than you would expect by chance, such as _autism_ and _epilepsy_.

Diagnostic criteria are points used by professional diagnosticians to judge whether or not a certain person should receive a particular diagnosis. Top professionals use their own _criteria_, which are normally made available to other diagnosticians after a trial period when the validity of the criteria is checked.

Dietary sensitivity is the tendency to react badly to certain foodstuffs even though there's no allergic reaction and the food is still digested, unlike an intolerance. You might recover from any dietary sensitivity by avoiding the foodstuff for three months and then gradually reintroducing it. Dietary sensitivities tend to be worse when you're stressed.

Dietary intolerance is an inability to digest a certain food or foods. Evidence for _intolerance_ is found by doing chemical tests on faeces. It's not the same as food _allergy_ or _dietary sensitivity_.

DPD usually stands for _dependent personality disorder_. Dependent personality disorder typically appears as a person who is very meek, agreeable, compliant, willing to have others make decisions for them, and who is afraid of having to make decisions for themselves.

DSM is the Diagnostic and Statistical Manual of Mental Disorders, published by the American Psychiatric Association (APA), is the official American handbook for diagnosticians. Currently in its fourth edition, known as DSM-IV, the fifth edition (DSM-5) is due to be published in 2013.

Dyscalculia is the limited ability to imagine numbers and do arithmetic, though people often say it's the limited ability to do maths, because a lot of the maths most people learn in school is arithmetic rather than "higher maths". Arithmetic is calculation with quantities, especially when just using the four basic functions (addition, subtraction, multiplication and division).

Dyslexia is the limited ability to recognise abstract symbols (which mostly means letters, numbers and punctuation). This affects reading and writing.

Dyspraxia is the limited ability to control certain movements, technically called voluntary motor movements, so it can make you clumsy and accident-prone. Less well-known are the effects of dyspraxia on speech, memory (especially short-term memory), sensory sensitivity and planning ability.

Early Intensive Behavioural Intervention (EIBI) is a behavioural teaching approach for individuals with an ASC. It involves reinforcing desirable behaviour and teaching alternatives to less desirable behaviour. In ASCs it's particularly helpful for challenging behaviour and self injurious behaviour.

Educational psychologists are professionals who work with children who have special educational needs. Most are employed by local authorities, and work in schools to set up individualised programmes for children who need extra support at school.

Emotionally unstable personality disorder is the *ICD* name for *borderline personality disorder*.

Empathy is a word that was originally coined by a psychologist to describe the human ability to put oneself in someone else's position, to work out what they might be thinking. These days, developmental psychologists usually split this concept into two, one called "(social) *imagination*" and one called "*theory of mind*". One of the consequences of being empathic is not wanting to hurt others, as you can imagine how they would feel.

Executive function describes how well you plan, control your impulses (such as stopping yourself from blurting out comments that will be perceived as rude), and control how your attention moves from topic to topic. You often need to plan and control some of your impulses, sometimes you need to keep your mind on a certain thing or things, other times you need to move your attention to something else: the ability to do all these things well is called having good executive function. Most people on the spectrum have poor executive function, though some have developed skills in one or two areas.

Functioning is a technical term that describes how well someone copes with life. Functioning is often split into categories like self-care (washing, cooking, and so on), employment and personal life (meaning sex, romance and relationships). If you aren't functioning well in one or more categories and the problems are persistent, a diagnosis in the *DSM* probably exists which describes you.

High-Functioning Autism (HFA) is a specific diagnosis used by some experts, although it's not in the *DSM* or the *ICD*. Strictly speaking, it's spelt with capitals to distinguish it from the general description, "*high-functioning autism*" (see the next entry). The *diagnostic criteria* for Asperger's says that there can only be a small *language delay* (the child should be using multi-word phrases by age three), so for people like the Goth, who first used phrases at three and a half, a diagnosis of Asperger's is wrong. Few diagnosticians would suggest that the Goth has *classic autism*, so the diagnosis of HFA is used.

High-functioning autism is used as a general description of anyone on the spectrum who functions well.

Hypersensitivity means you are very sensitive. Although it can refer to emotional sensitivity or any other sensitivity, it usually refers to sensitivity of your senses (sight, hearing, smell, touch, taste and the rest).

Hyposensitivity means you have reduced sensitivity. It usually refers to reduced sensitivity of one or more of your senses (sight, hearing, smell, touch, taste and the rest).

ICD — the International Classification of Diseases is a diagnostic "handbook" (it's massive) published by the World Health Organisation (WHO), but is not widely used in North America, where they use the *DSM*. The UK tends to use both. Currently, the ICD is in its tenth edition, referred to as ICD-10, with the eleventh edition due out in 2015.

Insensitivity is the lack of response by your senses to sensory stimulation.

Intolerance (sometimes called dietary intolerance just to be clear) is the inability to digest, and thus get nutritional benefit from, a food. You can be intolerant to any number of different foods. Evidence for intolerance is found by doing chemical tests on blood or faeces. It's not the same as food *allergy* or *dietary sensitivity*.

Language delay is a technical term meaning that a certain criterion in a child's development of language was missed. Language delay is a *sign* of some *ASC*s. Language development includes comprehension: if the child comprehends spoken words and the delay is purely in speaking then it's called speech delay. Speech delay isn't in itself a sign of any ASC. The standard *criteria* are: first real word (with understanding of its meaning) by one year, two-word phrases by two years and multi-word phrases by two-and-a-half years. If an earlier criterion is missed and a later criterion is achieved then the delay is said to have "resolved" (gone away).

Learning difficulty has a meaning that's intimately connected to *learning disability*. See the next entry.

Learning disability (LD) is defined in several different ways by different groups and organisations. In the USA it's defined as a mismatch between a particular skill (such as reading) and your IQ (this particular mismatch is *dyslexia*). You will come across this use of the term quite often, even in British books. In the UK, some mismatches are called *specific learning difficulties* (including dyslexia) and only a more widespread problem with learning and *functioning* is called learning disability.

Major depressive disorder (MDD) is the *DSM* name for *clinical* depression, which is depression which a doctor would consider severe enough to need treatment. However, a lot of GPs these days prescribe *antidepressants* for what some experts argue is *sub-clinical* depression (sub-clinical means almost clinical, almost severe enough to need treatment).

Major depressive episode is the *DSM* name for an acute depressive episode. These are usually between nine and eighteen months long. The *depression* is very severe (acute) and it's normally during one of these episodes that someone with *clinical depression* is first diagnosed. After an acute episode you might recover, or you might continue to suffer from *chronic* clinical depression or chronic *sub-clinical* depression.

Manic depression, bipolar disorder, bipolar *affective* disorder or bipolar *depression* are all names for the same thing, but manic depression and bipolar affective disorder are no longer used by professionals. People with *ASC*s are occasionally misdiagnosed with bipolar disorder, and it's possible to have both, but bipolar disorder isn't any more common in ASC than in anyone else.

Meltdowns are reactions to being severely overloaded with information and sensory stimulation. When this happens you reach a point where you can no longer cope no matter how hard you try. Then you are unable to stop yourself screaming, crying, gesticulating, or some combination of these.

Mentalising is the technical word for the ability to think about your thoughts and feelings and the thoughts and feelings of others. People on the spectrum aren't very good at mentalising: even mentalising their own thoughts and feelings can be extremely difficult.

Mentalising Behaviour Therapy (MBT) is a programme of treatment for *borderline personality disorder* which includes *cognitive behavioural therapy*, group therapy and careful monitoring and co-ordination of behaviour by the treatment team (doctors, nurses and *psychologists*).

Mood, technically, refers to your underlying emotional state. So watching a comedy programme might make you laugh and feel briefly happy even if your mood is depressed. If your mood is depressed, brief emotions can still be anything, including euphoric. Mood includes *signs* and *symptoms*; signs alone tell a professional about your *affective* mood, which is only a partial description of your mood.

Obsessive-compulsive disorder (OCD) is an *anxiety disorder* where your thoughts keep returning to a certain subject (called an obsession, such as germs). These intrusive thoughts cause anxiety, which may then prompt you to act to try to reduce the anxiety, such as by washing your hands. Some OCDs focus on taboo-breaking, such as having intrusive thoughts pushing you to hit random strangers or smash random windows.

Obsessive-compulsive personality disorder (OCPD) looks similar to OCD, but OCPD isn't an *anxiety disorder*. In OCPD the person enjoys the way their thoughts keep returning to the same things (obsessions) and gets comfort and a sense of purpose from their compulsive behaviour. When the obsession is with dieting, distinguishing between OCPD and *anorexia nervosa* can be very difficult.

Overload is when your brain is full and you can't take in any more information! Overload can be caused by the amount of thinking you need to do, so trying to hold a group conversation with six other people in peaceful surroundings might be overloading because of the mental effort of tracking the seven parts in the conversation. Sensory overload, where it's information coming in through your senses (such as background noise) that is overloading you is more common, and both causes can occur at the same time, of course! Extreme overload causes *meltdowns*, and people's experiences of what counts as extreme vary.

Panic attacks are the same as *anxiety attacks*, though some people use that term to mean less severe panic attacks. When you have a panic attack you might breathe hard, have a thumping heart, sweat, have a dry mouth, shake, feel detached from reality, feel sick, feel dizzy, have chest pain and in severe attacks you might wet yourself, soil yourself or collapse. People often fear that they are having a heart attack or are going to die, but these aren't ever a result of a panic attack.

PECS — the Picture-Exchange Communication System does pretty much what it says. The person wanting to communicate hands over an appropriate picture to communicate what they want, as well as or instead of words.

Personalisation (when you're talking about social care services and similar help) is the same as *person-centred planning*. Many people prefer the term "personalisation" because "person-centred planning" sounds like the plans are made by a paternalistic organisation for a person who has no control — this is not the case!

Pervasive developmental disorder (PDD) is the generic name used by the *DSM* and the *ICD* for all *autism-spectrum conditions*. PDD isn't a diagnosis but a category of diagnoses. PDD is sometimes also used as an abbreviated way of saying *PDD-NOS* (see the next entry).

Pervasive developmental disorder — not otherwise specified (PDD-NOS) is an *ASC* that does not fit the strict *criteria* for either classic *autism*, Asperger's or *CDD*. The *DSM* uses PDD-NOS as a catch-all diagnosis for anyone whose life is seriously affected by autism's *symptoms* but who doesn't meet the *diagnostic criteria* for any of the other forms. However, some researchers distinguish between atypical autism and PDD-NOS.

Photosensitivity is the technical name for being very sensitive to light. Usually it's sensitivity to any bright light, but some people have problems only with certain colours or have a problem with sunlight or are fine with sunlight but have a problem with any other bright light.

Proprioception is the sense of where each bit of your body is. Close your eyes and hold your hand up. Now move one of your fingers. You can "feel" exactly how much you've moved the finger; you don't need to look or touch anything. That's proprioception.

Psychotic means suffering from **psychosis**, which is a loss of contact with reality, often resulting in hallucinations (experiences of things that aren't there), delusions (beliefs that aren't true) and confusion as to whether your thoughts are inside your head or coming from outside. Psychosis is the principal *sign* of *schizophrenia* and *bipolar* disorder, and sometimes occurs in severe *clinical depression*.

PTSD — post-traumatic stress disorder is caused by a traumatic event (or a series of events) in susceptible people. It is an *anxiety disorder*. *Signs* and *symptoms* include *anxiety*, flashbacks, nightmares, avoidance of anything that might remind you of the event(s) (and thus cause anxiety), outbursts of anger, problems sleeping and extreme vigilance for possible threats (hypervigilance).

Regressive autism is where the first year or more of childhood is normal, language develops, social skills develop, motor skills develop, potty training is successful, and so on, then there is a significant regression in at least one of these areas of development. After regression the child often meets the *criteria* for classic autism and has the same expected course of development from then on. Regressive autism is not listed in the *DSM* or the *ICD*, and some researchers point out that many people on the spectrum show regression in certain circumstances, so it may not differ in any way from other forms.

Savantism is having a very special ability, such as being able to multiply six-digit numbers in your head, or being a brilliant self-taught pianist. Half of all savants have an *ASC*, and most others have a disability which affects the brain. It's widely believed that savants can just "do" what they do, but all savants who've been studied have spent many thousands of hours learning their subject and perfecting their abilities, just as anyone would have to do.

Seizures are the same as fits and convulsions. Seizures vary in severity, the mildest are often described as "not being home" for a few seconds (staring into the middle distance), although several reasons for this behaviour exist, including an *ASC*, so staring vacantly can't easily be diagnosed as a seizure.

Selective mutism is being able to speak only to certain people or in certain situations. A common example is only being able to speak to family members and only when at home. Rarely, selective *mutism* happens when someone is *unable* to speak to someone or some people instead of being unable to speak to most people. The cause is *anxiety* and low self-esteem. Then, without any practice in talking to people, the fear grows and the self-esteem drops — a vicious circle that can be hard to break. It used to be called elective mutism because the person was thought to be choosing (electing) to speak or not speak, rather than being physically unable to speak because of the fear.

Sensory confusion means having difficulty telling which sense is sensing what. So someone might hear something but think they have seen it, or they might be unable to tell which sense was hearing the sound. See chapter 9.

Sensory discrimination describes the ability to pick out details and subtleties. For example, someone with good tactile discrimination can distinguish between two fabrics which someone with less ability thinks feel the same. Discrimination can be poor as well as good.

Severe learning disability (SLD) is usually defined as having an IQ between 20 and 50 and a difficulty *functioning* compared to others with the same IQ. However, various definitions are used by different organisations, and in the USA they use the term to mean severe *specific learning difficulties*.

Shut downs are a response to *overload* where you block out the world in order to make it easier to think. Some people do this by closing their eyes, covering their ears, groaning and rocking (or maybe using only some of these techniques). Others have developed their ability so that they can shut down without obvious signs: they just go quiet and stare out of the window for a while. This type of shut down isn't as effective in very bright or noisy environments, so when pushed people who can do this type of shut down will also resort to closing their eyes, covering their ears, groaning and rocking.

Speech and language therapy (SALT, though SALT can also stand for speech and language therapist) is provided for people who have problems with speaking, reading and writing. SALT can help if the problem is due to physical problems with your lips, tongue, mouth, throat or breathing, or co-ordination problems (dyspraxia), or social problems with understanding when to speak, or other types of problem, which is why it's such an inclusive name (speech AND language).

Statements of special educational needs are legal documents produced by local authorities which outline the educational needs and school adaptations for children and young people with special educational needs.

Stereotypy describes repetitive movement. Rocking and hand-flapping are stereotypies, also called stereotypical behaviours. The word "stereotypy" can be used to describe all stereotypies, as in "stereotypy is very common in ASCs".

Synaesthesia is when sensory information is perceived in more than one way, such as seeing sounds as well as hearing them, or seeing all squares as green as well as whatever their real colour is.

Systemising is the ability to understand systems by breaking them down (often literally) and working out what all the components do and how the components fit together. It's an ability which is particularly useful for engineers, mechanics, computer programmers, physicists and mathematicians. Collecting things is also a form of systemising, especially if the collection is catalogued.

TEACCH — Treatment and Education of Autistic and related Communication-Handicapped Children is an educational approach widely used in special education classrooms that focuses on the role of structure in the learning environment of children with *ASCs*.

Theory of mind is what you use to work out what someone else would do. If you don't have a theory of mind, you won't be able to use your social *imagination* to work out what someone else might think. Imagination and theory of mind are closely related concepts and it's not always necessary to distinguish between them. Some authors, doctors and academics still use the word "*empathy*" when they don't need to distinguish, or when they mean both.

Tics are sudden bursts of muscle activity. They can be simple, like a twitch or shouting "ah", or complex, such as blurting out "hacking Margaret Thatcher" while pulling faces. As these examples show, tics can be motor (movement) tics, vocal tics or a combination.

Weak central coherence means having a detail-based style of experiencing the world, especially if you can't get the details to join together into the bigger picture. Details "cohere" when they join together. When all (or almost all) the details cohere the resulting coherence is called "central".

Index

• C •

• *F* •

• *S* •